Passport's Illustrated Trave

SINGAPORE
& MALAYSIA

FROM
THOMAS
COOK

PASSPORT BOOKS

NTC/Contemporary Publishing Company

Published by Passport Books, an imprint of
NTC/Contemporary Publishing Company,
4255 West Touhy Avenue, Lincolnwood
(Chicago), Illinois 60646–1975 U.S.A.

The contents of this publication are believed correct at the time of
printing. Nevertheless, the publishers cannot accept responsibility for
errors or omissions, or for changes in details given. We are always
grateful to readers who let us know of any errors or omissions they come
across, and future printings will be updated accordingly.

Published by Passport Books in conjunction with AA Publishing.

Written by Nick Hanna

Original photography by Nick Hanna and Ken Paterson

Library of Congress Catalog Card Number: on file
ISBN 0-8442-4817-7

Color separation: BTB Colour Reproduction, Whitchurch, Hampshire.
Printed by Edicoes ASA, Oporto, Portugal.

Cover picture: *Haw Par Villa, Singapore;* Back cover: *Raffles Hotel; Arab
Street, Singapore:* Title page: *Kek Lok Si, Pulau Pinang;* Above: *rickshaw
owner, Singapore*

Contents

About this Book

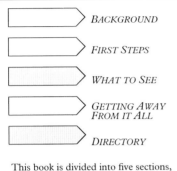

BACKGROUND

FIRST STEPS

WHAT TO SEE

GETTING AWAY FROM IT ALL

DIRECTORY

This book is divided into five sections, identified by the above colour coding.

Background gives an introduction to Singapore and Malaysia – their history, geography, politics, culture.
First Steps offers practical advice on arriving and getting around.
What to See is an alphabetical listing of places to visit, interspersed with walks and tours.
Getting Away From it All highlights places off the beaten track where it's possible to relax and enjoy peace and quiet.
Finally, the **Directory** provides practical information – from shopping and entertainment to children and sport, including a section on business matters. Special highly illustrated **features** on specific aspects of Malaysia and Singapore appear throughout the book.

> The mapping in this book uses international country symbols.
> RI Indonesia   MAL Malaysia
> T Thailand   BRU Brunei
> SGP Singapore

Sundry shop sun-shade, Pulau Pangkor

BACKGROUND

'Malacca fascinates me more daily. There is, among other things, a mediaevalism about it. The noise of the modern world reaches it only in the faintest echoes; its sleep is almost dreamless, its sensations seem to come out of books read in childhood.'

ISABELLA BIRD,
The Golden Chersonese (1883)

Introduction

*A*t the heart of Southeast Asia, Singapore and Malaysia are linked by a common heritage that started in the days of the great sea-trading routes of the spice traders, and continued through the colonial era to their current status as neighbouring economic powers.

For centuries, travellers have been drawn to their shores, creating a melting-pot of peoples and lifestyles – of Malays, Chinese, Indians and many other ethnic groups that live side by side in almost every corner of the region. For the present-day visitor, this diversity yields a rich and heady mixture of cultural attractions, of music, dance and arts from several countries, and an almost continuous calendar of festivals and feasts drawn from many different religious traditions.

Despite recent economic growth and modernisation, the soul of the Orient is never far from the surface. In Singapore, the tower blocks may be built according to the laws of structural engineering, but their design is still very much determined by the principles of Chinese geomancy or *feng shui,* which dictates where doors, windows and furniture are placed to ensure that good spirits and wealth stay within the building. A Singaporean executive might be trading worldwide via his mobile telephone, but his values are likely to be influenced as much by the Confucian precepts of filial piety, discipline and respect for the family as they are by currency markets.

In Malaysia the lifestyle is as varied as the landscape, although most of society is bound together by the common thread of Islam, the national religion. The call to prayer echoes five times a day from mosques everywhere, from the bustling streets of Kuala Lumpur, the capital, to the smallest village or *kampung,* where small wooden houses on stilts are surrounded by a cooling canopy of papaya, banana and palm trees. In both countries the vibrancy of street life will provide much

SOUTHEAST ASIA

to enthral and entertain. In one street you may come across a noisy and colourful celebration for a deity's birthday; in the next, a string of open-air restaurants where Indian cooks fling large circles of dough on to hot-plates to create sizzling snacks. In the markets of Sabah and Sarawak, tribal peoples display weird and strange fruits from the forest alongside brightly patterned basketware and other ethnic crafts.

Both Singapore and Malaysia are a gastronomic delight for the traveller. A mouth-watering variety of ethnic and international food is available at all times of day and night, often at a surprisingly low cost. A journey here is likely to be as much an exploration of taste sensations as it is a tour of the sights – a culinary adventure, whatever your budget.

There is a remarkable number of things to see and do, whatever your energy level. You can take it easy in Singapore, browsing by daytime in what must be the world's largest shopping bazaar, venturing out in the cool of the evening for a tour of the sights by bicycle-rickshaw. Alternatively, you can trace the roots of the city in the ethnic and colonial areas and catch up with today's generation in one of the many pulsating, hi-tech discos in the small hours of the morning.

Over the causeway to the north, the mountains, rivers and rain forests of Malaysia beckon to the adventurous. From jungle-trekking to scuba-diving, there are plenty of options for exploration and discovery in national parks and other wilderness areas. On the islands off the east and west coasts, you can recuperate beneath the coco-palms on coral beaches with the choice of

THOMAS COOK'S
Singapore and Malaysia

Thomas Cook first arrived in Singapore on his world tour of 1882/3. Raffles Hotel became a headquarters for Cook travellers, who subsequently travelled northwards through Malaya on the Federated Malay Railway System. The travel business in this part of the world was of such importance to Thomas Cook that a special Malay edition of the Thomas Cook magazine, The Travellers' Gazette, *was published in 1923.*

anything from a luxury hotel to a simple, thatched hut to stay in. A sense of history resonates from the smoke-filled temples of Pinang to the tribal long-houses of Sarawak, providing a range of travel experiences almost unparalleled in Asia.

SINGAPORE AND MALAYSIA

History

38,000 BC
Primitive man inhabits the Niah caves in Sarawak.

6–8,000 BC
The first Orang Asli ('original peoples') arrive from the Andaman Islands and settle in the northern Malay peninsula.

7th to 14th century
Seafarers from the Hindu Kingdom of Srivijaya settle the Malay archipelago.

1398
The port of Melaka is founded, quickly becoming a prosperous commercial centre for Arab and Chinese traders.

1511
Melaka is taken by the Portuguese navigator, Alfonso de Albuquerque, and becomes the central focus of European power in the region.

1641
Melaka falls to the Dutch after a bitter, six-month siege.

1785
The British East India Company is granted a lease on Pinang Island in return for protecting the Sultan of Kedah from his enemy, Siam.

1786
Captain Francis Light lands on Pinang and establishes a settlement, which quickly grows to rival Melaka as a free port.

1811
Singapore is annexed to the State of Johor.

1819
Worried by the increasing power of the Dutch in the region, Sir Stamford Raffles persuades the British East India Company to establish a settlement and port on Singapore to counter Dutch influence.

1824
Raffles persuades the Sultan of Johor and Prince Temenggong to cede Singapore to the British in return for an annual payment of 5,000 Spanish dollars.

1824
Britain acquires Melaka from the Dutch in exchange for territory in Sumatra.

1826
Singapore, Pinang and Melaka join together to form the Straits Settlements, under the control of the Governor of Bengal.

1840
A young adventurer, James Brooke, helps the Sultan of Brunei crush a rebellion and is awarded control of the province of Sarawak.

1841
James Brooke is installed as Rajah of Sarawak, marking the beginning of 100 years of rule by the white rajah.

1867
The Straits Settlements become a fully fledged Crown Colony, administered from Singapore.

1874
The great wave of immigration from South China begins, with tens of thousands arriving in Singapore.

1877
Rubber trees are introduced to Singapore; Dunlop invents the pneumatic tyre a year later and rubber plantations spread all over the Malay archipelago.

1888
Sarawak and North Borneo (Sabah) become British protectorates.

1895
The Federation of Malay States is established, consisting of Perak, Selangor, Negri Sembilan and Pahang.

1909
Siam cedes Kedah, Perlis, Kelantan and Terengganu to the British.

1914
The Sultan of Johor accepts British protection. The British now control the whole Malay peninsula.

1920
Malaya is producing half of the world's rubber and 60 per cent of its tin. The boom creates many millionaires and immigration continues to increase.

1921
Work begins on strengthening Singapore's coastal defences as concerns mount over Japan's growing military power.

1941
Japan outflanks 'Fortress Singapore' and invades Malaya on 8 December by land, instead of mounting the expected assault by sea. Japanese forces rapidly advance from Kota Bharu down the peninsula.

1942
Allied troops retreat across the causeway and the Battle for Singapore begins. Within seven days Singapore has fallen and the British surrender on 15 February. Singapore becomes Syonan-to. Thousands of Chinese are massacred.

1945
The Japanese surrrender to Allied forces on 21 August and the British are welcomed back.

1948
The first legislative council is elected in Singapore. In the post-war climate, the seeds of independence begin to take root in both Malaysia and Singapore. In June, attacks on Europeans by the Communist Party of Malaya marks the beginning of a 12-year guerilla war. A State of Emergency is declared.

1954
The young, Cambridge-educated lawyer Lee Kuan Yew founds the People's Action Party (PAP) with the aim of achieving full sovereignty for Singapore.

1957
Malaya is granted independence on 31 August.

1959
Singapore is granted self-government. The PAP sweeps the board in elections for the Assembly and Lee Kuan Yew becomes the first prime minister.

1960
The State of Emergency is officially ended on 31 July.

1963
Foundation of the Federation of Malaysia (including Singapore as a member) under the guidance of the first prime minister, Tunku Abdul Rahman.

1965
Singapore leaves the Federation to become a sovereign nation.

1970
Tunku Abdul Rahman retires, and is succeeded by his deputy, Tun Abdul Razak.

1981
The current Prime Minister of Malaysia, Dato' Seri Mahathir Mohamad, takes office.

1990
After 31 years at the helm, the 'Father of Singapore', Lee Kuan Yew, resigns as Prime Minister and is succeeded by Goh Chok Tong.

Sir Thomas
Stamford Raffles

Geography

Situated 136km north of the equator, Singapore is an island state lying off the southern tip of the Malaysian peninsula. The main island (covering some 580sq km) is what most people refer to as 'Singapore'; the state also encompasses around 58 smaller islands, most of which are scattered over the sea to the south in the Straits of Singapore. Singapore is a low-lying island with the capital occupying roughly a third of the total area.

Malaysia consists of two separate regions. Peninsular Malaysia extends from the Thai border down to the Selat Johor (Straits of Johor). East Malaysia comprises the states of Sarawak and Sabah on the northern half of Borneo, with the tiny country of Brunei Darussalam sandwiched between the two.

The regions of Peninsular Malaysia are defined by a mountainous spine (the Banjaran Titiwangsa) that runs down the centre of the country from the border with Thailand almost to the capital, Kuala Lumpur. The heavily forested and hilly interior is the most sparsely populated part of the peninsula. To the west of the mountains, the foothills and alluvial plains running down to the coast are carpeted in rubber and oil-palm plantations. On the eastern seaboard the coastal plains are not so extensive and rice cultivation predominates.

The most spectacular landscapes are in the East Malaysia states of Sabah and Sarawak. Sarawak is characterised by dense jungle and extensive river systems (the Rajang River flows for 563km through the heart of the country). Covering some 124,500sq km, Sarawak is the largest state in Malaysia.

Bordered by Sarawak and the Indonesian state of Kalimantan to the south, Sabah covers an area of 73,700sq km. Its shores are washed by three different seas: the South China Sea to the

west, and the Sulu Sea and Celebes Sea to the east. Gunung (Mount) Kinabalu, at the pinnacle of the Banjaran Crocker, is the highest peak in Malaysia.

Economy
Singapore's economy is based on tourism, trade, finance, shipping and manufacturing. It is now the world's second-busiest port, handling some 45,000 vessels and 6 million containers a year. Singapore is a clearing-house for trade and finance throughout the region in tin, rubber, coconut oil, rice, timber, jute, spices and coffee. Oil refining is also important, with several offshore refineries located on the islands in the Straits. Tourism is a key component of the economy, generating around S$8 billion annually and employing 100,000 people directly or indirectly.

Since 1968, Singapore has achieved an economic growth rate averaging an astonishing 9 per cent per annum, only dipping slightly below this figure during the recession of the early 1990s.

Malaysia has a prosperous economy and is one of the world's major exporters of rubber, tin, palm oil and cocoa. With the discovery of oil deposits off the east coast in 1978, the petroleum industry has added to the country's wealth and crude oil has now outstripped tin as the major export. Manufacturing industries include textiles, electronic goods,

Planting rice, an important crop in the northern states of Malaysia

jewellery, optical and scientific equipment, toys and sportswear. Malaysia is a major exporter of timber, principally from the eastern states of Sabah and Sarawak, a trade that has recently embroiled the country in considerable international controversy.

Climate

Singapore and the southern tip of Malaysia lie at latitude 1°N, with the northern provinces of Peninsular Malaysia extending up to latitude 7°N, putting both countries in the Tropical Humid belt with average annual rainfall of around 3,000mm. See **Climate** (page 180) for more details.

Population

The population of Singapore is 2.95 million. It is a multiracial society comprising around 78 per cent Chinese, 14 per cent Malays, 7 per cent Indians and small numbers of European and other nationalities. Malaysia is similarly multiracial, with a population of nearly 20 million comprising around 60 per cent Malays (including Orang Asli and the many different ethnic groups of Sarawak and Sabah), 30 per cent Chinese, 8 per cent Indians, and 2 per cent other diverse races. The majority (around 17 million) live in Peninsular Malaysia, with 1.7 million in Sarawak and 1.5 million in Sabah.

Limestone hills dot the rice fields of Perlis

Politics

*B*oth Singapore and Malaysia are parliamentary democracies. In Singapore, politics in the post-Independence period have been dominated until recently by the personality of Lee Kuan Yew, the country's first prime minister. Under his leadership, the country achieved remarkable economic growth and the foundations were laid for the stable, multiracial society that exists today.

Lee's party, the PAP (People's Action Party) has provided Singaporeans with a high standard of living, affordable housing (nearly 90 per cent of the population live in apartments built by the Housing and Development Board) and nearly full employment. These achievements have not been won without some cost to civil liberties. For 13 years (from 1968 to 1980) the PAP held every seat in Parliament, and the lack of any credible opposition meant that the government had free reign, effectively stifling criticism and silencing those few politicians who stood out against government policy. A draconian Internal Security Act has been used to imprison supposed radicals without trial. Even today, foreign publications that seek to criticise government policy are censored.

As Singapore became more affluent the government became more paternalistic, embarking on a series of campaigns to mould the nation into a well-behaved society and imposing numerous laws to further this aim. Government propaganda on how to behave, how many children to have, what languages to speak (Mandarin, not Chinese dialects) have all been backed up by lavish media campaigns. Foremost among them was the campaign to create a sense of national identity to prevent ethnic conflicts between the many racial groups in the country.

The stranglehold of the PAP on parliament began to decline in the early 1980s, when for the first time an opposition member, J B Jeyaretnam, was elected. In the 1984 elections there was a 13 per cent swing against the PAP, in response to which they began a programme of 'self-renewal', looking to politicians of a younger generation to take over. After 31 years in power, Lee Kuan Yew himself stepped down in 1990 to make way for his chosen successor, Goh Chok Tong. Under Goh's leadership the style of politics in Singapore has shifted slightly, to become more flexible and open to the aspirations of the younger generation. Goh has promised more consenus-

Coat-of-arms, the Sultan of Perak's Palace, Istana Iskandariah, in Kuala Kangsar

style government, and greater participation in decision-making at the town council level. He has even allowed the showing of 'blue movies' (to which Singaporeans flocked in great numbers) to try and counter authoritarian-style government as part of a drive towards artistic creativity – an area in which the country is notably lacking.

In the 1991 elections there were still only four opposition members of parliament, a small minority but none the less one which offers the population an alternative to the heavy-handed, paternalistic regime of the PAP.

Like Singapore, Malaysia has gone in for a degree of 'social engineering' to promote racial harmony and a sense of national unity. In the wake of Independence in 1957, the Chinese emerged as the main force in business and commerce in the country, leaving the *bumiputras* (literally, the 'sons of the soil' – native Malays) economically backward, even if they did hold many of the élite positions in government. After a series of bloody race riots in 1970 the government introduced the New Economic Policy, or NEP, a controversial attempt to help Malays 'catch up' and reduce economic disparities by introducing racial quotas in employment. Instead of promoting racial harmony the NEP was a recipe for corruption and antagonised the rest of the population. It was eventually dropped in 1990. Despite ethnic tensions such as these, which still rage beneath the surface, Malaysia has enjoyed considerable stability and peace.

The ruling party is the United Malays National Organisation (UMNO), headed by the current Prime Minister Dato' Seri Dr Mahathir Mohamad. The Supreme Head of State

Malaysia's first Prime Minister, Tunku Abdul Rahman, gazes out from Parliament House

is the Yang Di Pertuan Agong, a constitutional monarch elected from amongst the nine Malay sultans for a period of five years by his fellow rulers.

Prior to the British colonial period the sultans reigned supreme in their sovereign states, their power unchallenged since they were answerable only to God. Although these powers were diluted by the British, their sovereignty was eventually guaranteed in the constitution following Independence. However, the position of the monarchy has recently come under scrutiny following charges of assault by the Sultan of Johor on members of the public. For centuries the sultans have enjoyed immunity from prosecution, but in 1993 parliament approved a bill to strip them of these rights.

PEOPLES OF MALAYSIA

Wander through any market in Malaysia and you will hear a babel of tongues as traders and customers converse in Chinese, Bahasa, Malay, Tamil and quite likely English as well. The peoples of Malaysia are a highly diverse mix of races and cultures.

The 10 million Malays comprise the majority of the population, although they are by no means a homogeneous group. Malays are sometimes referred to as the *bumiputras*, which means the Sons or Princes of the Soil. As the name implies, the *bumiputras* have traditionally been farmers or fishermen, the Malays. The first Chinese traders set up their warehouses in Melaka around the time of Admiral Cheng Ho's visit in the 15th century but the majority arrived during the 19th century. Escaping hard times in China, people from the southern provinces (principally Hokkiens, Hakkas, Teochews, Cantonese and Hainanese) came seeking their fortunes. The Chinese constitute the majority of Malaysia's traders, merchants and industrialists.

Malays and Chinese live side-by-side in almost every corner of Malaysia

but just as many now lead an urban life, particularly since Malays dominate in the civil service and government.

The tribal peoples of Sarawak and Sabah (see opposite) are also classed as *bumiputras*, as are the Orang Asli (see pages 60–1).

There are some 6 million Chinese in the country, the largest group after

Like the Chinese, the Indians had been coming to Malaysia for centuries, but it was not until the 19th century that they arrived in significant numbers. Most came to work on the plantations, and the majority were from southern India. Malaysian Indians mostly live on the west coast.

With 25 different ethnic groups in

Faces of Malaysia: a healer in Sabah (left), a Chinese man collecting cardboard (below) ...

... shoppers Kuala Lumpur (below left)

Sarawak and Sabah (including Malays and Chinese), the picture is far more complex. In Sarawak, the largest group are the Iban, who number around half a million. Although they live inland, Europeans named them 'sea dyaks' because of their frequent forays downriver to raid coastal areas. The Bidayuh, who built their houses on steep hillsides, became known as 'land dyaks'. Other tribes include the Melanau and the Orang Ulu ('up-river dwellers'), which includes the Penan, Kayan, Kenyah, Kelabit and Lun Bawan peoples.

In Sabah, the population comprises approximately 30 different ethnic groups and races, with the major indigenous peoples consisting of the Kadazan/Dusuns, the Bajau and the Murut (see pages 106–7).

Culture

*F*or centuries traders, immigrants and conquerors from all over the world have passed through Singapore and Malaysia, bringing with them their traditions, religions and lifestyles. The people of the region learned to change and adapt to new ways, and to live in tolerance with other races and creeds. Nowhere is this more obvious than in streets such as Jalan Tokong in Melaka, Telok Ayer Street in Singapore or Jalan Masjid Kapitan Kling in Georgetown, Pinang, in all of which you can find Taoist temples next to Islamic mosques and Hindu shrines.

In Singapore and Malaysia the Chinese populations contribute a wealth of festivals to the local lifestyles, the biggest one being the Chinese New Year in February. Chinese temples often combine different shrines to different gods, much as Chinese philosophy is a blend of Confucianism, Taoism and Buddhism. It is just as common to see young office workers throwing fortune sticks to divine the future as it is to see the older generation offering joss-sticks, fruit and flowers to the temple gods. Luck or 'joss' is an important part of everyday life, as is ancestor worship.

Malays are usually Muslims. They are expected to pray five times a day either at home, at work or in the *surau* – the village mosque, centre of Malay neighbourhoods. The most important event in the Islamic calendar is the month of Ramadan, during which Muslims fast from sunrise to sunset every day. At the conclusion of Ramadan, the festival of Hari Raya Puasa is a whirl of socialising and feasting.

The majority of the Indians in Singapore and Malaysia are Hindus. Major Hindu festivals range from the gentle, family-orientated Deepavali (or Festival of Lights) to the dramatic and gruesome Thaipusam Festival.

Offerings to the gods are a part of everyday life

FIRST STEPS

'Flat, steamy, thickly humid, the island lies there in its hot seas, fringed with mangrove swamps, and from the air it looks as it always did, a slightly desperate place that ought to be uninhabited. It looks like an invented place, and so of course it is.'

JAN MORRIS,
The City State (Singapore), an essay in Travels (1976)

First Steps

Singapore and Malaysia are both easy destinations for first-time visitors to Asia, with good transport links, telephones and other services that work, and a range of accommodation to suit all pockets. English is the only widely spoken western language in Singapore and in the tourist destinations in Malaysia (outside the resorts and cities a few words of Bahasa Malaysia, the national language, can be helpful).

Avoiding offence

Singapore is an extremely cosmopolitan city and residents are generally relaxed about visitors' behaviour. The two things most likely to cause offence in Malaysia are pointing at someone or touching them (see **Etiquette**, page 183). If you are sitting on the floor, whether inside a house or at a village function, men can sit cross-legged but women should sit sideways, with their feet tucked under them.

Wherever or whatever you are eating, the most important thing to remember is never to handle food or eat with your left hand – or worse still, offer someone food with your left hand. Food is always eaten with the right hand (the left hand is 'unclean' since it is normally used for personal ablutions).

Take it slowly while you find your feet and adjust to the tropical heat

Coping with the heat

Both Singapore and Malaysia are hot and humid for most of the year. If you are not used to the heat the best advice is to take it easy and start off by venturing out either in the early mornings or late afternoons, when temperatures are lower. An umbrella is excellent protection against both the fierce tropical sun and the sudden downpours that occur even in the so-called dry season. If you haven't brought one with you, cheap, folding umbrellas can be bought almost anywhere.

It's tempting to keep hopping into air-conditioned restaurants or shopping malls to cool off when you find yourself flagging, but be warned that the constant change of temperature is likely to give you a cold.

Culture shock

No-one is likely to suffer culture shock on landing in Singapore unless, of course, you have been travelling elsewhere in Asia and are not prepared for a futuristic city with a first-class infrastructure, well-planned, tree-lined streets and the almost total absence of crime and litter.

This pleasant environment has not been achieved without Singaporeans – and visitors – being subjected to a barrage of laws concerning litter and public behaviour (see **Etiquette**, page

Colourful processions are an everyday occurrence on the streets

183) of which you should be aware.

Culture shock is much more likely to hit you if you arrive in Kuala Lumpur and immediately set out to see the sights, only to find yourself over-whelmed by noise and vehicle fumes from the rush-hour traffic. Allow time to recover from jet-lag – spending the first day beside a hotel swimming-pool is always a good remedy – and only set out to explore when you feel full of energy again.

Greetings

Hand-shaking is normal when you are being introduced in either Singapore or Malaysia, although in the latter case men customarily do not shake hands with women, but instead bow respectfully. Nowadays women do tend to shake hands more, but if you are introduced to a Malaysian woman it is best to watch her behaviour first and take your cue from that. If she clasps her hands in front of her, stick to a bow.

Hassles

On the whole, Malaysia is a safe country for tourists and you are unlikely to encounter many problems provided you take normal, common-sense precautions.

Bag-snatches by thieves on motor-bikes have been reported in Kuala Lumpur, but it is fairly unusual. The most harassment you are likely to encounter is from an overly persistent salesman. There are very few beggars in Malaysia. Foreign females may provoke verbal harassment from Malay youths (particularly in beach-resort areas), but violence is rare. Singapore is generally acknowledged to be one of the safest cities in the world.

THE STRAITS CHINESE

In the ethnic melting-pot of the old Straits Settlements one of the most unusual cultural minorities to evolve were the Straits-born Chinese, or Peranakans ('local born'). Their origins date back to the early Chinese traders and settlers who intermarried with local Malay women (particularly from the west coast around Melaka), creating a new generation with their own unique heritage.

Peranakan men are referred to as Babas, unmarried women as Nyonyas, and older, married women as Bibis (as a group, they are also known as 'Baba Nyonyas'). Over the centuries the Peranakans prospered, creating their wealth in timber, tin, spices and, later on, rubber plantations. They evolved a luxurious lifestyle that flourished as a result of combining gracious Malay pastimes with Chinese business acumen. They speak their own dialect of Malay, with the addition of many Chinese colloquialisms, and developed their own style of cooking, which relied on unusual mixtures of piquant spices, coconut milk and *belacan* (dried shrimp paste).

The Peranakans are renowned for their taste in porcelain, which used to be specially commissioned from China. Known as Nyonyaware, it is characterised by bright colours and exuberant decorative motifs. Special sets of blue-and-white ceramics were also ordered for use during times of mourning and ancestral worship. Intricate beadwork and delicate, filigree silverware are also Peranakan hallmarks.

Peranakan culture was at its height during the colonial era, from the mid-19th century onwards. Not only did they show tremendous loyalty to the British Crown (to the extent that they were also known at one time as 'the King's Chinese'), but they also emulated the British lifestyle and adopted European clothing.

The art of living, Peranakan-style: tempting foods and lavish décor

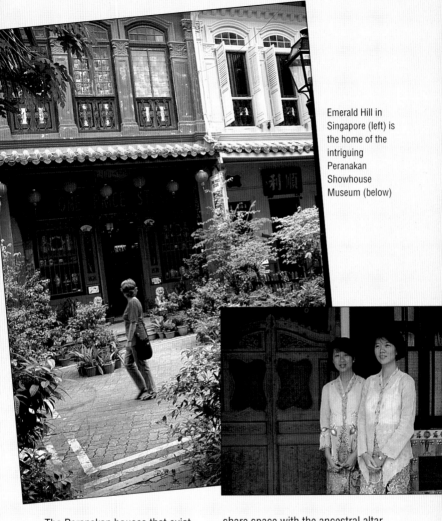

Emerald Hill in Singapore (left) is the home of the intriguing Peranakan Showhouse Museum (below)

The Peranakan houses that exist today give a fascinating glimpse into this unique fusion of cultures and lifestyles. Intricate Ching-dynasty tables and chairs, inlaid with mother-of-pearl, sit side-by-side with massive English-style sideboards and cupboards laden with crystal and the finest old brandies. Colonial 'planter's chairs', with their wicker seats and foot-rest extensions, share space with the ancestral altar covered in dragon carvings. Roll-top desks and pedestal-type telephones co-exist with embroidered Chinese wall-hangings and mah-jong tables. The houses themselves (which were built in a style known variously as Chinese palladian or Chinese baroque) are a riot of intricately carved screens and doors overlaid with gold leaf.

Skyscrapers in the business district overshadow the historic Singapore river basin

Hospitality

Singaporeans are well mannered and polite to visitors, although generally they keep their distance. It is unusual to be invited into someone's home on first acquaintance. None the less, you will be made to feel welcome. Malaysians tend to be more generous with their hospitality and it is important to remember that whenever you enter someone's home, be it a suburban apartment or a rural fisherman's hut, you should take off your shoes and leave them at the door. Never walk in anywhere uninvited.

What to wear

Although the old Chinese shopkeepers might prefer baggy shorts, sandals and a grubby T-shirt, young Singaporeans like to look smart and dress well. The same is true in Malaysia, although the young don't have the spending power of their contemporaries across the causeway. In neither case are they surprised if visitors fit the stereotype of the typical tourist, and informal attire is acceptable. However, in Malaysia in particular, bear in mind at all times that it is a Muslim society. A Muslim woman is expected to cover her arms, legs and head; non-Muslim women should dress appropriately, preferably with short or long sleeves (no bare shoulders) and knee-length skirts or shorts. Shorter skirts and more revealing clothes are acceptable in discos or clubs in Kuala Lumpur, but not necessarily in the daytime, and definitely not in small towns and villages. Topless bathing is absolutely out. The east coast of Malaysia is more strictly Muslim than the rest of the country.

Temples and mosques

Visitors are normally welcome in mosques outside prayer times, although you should not enter the inner prayer

Walking around Singapore is no problem

hall unless you are a Muslim. Both men and women will need to have their arms and legs covered, and robes are usually provided if you are not suitably dressed already. Never photograph people at prayer. Shoes should always be removed before entering mosques. The same applies to Indian temples, although not to Chinese temples.

EXPLORING SINGAPORE
City centre
The city of Singapore overlooks the Straits of Singapore on the southern side of the island. It is divided by the Singapore River, the heart of its historic development as a port. To the south of the river is the bustling area of Chinatown and the ever-growing skyscrapers of the financial district.

Immediately to the north of the river is the colonial heart of Singapore, with many of the most imposing buildings from that era centred around a large open space known as the Padang. Beyond the Padang is Raffles City, overshadowing the venerable Raffles Hotel. Continue northwards and you will reach Little India and Arab Street. Turn left and you will come to the start of Singapore's Golden Mile, the ever-open shopping malls and numerous luxury hotels centred on Orchard Road and Scotts Road.

Around the island
The majority of Singapore's residents live outside the city centre in satellite dormitory towns such as Queenstown, Kallang, Toa Payoh and Jurong. Most of Singapore's manufacturing industries are on the north coast. Many of the large theme parks, wildlife parks and similar attractions are outside the city centre to the west, in areas such as Jurong, but with comfortable, regular and cheap public transport, nowhere on the island is hard to reach. Remnants of the island's natural heritage can still be found outside the city centre. The last patch of the primary rain forest that once covered the island surrounds the highest hill, Bukit Timah.

Shoes must stay outside when visiting mosques

EXPLORING MALAYSIA
Kuala Lumpur

Usually referred to as simply 'KL', Kuala Lumpur is a sprawling city with a confusing street plan. From the visitors' point of view it can be roughly divided into two or three parts. Most of the international-class hotels are scattered over the eastern half of the city, with a cluster centred around Jalan Sultan Ismail. The majority of the cultural sights and tourist attractions are in the downtown area, some distance away. On the east side of the Klang River is Chinatown and the Central Market, while many of the city's historic buildings are on the west side of the river.

Statues outside a Chinese temple, Kuala Lumpur

The west coast

For centuries the west coast has been the centre of commerce in Malaysia, and this has given it some of the Peninsula's most intriguing historical towns and cultural sights. A popular excursion from Kuala Lumpur is to the port of Melaka on the southwest coast. Most of the country's top beach hotels are on the west coast islands, the best known of which is Pulau Pinang. To the north of Pinang is Pulau Langkawi and, further to the south, Pulau Pangkor, both of which are quieter and more unspoiled than Pinang.

Hill resorts in the highlands

The mountains of the Central Highlands are visible to the north of Kuala Lumpur on a clear day, beckoning to those intent on exploring the wilderness. The 'hill stations' of the highlands were established in colonial times so that Europeans could benefit from the cooler climate of the mountains, and they are still popular with both visitors and locals as a cool retreat from the heat of the plains and the coast. A hire car is a good idea if you want to visit several of the hill resorts or explore once you are there.

The east coast

Malaysia's east coast is less developed and more traditional in character than the west coast. Here you will find miles and miles of sandy beaches linking numerous fishing villages and coconut groves. Off shore, there are a number of small-scale, laid-back resorts on a string of islands which are accessible by ferries from the mainland. There is one main highway down the east coast and driving is easy, with very little traffic compared to the west coast.

Eastern Malaysia

Just over an hour's flight across the South China Sea, East Malaysia (comprising Sarawak and Sabah) is more of a challenge for the independent traveller, although package tours are available for those who don't feel confident enough to tackle it on their own. Although travel is more difficult, tourism is a fast-growing industry and there are plenty of first-rate hotels. Travelling costs are generally higher than on the peninsula.

WHAT TO SEE

'Penang has a certain Sicilian air.
It is a sort of Palermo, lacking
indeed the architecture and the
orange groves, but rich in a tropical
wealth of wicker huts and naked
children, of coco palms and jungle.'
ALDOUS HUXLEY,
Jesting Pilate (1926)

Singapore

*F*or many people Singapore is synonymous with gleaming skyscrapers and endless shopping malls. They have a vision of a modern and efficient city of air-conditioned concrete and glass buildings. Is this really all there is to Singapore? A decade ago the answer might have been 'yes'. While economists praised the achievement that has made Singapore the wealthiest country in Southeast Asia, visitors went elsewhere in search of the authentic Orient.

As visitors elected to spend fewer days in Singapore than elsewhere, the Government realised that it was losing income from an important sector of the economy and set up a special task force to tackle the problem. Its solution was an ambitious restoration programme for local architecture and historic buildings. The first project was the restoration of Emerald Hill, a small terrace of colourfully painted houses just off Orchard Road. Emerald Hill was an enormous success and became the prototype for a host of similar schemes.

Not only has much of old Singapore been saved but new attractions are constantly opening up and older ones are being upgraded. Many of these are theme parks where you could easily spend half a day or more, such as the old Haw Par Villa, re-opened in 1985 as a Chinese mythological theme park, or the Tang Dynasty Village, a hugely ambitious cultural and historical theme park. Not to be outdone, long-standing and popular attractions such as the Singapore Zoo and the Jurong Bird Park have recently invested millions of dollars in upgrading their already excellent facilities. Underwater World on Sentosa Island is one of Southeast Asia's largest and most impressive tropical sea-life centres.

Alongside these attractions the old cosmopolitan atmosphere of the city still

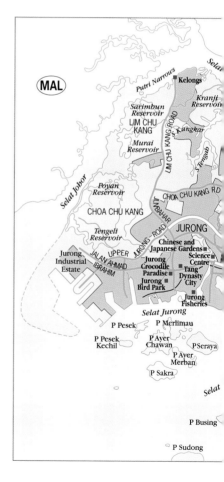

remains. In Little India, sari-clad women cluster over display cases of gold jewellery, while next door tantalising aromas waft from the open-fronted shop of the local spice-grinder. In nearby Arab Street, bales of multicoloured fabrics from all over the world are unloaded on the pavement and the plaintive wail of the *Bilai* calling the faithful to prayer can be heard echoing from the Sultan Mosque. In Chinatown, fortune-tellers and tailors are as much part of the street scene as temples and tea-houses. And when you have had your fill of all this, there is a fabulous range of restaurants to choose from, covering the whole spectrum from colonial elegance to noisy jazz cafés.

SINGAPORE ISLAND

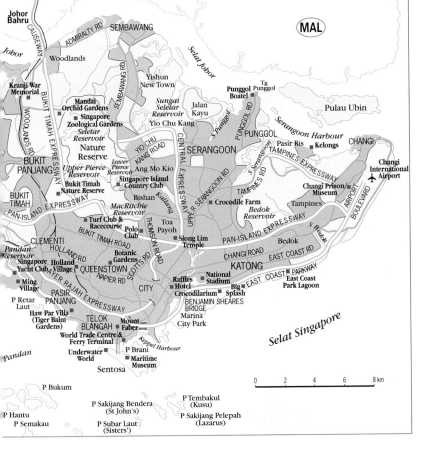

ARAB STREET

In the 19th century, merchants and traders from Malaya, Java, India and Arabia created a bustling community centred around Arab Street and the nearby Sultan Mosque on North Bridge Road. Arab Street is now the main centre for the textile trade, with Javanese batiks, Thai and French silks, sarongs, lace, brocades and colourful cottons piled to the ceilings in the shops down either side of the road. Leatherware and basketware shops also line the covered walkways, while nearby restaurants turn out tasty *murtabak* (savoury pancakes) and other snacks.

Bussorah Street, leading down from the Sultan Mosque, has become a pedestrian zone with more shops; many of the old houses surrounding Arab Street are being restored as part of the Kampung Glam Conservation Area. Near by on Beach Road is the Hajjah Fatimah Mosque, less grandiose than the Sultan Mosque, built by a Malay woman called Hajjah Fatimah in honour of her late husband.
Both mosques can be visited outside of prayer times. MRT: Bugis.

ARMENIAN APOSTOLIC CHURCH OF ST GREGORY (1835)

Considered to be one of the finest works of the colonial architect George Coleman (who also designed Parliament House and the Supreme Court), the Church of St Gregory the Illuminator was commissioned by Singapore's once-thriving Armenian community, refugees from Turkey. In the graveyard are the weather-beaten tombs of many of the Armenian settlers, including that of Agnes Joaquim, after whom Singapore's national orchid, the *Vanda* 'Miss Joaquim', is named.

The oldest surviving church in the country, St Gregory's is now a national monument and no longer used as a place of worship.
Hill Street, below Fort Canning. MRT: City Hall. Bus: 124, 173, 174.

BIRD CAFÉ

Every Sunday morning from 8am onwards bird enthusiasts congregate in this small outdoor café for breakfast and a little friendly singing competition between their feathered charges. In their bamboo cages suspended on a grid above the café, melodious *merboks* and *sharmas* trill away while their owners compare diets and handling techniques. Every so often the owners move their birds around, hoping that proximity to a different neighbour will produce sweeter sounds. Some of the bamboo cages, which are decorated with porcelain or jade ornaments, are over 80 years old.
Junction of Tiong Bahru and Seng Poh Roads. MRT: Either Tiong Bahru or Outram Park. Bus: 103, 123.

BOTANIC GARDENS

Just a short distance past the northern end of Orchard Road, the attractively landscaped Botanic Gardens contain some 2,000 tropical and sub-tropical species of plants and trees. The grounds are popular with joggers and walkers at the weekends, with well-maintained paths meandering between lakes, gazebos, fountains and rose and fern gardens. The 52-hectare site also includes a small patch of primary jungle and the spectacular National Orchid Garden with over 60,000 specimens. A 'reverse greenhouse' enables alpine and cold-climate plants to flourish.

The garden's genesis lies with Sir Stamford Raffles, himself a keen naturalist, who established the first 'Botanical and Experimental Garden' in 1822 on Fort Canning Hill (then known as Government Hill) with the aim of introducing crops yielding spices, timber and raw materials to the island. The present gardens were established in 1859 and continued their role in fostering potentially useful plants. One of their earliest successes was the introduction from Brazil in 1877 of rubber trees, using seeds sent out by London's Kew Gardens. Henry Ridley, one of the early directors, conducted a relentless campaign to convince local planters to grow rubber, but once the pneumatic tyre was invented his perseverance paid off.

Today, the gardens continue to serve as an important centre for botanical and horticultural research, particularly in orchid breeding. Trail leaflets indicate where some of the more interesting and unusual or economically significant plants can be found in the gardens. *Main entrances: Main Gate, junction of Cluny and Holland roads; Tyersall Avenue (opposite the Orchid Garden). Open: daily, 5am–midnight. Admission free. SBS bus: 7, 105, 106, 123 and 174 from Orchard Boulevard.*

Colourful blooms in Singapore's Botanic Gardens

SINGAPORE – THE GARDEN CITY

One of the first things you notice in Singapore is the tropical greenery which flourishes everywhere, disguising concrete bridges and brightening up the roadside verges. This is not simply nature taking over, but part of a concerted strategy which began in the 1960s to turn Singapore into a Garden City. In the early days, the plan was limited to roadside tree-planting and creating parks. In the 1970s and 80s the scheme developed further with the introduction of fruit trees, ferns, vines and more colourful and fragrant plants. In the 1990s, the concept has grown to include a network of walkways, cycleways and canal-side paths which are currently being developed to link together reserves, residential areas and parks.

Even in the tropical humidity, this luxuriance means that Singapore has become one of the most enjoyable cities in Asia to visit.

BUKIT TIMAH NATURE RESERVE

This 81-hectare reserve is all that remains of the rain forests that once covered the island. It encompasses Singapore's biggest hill, Bukit Timah, a granite outcrop 162m high, which affords good views. From the Visitor Centre, well-marked trails branch off and thread their way around the hillsides (see **Bukit Timah walk**, pages 44–5).
Just off Upper Bukit Timah Road, at the end of Hindhede Drive (12km from Orchard Road). Open: daily, 8.30am– 6pm. Admission free. MRT: Newton, then TIBS bus 171 or 182.

CHANGI PRISON CHAPEL AND MUSEUM

Situated in the grounds of the current Changi Prison, the museum is a moving testimony to the lives of the Allied prisoners-of-war who were incarcerated here during the Japanese occupation of Singapore.
Changi Prison, Upper Changi Road North. Open: Monday to Saturday, 9.30am–4.30pm. Closed: Sundays and public holidays. MRT: Tanah Merah, then SBS bus 2. Bus: 2, 14.

CHETTIAR TEMPLE

Dedicated to the six-headed Hindu deity Lord Subramaniam, the original temple (built in 1860) was financed by local *chettiars*, or money-lenders. Rebuilt in 1984, the entrance features a typical South Indian *gopuram* (gateway), but its most unusual feature is a series of 48 glass panels in the ceiling engraved with images of the deities, which are designed to catch the light of the rising and setting sun. The temple is the starting point for the Singaporean Thaipusam festival (see **Festivals**, pages 142–3).

Tank Road. Open: daily, 8am–noon, 5.30–8.30pm. MRT: Dhoby Ghaut. Bus: 123, 143.

CHINAMAN SCHOLAR'S GALLERY

An interesting little museum assembled by antique dealer Vincent Tan, who has re-created a typical Cantonese scholar/merchant's house from the 1920s and '30s. The house contains a collection of embroideries, calligraphy and traditional Chinese stringed instruments. Mr Tan will demonstrate the instruments and perform a tea ceremony for groups.
14-B Terengganu Street (tel: 222 9554). Open: 9am–4pm, but call to check first. Admission charge.

CHINATOWN

Bounded by the Singapore River to the north and the financial district to the east, Chinatown is no longer the maze of crumbling façades and run-down shop-houses that used to exert such charm. Many areas have been or are in the process of being restored, and the new occupants are design consultants, software suppliers and architectural firms rather than the clog-makers and reflexologists who once lived here (and are now unable to afford to move back in). However, Chinatown still manages to convey something of the flavour of old Singapore and is well worth visiting (see **Chinatown walk**, pages 42–3).

CHINESE AND JAPANESE GARDENS

Linked by the 65m Bridge of Double Beauty, the two gardens have been created on adjoining islands in the Jurong Lake. The Chinese Garden ('Yu Hwa Yuan'), covering 13 hectares, re-creates the exuberant style of the Sung

SINGAPORE CITY

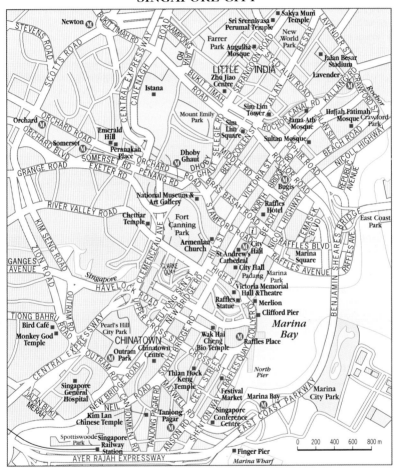

Dynasty and Beijing's Summer Palace gardens, and includes the Penjing Garden ('Yun Xiu Yuan'), the largest Suzhou-style garden outside China, with over 3,000 bonsai specimens.

In contrast, the Japanese gardens are in a minimalist style emphasising the spatial relationships between rocks, gravel, water, shrubs and a tea-house to create the calm, reflective atmosphere in keeping with its name, 'Seiwaen', the Garden of Tranquillity.

1 Chinese Garden Road, Jurong (tel: 264 3455). Open: daily 9am–6pm. Admission charge. MRT: Chinese Garden. Bus: 82, 154, 335, 951.

COLONIAL SINGAPORE

When Raffles first landed in Singapore the only part of the island not then covered in swampy mangroves was a small area that became known as the Padang (Malay for 'open space'), and which eventually became the central focus of the colonial administration. The Padang is still the seat of judicial and parliamentary rule.

City Hall

Built in 1929, this imposing building housed the Municipal Offices until King George VI granted Singapore the status of a city in 1952, after which it became known as City Hall.

Empress Place Building

This impressive neo-classical building was built in 1865 as the East India Company court house and was originally much smaller than it is now. Five

different extensions were added to accommodate government departments, and fortunately none of these additions departed from the original design. The whole building eventually fell into a state of considerable disrepair and has recently been painstakingly renovated. It is now a world-class exhibition centre, largely focusing on Asian material, particularly Chinese culture. The museum has an agreement with China to feature a series of rotating exhibitions of priceless and rare artefacts from various Chinese dynasties, many of which have never been seen outside China before, combined with an extremely high standard of interpretative material.

1 Empress Place (tel: 336 733). Open: daily, 9am–7.30pm. Admission charge.

Merlion Park

This small park is on the promontory where the Singapore River flows out into the harbour. The Merlion was adopted in the 1960s as the emblem of Singapore. According to legend the Merlion is a mythical beast, said to be half-lion, half-fish, which appeared to Prince Sri Tri Buana around 700 years ago.

Open: daily.

Padang

The cricket and parade ground is the traditional setting for ceremonies on National Day (9 August). At one end lies the Singapore Cricket Club, at the other the Singapore Recreation Club. Cricket matches take place on the Padang at weekends between March and October.

The immaculately restored Empress Place Building, now an exhibition centre

Parliament House
Originally a private mansion of 1827, designed by George Coleman, who stamped his mark on much of Singapore's colonial heritage. Parliament House is Singapore's oldest government building.

Raffles Statue
Located near where Sir Stamford Raffles is thought to have landed in 1819, this is one of two Raffles statues: the original bronze cast (of which this is a replica) is in front of the Victoria Theatre in Empress Place.

St Andrew's Cathedral
Completed in 1861 by Indian convicts (see **Little India**, page 36–7) who used a special plaster known as Madras Chunam (incorporating shell lime, egg white, sugar and coconut husks), St Andrew's withstood the elements for nearly 125 years before needing refurbishment. The neo-Gothic building, with a cool blue-and-white inside, has now been completely renovated.
Open: daily.

Supreme Court
Built in 1939 and adjacent to City Hall, the classically inspired Supreme Court occupies the site of the old Europe Hotel, a renowned watering-hole for the colonial élite.
Open: Monday to Friday, 8am–5pm. Tel: 336 1544. Admission free.

Victoria Memorial Hall and Theatre
Situated opposite Parliament House, this was once the Town Hall. It was later converted into a ballroom and theatre, and is now home to the Singapore Symphony Orchestra (see **Entertainment**, page 137).

SIR STAMFORD RAFFLES
The founder of Singapore, Stamford Raffles, was born in 1781 aboard the ship that his father captained off the coast of Jamaica. It was an auspicious beginning for the man who was to establish one of the world's greatest seaports.

At the age of 15, Raffles started work in the East India Company and rose up the ranks to become Lieutenant Governor of Java by the time he was 30. Posted to Sumatra, he chafed as he saw the Dutch take control of regional trade, using Melaka as their base. He urged Lord Hastings, the Governor General of India, to establish a colony that could compete with the Dutch for supremacy.

He landed in Singapore on 29 January 1819, and negotiated a treaty with the Sultan of Johor giving the East India Company permission to establish a trading post. Traders were soon attracted by the novelty of free-port status, and Singapore grew quickly.

Three years later Raffles, returning from Sumatra, was dismayed to discover the ramshackle development of the port; he immediately set out to rectify this by drawing up detailed plans allocating different areas for government offices and for the many ethnic groups who had settled there. Raffles left Singapore in 1823 and died soon after, but the legacy of his master plan is still evident today in the communities of Little India, Chinatown and Arab Street.

Cavorting with crocs draws crowds at Jurong Crocodile Paradise

CROCODILE PARKS

Singapore has three crocodile farms, all of which are open to visitors. They are not all good. At the worst, you are likely to see no more than a sad display of dozens of crocodiles penned into small concrete enclosures waiting to be turned into handbags and other fashion accessories. At the Crocodilarium, on the East Coast Parkway, the only information available is on the price tags attached to the crocodile-skin products on sale in the adjoining handbag emporium.

Of them all, the least like a crocodile-handbag factory is Jurong Crocodile Paradise, next door to the Jurong Bird Park, where over 2,500 crocodiles of various species are on display. There is also a Crocodile Underwater Viewing Gallery, a Golden Pythons Display, and regular crocodile wrestling and feeding shows.

Jalan Ahmad Ibrahim (tel: 261 8866). Open: daily, 9am–6pm. Admission charge. MRT: Boon Lay, then bus 194, 251 or 255.

FORT CANNING

Originally known as Bukit Larangan, or the 'Forbidden Hill', legend has it that the last Malay ruler of the kingdom of Singapura, Sultan Iskandar Shah, was buried here after his kingdom was destroyed by the Sumatran Majapahites in 1391. Consequently, Malays considered it sacred ground and access was banned long after the last Malay king had died. Ignoring this taboo, Sir Stamford Raffles built his own bungalow, Singapore's first Government House, at the top of the hill. Misfortune struck: Raffles lost three of his four children and was only 42 when he himself died of a brain tumour.

In 1859 the house was demolished to make way for Fort Canning. During the 1930s an underground bunker system was built inside the hill, and it became the Far East Command and Control Centre during World War II. Said to be the largest underground bunker system in the world (more extensive than Hitler's), it was from here that the British High Command made the decision to surrender Singapore. Although the British destroyed as much as they could before the Japanese arrived, old photographs of the interior survived and the bunker system is now being re-created in authentic detail by the National Parks Board as a tourist attraction.

On the east slope of the hill a Christian cemetery holds the weathered tombstones of many Singapore pioneers. Just above here is the Fort Canning Centre, home to the Singapore Dance Theatre and an art gallery. *MRT: City Hall.*

GUINNESS WORLD OF RECORDS

The usual waxworks and other exhibits portray people with extremely tall, fat or small bodies and firsts in human achievements. The Asian section includes record-breaking facts from the region. It is worth a quick glance if you happen to be waiting for a ferry at the World Trade Centre.

02–07 World Trade Centre, 1 Maritime Square, Telok Blangah Road (tel: 271 8344). Open: daily, 9.30am–8.30pm. Admission charge. Bus: 65,143, 167.

HARBOUR AND RIVER

A sheltered, deep-water harbour was one of the island's main assets when Raffles spotted its potential as a strategic trading post. Flowing into the natural harbour, the Singapore River soon became the commercial and historical hub of the new colony.

The low-slung, sturdy craft that plied back and forth were known as bumboats, traditionally painted with eyes on the bows to enable them to see the way ahead. Until just a few years ago hundreds of bumboats could be seen moored at Boat Quay in front of the business district. However, as part of a major programme to clean up pollution in the Singapore River, the bumboats were relocated to wharves west of the city centre. A few dozen can still be seen moored off Clifford Pier, from where they ferry crew to and from ships at anchor. You can also take a 30-minute bumboat cruise, with taped commentary on the historic sights of the river and its many bridges. Harbour cruises are popular and an enormous range of tours is available, from basic trips round the bay to a full-blown dinner extravaganza on a Chinese junk, or *tongkang.*

Bumboat river cruises leave from the landing steps next to Parliament House at regular intervals between 9am and 7pm. Tongkang *trips start around 10.30am and last approximately 2½ hours. Dinner cruises start at 6pm and last around 2–2½hours.*

Contact Eastwind Organisation (tel: 533 3432); Watertours (tel: 533 9811); or your hotel tour desk.

HAW PAR VILLA DRAGON WORLD

The Haw Par brothers (Aw Boon Haw and Aw Boon Par) inherited a fortune based on the invention of Tiger Balm, a cure-all ointment still widely sold throughout Asia. Haw Par Villa was one of the Aw family's three residences in Singapore and originally had a zoo in the grounds until the Government brought in licensing for zoos. The Haw Par brothers replaced the animals with over 1,000 statues depicting scenes from popular Chinese myths and legends. By the 1980s these gaudy displays had become tawdry and uninteresting, and in 1988 the park closed. It has now re-opened, covering five times its original size, as a Chinese mythological theme park. The original statuary has not been overlooked and a 'Tales of China' boat-ride floats past the tableaux which demonstrate the various punishments awaiting sinners in the Chinese underworld.

New attractions at the park include a flume ride, a large outdoor amphitheatre with dragon dances, acrobats and other regular performances, and three further theatres with special-effect videos, lasers and computerised shows. A variety of 'fringe' performances take place throughout the park, among them a highly entertaining story-telling show at the Four Seasons amphitheatre where members of the audience are enrolled to enact myths and fables.

262 Pasir Panjang Road (tel: 774 0300). Open: daily, 9am–6pm. Admission charge, includes all rides and shows. MRT: Buona Vista, then bus 200. Bus: 10, 30, 51, 143.

Colourful macaws, kings of the parrot family, greet visitors at the entrance to Jurong Bird Park

JURONG BIRD PARK

Set in 20 hectares of grounds, the Bird Park houses one of the largest and most spectacular collections of exotic birds in the world, with over 8,000 birds from around 600 different species in spacious enclosures. You can walk around for a close look at their beautiful plumage in the larger aviaries, such as the Southeast Asian Birds enclosure (which simulates a rain forest environment, complete with rainshowers) and the Waterfall Aviary (which has over 1,200 free-flying tropical birds and a 30m waterfall).

The park has a monorail that glides round at tree-top level and passes through the Waterfall Aviary. Other attractions include Pelican Lake, a Hornbill and Toucan exhibit and the Penguin Parade with an underwater viewing chamber. Shows staged at intervals throughout the day include a magnificent Birds of Prey show, Penguin and Pelican feedings, and the All Stars Birdshow.

Jalan Ahmad Ibrahim (tel: 265 0022). Open: daily, 9am–6pm. Admission charge (excluding monorail charge). MRT: Boon Lay, then bus 194 or 251.

LAU PA SAT FESTIVAL MARKET (TELOK AYER MARKET)

This ornamental, Victorian cast-iron building, which used to be known as the Telok Ayer Market, had to be moved because the structure was unable to withstand the rigours of nearby work on the MRT (Mass Rapid Transit). It has been reborn as the Lau Pa Sat Festival Market ('Lau Pa Sat' means the 'old market' in Hokkein).

Built in 1894, the octagonal-shaped market was constructed using cast-iron frames specially shipped over from Glasgow, Scotland. The intricate filigree ornamentation and tall pillars supporting the roof have been restored and painted white, creating a sense of light and space within the structure. A popular hawker centre for many years before renovation, it is now an up-market Food Hall. There are a number of craft stalls and regular performances by dancers, stilt-walkers, magicians and musicians.

18 Raffles Quay (tel: 222 9930). MRT: Raffles Place.

LITTLE INDIA

Although not as extensive as Chinatown, Little India is an interesting area to explore on foot (see **Little India walk**, pages 46–7). The central focus of Little India is Serangoon Road. Along here and in the streets off to either side, the

sari-sellers, fortune-tellers and spice-millers evoke the sights and sounds of the Indian sub-continent. Although Indian traders had crossed the ocean to Malaysia over a 1,000 years ago and founded coastal settlements, most of the Indians who arrived in Singapore in its founding years had little choice. The British East India Company in Calcutta decided Singapore was a convenient place to send convicts, and thousands were sent over to build roads and canals and clear the mangrove swamps. St Andrew's Cathedral and the Istana (home of the President) are among the buildings constructed by convict labour. When a penal colony was built on the Andaman Islands in the 1860s those with life-sentences were transferred from Singapore, but many other prisoners were pardoned and given land around Serangoon Road, near their former ´ prison. With the continuing influx of voluntary immigrants the community expanded and developed, creating the basis for what is now known as Little India.
MRT: Bugis. Bus: 64, 65, 92, 106, 111.

MANDAI ORCHID GARDENS

Covering 4 hectares of landscaped grounds, the Mandai Orchid Gardens are the largest on the island with a huge variety of species to admire. A visit here can be combined with the Zoological Gardens next door (see page 41).
Mandai Lake Road (tel: 269 1036). Open: daily, 8.30am–5.30pm. Admission charge. MRT: Ang Mo Kio, then bus 138. Bus: 171 from Orchard Road or the Zoo Express shuttle bus, which picks up from major hotels (tel: 235 3111 for schedules).

NATIONAL MUSEUM AND ART GALLERY

Opened in 1887 in honour of Queen Victoria's Golden Jubilee, this splendid building was formerly the Raffles Museum. It now houses permanent exhibits, which include a series of 'dioramas' on the ground floor (with waxwork tableaux illustrating early lifestyles and historic scenes), the Straits Chinese Collection in the Sireh Gallery (first floor), and the renowned Haw Par collection of magnificent jade, agate, jasper and crystal carvings.

Temporary exhibits highlight a wide range of Asian arts and crafts. Daily multi-slide shows (between 10.15am and 3.45pm) focus on topics such as the Singapore River, Malay *kampungs*, Chinatown and the development of Singapore as a nation.

The adjacent Art Gallery features exhibitions of Singaporean and Asian artists drawn from their permanent collections, as well as local exhibitions.
Stamford Road (tel: 1800 336 1460). Open: Tuesday to Sunday, 9am–5.30pm. Admission charge. MRT: City Hall or Dhoby Ghaut.

Cultivating and exporting orchids is big business in Singapore

The resplendent façade of the Raffles Hotel, one of Singapore's most well-known sights

PERANAKAN PLACE AND MUSEUM

Situated on the corner of Orchard Road and Emerald Hill, Peranakan Place is a complex of old Straits-Chinese shop-houses now containing restaurants and coffee-shops, with the museum just next door. The house containing the museum was lived in by a Peranakan family until as recently as 1985, and displays a collection of Peranakan furniture, bridal gowns, porcelain and embroidery. See **The Straits Chinese**, pages 20–1.
Emerald Hill, off Orchard Road (tel: 732 6966). Open: Monday to Friday, 10.30am–3.30pm. Admission charge. MRT: Somerset.

RAFFLES HOTEL AND MUSEUM

Between 1989 and 1991 the revered Raffles Hotel underwent a major face-lift and was extended to include the Raffles Arcade, with three floors of chic, up-market boutiques. The hotel rooms have been converted to suites, decorated in 1920s style; the famous Long Bar has been moved and now occupies two floors to accommodate the coachloads of tourists who pour in for their obligatory gin sling. Traditionalists will no doubt mourn the loss of the old-style Raffles, but if you haven't been there before you will enjoy the atmosphere in the Raffles Grill or the Tiffin Room.

One of the bonuses of the new Raffles is the intriguing and delightful Raffles Hotel Museum, where artefacts and memorabilia from the 'Golden Age of Travel' (roughly the period 1880 to 1939, which corresponded with the opening of Raffles and its rise to prominence as the 'Grand Old Lady of the East') are on display. As well as letters, postcards and photographs bearing witness to its many illustrious visitors, from Charlie Chaplin through to US Presidents, there is also a collection of wonderful shipping and luggage labels, period photographs of Singapore, and old travel guides.

Possibly Raffles' most well-known

patrons were writers such as Rudyard Kipling, Joseph Conrad and Somerset Maugham. The hotel's original owners, the Armenian Sarkie brothers, used these connections shamelessly, quoting Kipling in their advertising as having written: 'Providence led me to a place called Raffles Hotel, where the food is as excellent as the rooms are good. Let the Traveller take note: Feed at Raffles and Sleep at Raffles'. In fact, what Kipling actually wrote in *Sea to Sea* was: '...Raffles Hotel, where the food is as excellent as the rooms are bad. Let the Traveller take note: Feed at Raffles and sleep at the Hotel de L'Europe'!

1 Beach Road (tel: 337 1886). Museum open: daily, 10am–9pm. Admission free. MRT: City Hall.

SAKYA MUNI TEMPLE

This simple Buddhist temple, built in the style of a Thai *wat*, was constructed by a Thai monk, Vutthisasara, who came to Singapore in the 1880s determined to erect a monument to the Enlightened One. He built the entire temple with his own hands and died in the 1970s, aged 94, his task complete. It is also known as the Temple of a Thousand Lights since the central, 15m-high statue of a seated Buddha is surrounded by a halo of lights. Around the base of the statue, scenes depict the life of Buddha.

366 Race Course Road. Open: daily, 7am–4.45pm. Bus: 64, 65, 106 or 111.

SENTOSA ISLAND, see **Excursions**, pages 48–9.

SINGAPORE SCIENCE CENTRE

There is almost no such thing as a dull museum in Singapore, especially where families and children are the main targets, and if it can be made more

interactive – and more fun – then it will be. The Science Centre is no exception, and it's a great place to let children loose to prod, poke, peer, press and play with everything in sight, which they can and will do – meanwhile, possibly learning a thing or two about the principles of flight, the workings of the human body, or computers and lasers.

Next door is the Omnimax cinema, where films are projected through a 180-degree fish-eye lens on to a huge domed screen, giving a complete wrap-around image. Film shows change regularly.

Science Centre Road, Jurong. Open: Tuesday to Sunday, 10am–6pm. Admission charge. Films are screened from noon to 8pm (tel: 560 3316 for details); admission charge. MRT: Jurong East and then bus 335. Bus: 66, 178, 198, 336.

SIONG LIM TEMPLE

Built between 1898 and 1908, this is one of the largest Buddhist temples in Singapore and is now a National Monument. Thought to have been founded by a Seow family from China, the original construction was funded by two Hokkien merchants. It houses numerous shrines and works of religious art, including carved marble Buddha statues from Thailand.

184-E Jalan Toa Payoh. MRT: Toa Payoh.

Aviation explained at the Science Centre

SRI MARIAMMAN TEMPLE

The oldest Hindu temple in Singapore, originally built by Nariana Pillay, an early Indian pioneer who arrived with Raffles in 1819. The initial wood and *atap* (thatch) structure was replaced by the present building in 1843, which was extensively refurbished in 1984 by South Indian craftsmen. The South Indian Dravidian influence is evident in the colourful towering *gopuram* (gateway) with its mass of sculptured figures depicting mythological scenes. It is now a National Monument.

Early morning or early evening is the best time to visit, when devotees make their prayers to the accompaniment of temple music. In October/November the temple is the setting for the annual Thimithi, or Fire-Walking Festival (see **Festivals**, page 143).
244 South Bridge Road. MRT: Raffles Place. Bus: 124, 174.

The Dravidian-style Sri Mariamman Temple

TANG DYNASTY CITY

This large new theme park in the Jurong suburb is a re-creation of the 7th-century capital city of Tang Dynasty China, Chang 'An, which flourished as the starting point for the Silk Road across Asia. Built by the same company that runs the Sung Dynasty Village in Hong Kong, this 'living museum' is spread over 12 hectares and incorporates replicas of the six palaces of the Imperial City, a five-storey pagoda, 1,100 Terracotta Warriors in an Underground Palace, a Silk Road Market Place with tea-houses, medical halls, fortune-tellers, calligraphers, potteries, a court house, and the House of a Thousand Pleasures brothel (although all you will receive there is a history lesson on how consorts lived at the time).

Actors in period costumes bring the scene to life, staging festivals, events and acrobatics throughout the day. The park also incorporates three film studios (in which you can star in your own *Kung Fu* movie) with regular stunt-show performances.
2 Yuan Ching Road (tel: 261 1116). Open: daily, 10am–6.30pm. Admission charge. MRT: Lakeside, then taxi or bus 154, 240.

THIAN HOCK KENG TEMPLE

Completed in 1841, the Temple of Heavenly Happiness is one of the most ornate in Singapore, and the oldest Hokkien temple on the island. The present temple replaced an earlier josshouse (shrine) on the same site, then on Singapore's waterfront, which grew wealthy with the offerings of grateful immigrants for their safe arrival. The shrine of Ma Chu Por, the Mother of Heavenly Sages and Goddess of the Sea, dominates the central courtyard.

Orang-utans are among the thousands of animals kept in 'open' enclosures at the Zoo

Telok Ayer Street. MRT: Raffles Place.
Bus: 124, 167, 174, 179, 182, 190.

ZOOLOGICAL GARDENS

Founded in 1973, the Singapore
Zoological Gardens were designed from
the start to avoid cages as much as
possible. Instead, the emphasis has
always been on providing the animals
with as natural a habitat as possible,
keeping them in breeding groups or
landscaped enclosures where different
animals live together as they might do in
the wild. The zoo says that the success
of its breeding programme is proof that
this has worked.

The zoo is often hailed as one of the
most beautiful in the world, and it is not
hard to see why, given the combination
of well-landscaped grounds on the edge
of the Seletar reservoir and healthy-
looking animals roaming in spacious
enclosures.

From their original collection of just
270 animals, the zoo has expanded to
accommodate over 2,000 animals of
nearly 200 species. The captive breeding
programme of rare species has included
polar bear cubs, orang-utans, Cape
hunting dogs, Indian rock pythons,
rhinoceros iguanas, ruffed lemurs,
pygmy hippos, Malayan tapirs, oryx and
Himalayan thars.

Animal feedings and shows are
almost continuous throughout the day.
Breakfast with Ah Meng, a Sumatran
orang-utan, is particularly popular.
There are also underwater viewing areas
for polar bears, sea-lions and penguins,
crocodiles and pygmy hippos, as well as
elephant, camel and pony rides. A
recent addition is Children's World,
with a miniature railway, play area and
'animal contact' area.

80 Mandai Lake Road (tel: 269 3411).
Open: daily, 8.30am–6pm. Admission
charge. MRT: Yishun, then bus 171 or
Ang Mo Kio, then bus 138. The Zoo
Express leaves twice daily from major hotels
(tel: 235 3111 for information).

Chinatown

This walk encompasses many of the older streets
in Chinatown, several temples, shrines and
mosques, and the newly smartened-up
conservation areas with their pastel-coloured
façades in the vernacular Singapore style. *Allow
2–3 hours.*

*From the Raffles Place MRT station, head north and turn left in
Chulia Street, then take the first right which leads to Boat Quay.*

1 BOAT QUAY

One of the most recent areas to be spruced up, Boat Quay
is now a pleasant waterfront promenade with views of the
Raffles Landing Site. The river basin in front of Boat Quay

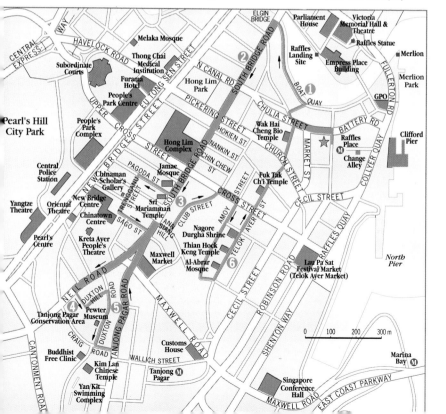

was once the hub of this busy port.
Walk along Boat Quay towards Elgin Bridge. At the bridge, turn left and proceed down South Bridge Road.

2 SOUTH BRIDGE ROAD

The side streets off to your left – such as Hokkien Street, Nanking Street and Chin Chew Street – are worth exploring to see some of the traditional, pre-renovation Chinese family houses.
Continue down South Bridge Road, across Cross Street, until you come to the Sri Mariamman Temple (see page 40).

3 SRI MARIAMMAN TEMPLE AREA

Wandering around in the streets behind the temple you will come across some fine examples of restored Chinese town houses, resplendent in their pastel-coloured paintwork. Alongside the shops selling Chinese knick-knacks and souvenirs some old businesses still survive. Tucked away up two flights of stairs above a herbal medicine shop in Trengganu Street is the Chinaman Scholar's Gallery (see page 30).
Re-enter South Bridge Road and head south, crossing over where it becomes Neil Road, to reach the Tanjong Pagar Conservation Area.

4 TANJONG PAGAR CONSERVATION AREA

The area includes many old ornamental shop-houses with intricately decorated façades restored to their former vibrancy. In the arcade at 51 Neil Street, the small Tanjong Pagar Heritage Exhibition traces the history of the community back to the days when it was a Malay fishing village, later to become the centre for nutmeg plantations owned by European settlers.

Make your way up Duxton Hill, at the heart of Tanjong Pagar, and turn right down Duxton Road.

5 PEWTER MUSEUM

Set in three restored shops at 49a Duxton Road is a Pewter Museum and showroom, with exhibits including the traditional tools and antique items dating back to the beginnings of the pewter industry.
Turn left into Craig Road and left again into Tanjong Pagar Road. Cross Maxwell Road, then turn right up Ann Siang Hill and left into Club Street. At Cross Street, turn right and then right again into Amoy Street. Follow this to the end, doubling back down Telok Ayer Street.

6 TELOK AYER STREET

Since Telok Ayer Street was once on the waterfront it was a natural site for places of worship, hence several mosques and Chinese temples were built here. The first mosque is the Al-Abrar Mosque, which began life as a thatched hut; the present building was erected between 1850 and 1855. Just past here lie the Thian Hock Keng Temple (see page 40) and the Tamil Nagore Durgha Shrine. Beyond Cross Street is the Fuk Tak Ch'i Temple, also known as the Temple of Prosperity and Virtue.
Continue to the end of Telok Ayer Street and turn right to return to Raffles Place.

Tanjong Pagar Heritage Exhibition, 51 Neil Road. Open: daily, 11am–6pm. Admission free.
Pewter Museum, 49a Duxton Road (tel: 221 4436). Open: daily, 9am–5.30pm. Admission free.

Bukit Timah Nature Reserve

This walk links together several of the signposted trails in the reserve. It is an easy walk for most of the way, apart from one section of the aptly named Rock Path, where you have to scramble over boulders for a short way (this is easily by-passed if necessary). There are plenty of rest benches and hut shelters on the trails. *Allow 2–2½ hours.*

From the Visitor Centre, head uphill and take the first right-hand fork, marked Lower Path.

1 DIPTEROCARP FOREST

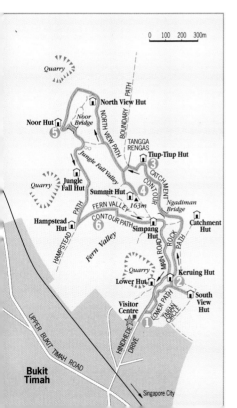

The reserve is a good introduction to the ferns and trees of the dipterocarp forests characteristic of the region. Many of the more common forest trees are labelled on this track for easy identification. Of particular note here are the towering seraya (*Shorea cutisii*), one of the most common dipterocarps. The older trees are supported by strong, thick buttresses at the base.
Keep straight on where the path forks right to the Taban Circle. At the top of the next gradient, you can detour right to South View Hut. Back at the junction, continue along Keruing Path.

2 GIANT KERUINGS

This path is named after another of the more abundant and typical dipterocarp species, the keruing. A commercially valuable species, keruings grow to great heights, like the seraya, with their topmost branches pushing out above the general forest canopy 50m up. Another giant species seen along this path is the barking deer mango, so called because barking deer are said to be partial to its fruits.

Where the path meets the road again at Keruing Hut, turn right where it is signposted Rock Path and Catchment Contour. To avoid the Rock Path, keep on up the road to the Summit Hut. Continue right along Contour Path. At the junction with Boundary Path follow the signs to Jalan Tiup-Tiup.

3 FERNS

The slopes leading off to the right of the path are typical of secondary forest, where clearings have been entirely colonised by a blanket of sun-seeking resam ferns (*Dicranopteris linearis*), preventing anything else from growing. Other secondary species to look out for include macaranga, which has ants living in hollows inside its leaf stems.

Away from the city centre, peace and quiet can be found in the island's nature reserves

After 5 to 10 minutes, take the steps to your left signposted Tangga Rengas – Summit.

4 SUMMIT

From the summit there are good views to the northeast across the Lower Pierce and Upper Pierce reservoirs that form part of the central water catchment area, one of the largest tracts of wilderness on the island.

Retrace your steps back down and follow the signs for North View Path. Follow this all the way around the northern slopes of Bukit Timah to the Noor Hut.

5 BIRD-SPOTTING

The northern slopes are a good place to listen for the calls and songs of birds such as the short-tailed babbler (*Trichastoma malaccense*), which chatters away on the forest floor, or the stripe-throated tit-babbler (*Macronous gularis*), which sounds a loud and repetitive 'chonk-chonk-chonk' at mid-forest level. In the upper canopy, one of the easiest

birds to spot is the greater racquet-tailed drongo (*Dicrurus paradiseus*) with its conspicuous racquet-tipped tail and metallic black body.

Immediately past the Noor Hut, take the right-hand track, crossing the small Noor Bridge, and turn right again at the next T-junction. At the junction with the Jungle Fall Path turn right, take the next right again down the Hampstead Path, and left at the Hampstead Hut to follow the Fern Valley Contour Path.

6 THE FERN VALLEY CONTOUR PATH

This is one of the loveliest sections of track in the park, with views down the forest slope and through the trees at mid-forest level. Of the 100 or so species of ferns that still exist on the island, around 80 are now found only in the reserve, with Fern Valley being one of the best places to see them.

At the Simpang Hut, take the road back down to the Visitor Centre.

Little India

While not as extensive as Chinatown or as distinctive architecturally, Little India is still an identifiable community where street life echoes the sights and sounds of the Indian sub-continent. This is an easy walk. *Allow 2 hours.*

From Bugis MRT, head up Rochor Road, turn right into Jalan Besar and second left into Dunlop Street.

1 DUNLOP STREET

The beginnings of Little India became evident the closer you get to Serangoon Road. The covered walkways are strung about with glittering fabrics, luring customers inside where bolts of sari material line the shops almost up to the ceiling. Alongside, other stores are piled high with brass incense-holders, peacock feathers (considered lucky by Hindus), multi-tiered 'tiffin' containers (the Indian equivalent of a lunch-box), Hindi pop cassettes and temple knick-knacks. Near by, stallholders string together fragrant garlands of jasmine and marigolds, to be used for wedding celebrations or simply as daily offerings in the temple.

At the end of Dunlop Street, cross over Serangoon Road to the Zhu Jiao Centre.

2 ZHU JIAO CENTRE

This the largest fresh-produce market in the city, a feast for the eyes and the appetite, serving not only the local community but also shoppers from further afield drawn by the vast array of fresh produce.

Turn back up Serangoon Road and you will soon reach the Veerama Kali Amman Temple.

3 VEERAMA KALI AMMAN TEMPLE

Dedicated to the Goddess Kali, this

The busy Sri Sreenivasa Perumal Temple

Shaivite temple is at its busiest in the early evenings, when dozens of worshippers mill around outside, the day's work done, exchanging news and waiting to perform their *puja* (prayers).
Continue up Serangoon Road. After passing a dull section of housing estates and open paddocks you will eventually reach the Sri Sreenivasa Perumal Temple on your left.

4 SRI SREENIVASA PERUMAL TEMPLE

The spacious interior courtyard of the Hindu temple houses numerous shrines, the main one being Lord Vishnu's, with others dedicated to Sri Anjanepar, Sri Vinayagar and Sri Mahalakshmi. The original temple dates back to 1855, but it was completely rebuilt in the 1960s, with the towering *gopuram* (gates) only being completed in 1979. The whole temple is a joyous riot of brightly painted friezes and sculptures.
Immediately after the temple, take a path to the left and turn right into Race Course Road. On your right is the Sakya Muni Temple (see page 33), while facing it is the Leong San See Temple.

5 LEONG SAN SEE TEMPLE

Nestling incongruously beneath the apartment blocks behind it, this temple, dedicated to Kuan Yin (the Goddess of Mercy), houses some interesting frescos, carved lions, and a splendid altar with carvings of birds, flowers and the mythical phoenix.
Retrace your steps and proceed back down Serangoon Road on the opposite side.

6 SERANGOON ROAD

Once past the Serangoon Plaza, it is rewarding to linger along this section of Serangoon Road and the side-streets off to the left. Some of the old trades carry on regardless of your presence: a Tamil at his miller's wheel, for instance, grinds spices for his customers, sending aromatic clouds wafting into the air. Other traders have adapted to modern ways, such as the fortune-teller whose parrot, on being told your name, picks out a card with your future written on it. Although this is theoretically Little India, the Chinese influence is never far away, and you may well come across a fast and furious game of checkers on the sidewalk, with money surreptitiously changing hands.
At the end of Serangoon Road, turn left into Sungei Road, and eventually retrace your steps back to Bugis MRT.

Basketware piled high in a Little India shop-front

Excursions

SENTOSA ISLAND

Just 0.5km off shore from the city, Sentosa Island is a popular recreation spot and attracts around 3.5 million visitors a year. The island is one of the largest in Singapore harbour and was converted from a British military base into a holiday resort in the 1970s.

Cable-cars (which run from Mount Faber or the World Trade Centre) are one of the most popular ways of getting there, with the added bonus of extensive views across the harbour. Alternatively, shuttle ferries operate regularly from the World Trade Centre; and with the completion of a bridge to the shore, Sentosa is now also accessible by bus, taxi, bicycle or on foot.

Scattered over Sentosa's 375 hectares are a wide variety of things to see and do for all age groups, including golf courses, three museums, nature trails, a butterfly park, musical fountains, a cycle track, monorail, roller-skating rink, a tropical-fish oceanarium, and a range of restaurants and food centres.

On Sentosa's sea-facing coast the 3km beach-front has been upgraded and the two beaches (replenished regularly with sand from Indonesia) and swimming and leisure lagoons have facilities for aquabiking, windsurfing and canoeing. At one end of the beach is the Shangri-La Rasa Sentosa resort, Singapore's first 'beach hotel'; the island has one other hotel, the deluxe Beaufort Singapore, located near the golf courses and a luxury campsite, the NTUC Sentosa Beach Resort.

Further attractions include an Asian Village, a water theme park and various multimedia displays. Avoid weekends on Sentosa if you can, when there can be a crush on the ferries and at the attractions.

Butterfly Park and Insect Kingdom Museum

The collection includes over 2,500 live butterflies from 50 species and 4,000 mounted specimens of butterflies and insects from all over the world.
Open: Monday to Friday, 9am–6pm; weekends and public holidays, 9am–6.30pm. Admission charge.

Fort Siloso

Originally built by the British in the 1880s, this 4-hectare complex of tunnels, bunkers and gun emplacements, Sentosa's only authentic site, also includes a display on the history of the fort.
Open: daily, 9am–7pm. Admission charge.

Images of Singapore

This three-part exhibition is a multimedia presentation of Singapores' history and culture.

The **Pioneers of Singapore** highlights the lives of the immigrant groups who helped build the colony, with 'dioramas' (waxwork tableaux) illustrating historic moments and the day-to-day lives of Chinese coolies, colonial plantation owners and Indian merchants.

The **Surrender Chambers** continues the story, illustrating – with the addition of contemporary photographs and taped commentaries – the war years in Singapore from 1941 to 1945.

Festivals of Singapore re-enacts

some of the customs of Singapore's multicultural society with animated models.
Open: daily, 9am–9pm. Admission charge.

Maritime Museum

This attraction includes a wide range of displays from the development of canoes and early sailing ships through to merchant sailing ships and the port of Singapore today.
Open: daily, 10am–7pm. Admission charge.

Nature Walk/Dragon Trail

This is a 1.5km walk through forest foliage, with various dragon models, fossils and skeletal remains.
Open: all day. Admission free.

Sentora Orchid Gardens

An orchid theme garden with permanent exhibits including a flower clock made from orchids, a carp pond and a Japanese tea-house.
Open: daily, 9am–7pm. Admission charge.

Underwater World

Underwater World is Southeast Asia's largest tropical oceanarium. The most impressive feature is a 100m-long acrylic tunnel with a moving walkway running through it, which conveys you underneath two large marine aquarium tanks. The first of these is a coral-reef community tank, where typically colourful shallow-reef species such as parrotfish, angelfish, batfish and butterflyfish swim around and above you. The second tank – separated from the first for obvious reasons – contains carnivores and predators such as black-tipped and white-tipped reef sharks.

Other well-designed displays focus on tidal pools, schooling fish, sea

sponges, hard and soft corals, cave habitats and poisonous marine creatures. There is also a turtle pool and a touch-pool where you can handle sea-cucumbers, starfish and other invertebrates. In the small theatre an audio-visual show (every 10 minutes) focuses on marine life and marine conservation. Feeding times (11.30am and 4.30pm) ae a popular draw.
Open: daily, 9am–9pm. Admission charge.

VolcanoLand

Watch a volcano erupt, every half hour. This multimedia entertainment involves a journey to the centre of the earth and an exploration of the evolution of life.
Open: daily, 10am–8pm. Admission charge.

Sentosa Development Corporation, 1 Garden Avenue (Information Hotline: 275 0388). Basic admission charge includes bus transfers (Service A runs from the World Trade Centre, Service from Tiong Bahru MRT, 7am–11pm, daily) and monorail ride. If you walk or cycle across the causeway or take the ferry or cable-car, admission charge includes free return bus transfer. Ferries from the World Trade Centre run at 15-minute intervals, 9.30am–9pm weekdays, 8.30am–9pm weekends and public holidays. Cable-cars operate 8.30am–9pm, from either Mount Faber or the World Trade Centre.

The majority of indoor attractions open between 9am and 10am and close between 9pm and 10pm, with varying admission charges.

The World Trade Centre is served by buses 10, 30, 61, 65, 84, 97, 100, 125, 143, 145, 166 and 167.

Popular for weekend picnics, St John's Island is one hour from Singapore by ferry

PULAU SI-KIJANG (ST JOHN'S) AND PULAU TEMBAKUL (KUSU ISLAND)

The two most popular and easily accessible of the southern islands after Sentosa have regular ferry services from the World Trade Centre. The first ferry stop is Pulau Tembakul (Kusu Island), the smaller of the two, which has many myths and legends associated with it. Several of these involve rescues by turtles or tortoises ('Kusu' means 'place of the turtle' in Malay). In one, sailors shipwrecked at this spot centuries ago were rescued by a giant turtle that turned itself into an island. Another relates how two fishermen were shipwrecked near by, although this time it is a tortoise that becomes an island. In another, an Arab named Syed Abdul Rahman left Singapore with his wife and daughter in a sampan, which capsized in a storm. A giant tortoise spotted them and brought them to safety on the island. The interesting Malay *kramat* (shrine) on the island commemorates this man and his family.

As well as the *kramat*, there is a Chinese temple (dedicated to Da Bo Gong, the God of Prosperity), a tortoise sanctuary, turtle pool and pavilion. During the Ninth Lunar Month (October/November) thousands of devotees make a pilgrimage to the island to pay homage to their deities.

The first recorded mention of the island dates from 1616, when Dom Jose de Silva, Spanish Governor to the Philippines, ran aground on Kusu Reef while homeward bound with his fleet of 10 galleons and two galleys. Kusu was no more than two tiny outcrops on the reef until 1975, when it was filled in and expanded to its present size of 8.5 hectares.

Pulau Si-Kijang (St John's) is another popular picnic spot at the weekends, with three swimming lagoons. Don't expect shimmering tropical sandy beaches with clear blue waters on either island. The beaches are fairly minimal and the water is not particularly clear.

Both islands have grassed picnic areas, shelters, changing rooms and toilets. There is a canteen on St John's. *Ferries leave from the World Trade Centre, taking 40 minutes to reach Kusu and a further 20 minutes to reach St John's. On Sundays and public holidays, ferry schedules allow both islands to be visited in the same day when there are more sailings.*

PULAU UBIN

Ten minutes by boat from Changi Village on the northeast tip of the Singapore mainland, Pulau Ubin is a peaceful little island where life is closer in spirit to rural Malaysia (the coastline of Johor is just across the sea on the north coast) than to Singapore, whose downtown skyscrapers can be glimpsed in the distance. It is best explored by bike or on foot.

The island is still home to agricultural and fishing communities – the latter mostly relying on traditional *kelongs*, the V-shaped fish traps that you can see strung out along the coast. Pulau Ubin ('stone island') is also an important source of granite. Some of the quarries are still being worked, but many of the disused quarries scattered around the island are now filled with water and overrun with jungle vegetation, providing picturesque settings for a spot of fishing or even canoeing.

Within a few metres of the jetty in the village are several hire shops renting out mountain bikes (and canoes), which is how most people choose to explore the island. The island is mostly flat, with very little traffic on its bumpy, pot-holed roads. The most popular route is over to the north coast, where there is an excellent seafood restaurant and a Buddhist meditation centre.

Just outside the village the road winds along with bananas, papaya and coco-palms crowding the verges. Elsewhere, there are extensive rubber and coconut plantations, with abandoned plantations providing a haven for wildlife that is now absent elsewhere (such as the purple jungle fowl, ancestor to the domestic chicken). There are large areas of mangrove where monitor lizards are common.

Unlike the manicured resort islands to the south, Pulau Ubin has no swimming beaches, but is much more interesting if you want to experience a typical tropical island and the communities who live and work there. It is best explored on weekdays when there are few other people about. There are a couple of basic guesthouses.

Take the MRT to Tampins and change to bus 29. Alternatively, take bus 2 (which goes past Changi Prison). From the jetty in Changi Village the small ferry boats leave roughly every 15–30 minutes, depending on when they fill up. Mountain bike hire is relatively cheap.

Chinese pavilion on Kusu Island, where legends tell of ship-wrecked sailors rescued by turtles

Malaysia

KUALA LUMPUR

Founded in 1857 as a trading post for miners, Kuala Lumpur (roughly translated as 'muddy estuary') has grown rapidly to achieve its present status as the federal capital of Malaysia and is still expanding – although now progress is skywards. The modern high-rise buildings contrast sharply with the jumble of temples, markets and crowded streets at ground level. Bisected by fast-moving freeways, Kuala Lumpur is a cosmopolitan city with facilities (such as deluxe hotels) to match, but it is also a city of great character with a multiracial population and an interesting mix of architectural styles, from colonial British to contemporary Islamic.

Kuala Lumpur began as a cluster of makeshift buildings at the confluence of the Klang and Gombak rivers. The early Chinese traders found they could pole no further upriver than this point, and so established a settlement to supply the tin mines at nearby Ampang. In the first few months 70 of the original party of 87 had died of fever, but the population of Kuala Lumpur grew rapidly as more tin deposits were discovered.

The outpost developed into a boom town where gang wars, brawls and epidemics were a normal part of the pioneers' lives. The Sultan of Selangor, Abdul Samad, put the settlement under the control of Yap Ah Loy, the *Kapitan China* (Chinese headman), but it progressed little beyond a squalid shanty town.

The major change came when Frank Swettenham, the British Resident in Selangor, moved his administration to Kuala Lumpur and rebuilt it from scratch, pulling down the wooden huts and replacing them with stone and brick structures.

In 1886 a railway line was constructed connecting Kuala Lumpur to the port of Klang, and in 1896 it became the capital of the Federated States.

Wealth started to flood in from tin revenues, and the new tin millionaires built themselves impressive mansions along Jalan Ampang. Development proceeded rapidly and the population grew – augmented by many thousands

Moorish-style minarets on the Central Railway Station with modern Kuala Lumpur backdrop

of Indians who arrived at the beginning of the 20th century to work as labourers on the rubber plantations. After Independence in 1957 the city soon established its pre-eminent role as the business and commercial capital of Malaysia.

Getting around the city is not hard, particularly in the downtown areas where most of the sights are within walking distance of each other. Make sure you protect yourself from the sun and try to avoid the morning and evening rush hours, when the congestion and belching fumes make walking unpleasant. For travelling to and from your hotel, or for journeys elsewhere in the city, taxis are the best bet. The distances can be considerable, but taxis are plentiful and inexpensive.

Kuala Lumpur is not a city to be rushed through (the traffic will see to that), so allow plenty of time for sightseeing or shopping.

KUALA LUMPUR

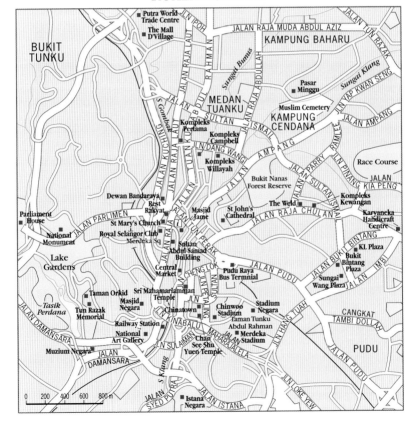

Watching the world go by above the busy streets of Chinatown

CENTRAL MARKET AND CENTRAL SQUARE
Sited on the banks of the Klang River, the Central Market is one of the focal points of downtown Kuala Lumpur. Built in 1936, this handsome art deco building was originally a produce market until it was converted in 1984. It is now a 'festival hall' with craft shops, restaurants and cultural performances and Kuala Lumpur's main outlet for craftspeople, painters and musicians. Surrounded by pedestrianised areas, it offers a pleasant retreat from city traffic and is a good place to while away an hour or two browsing among the stalls, listening to the buskers or watching outdoor performances in the evenings. See **Shopping** (pages 132–5) and **Entertainment** (pages 140–1) for more details. Next door is Central Square, a colourfully decorated building housing more shops, restaurants, photographic exhibitions and a multi-screen cinema. *Jalan Hang Kasturi (tel: 274 6542). Open: daily, 10am–10pm.*

CHAN SEE SHU YUEN TEMPLE
Right on the southern boundary of Chinatown (see below), this typical clan-house and temple (built in 1906) is embellished with ornate ceramic friezes and sculptures on the outside, with elaborate wall-paintings and wood-carvings decorating the interior. *Jalan Petaling. Open: daily.*

CHINATOWN
You really need to visit the bustling streets of Chinatown twice. During the day you can wander around and peer into old shop-houses where sign-painters, shoe-repairers and basket-makers carry on in time-honoured fashion. Chinatown then has to be seen by night, when the central area around Jalan Petaling is transformed into a *pasar malam* (night market), with stalls selling everything from hot chestnuts to calculators. See **Shopping** (page 132–5) and **Food and Drink** (page 156–63).

JALAN AMPANG
Many of the grandiose mansions of the early tin magnates still survive, although few are private homes any more. Most have been taken over by foreign embassies and consulates (hence Jalan Ampang is also known as Ambassador's Row), while others have been converted to different uses, such as Tunku Abdul Rahman Hall, which is now the Malaysia Tourist Information Complex.

LAKE GARDENS
The Lake Gardens are the only significant swath of greenery in Kuala Lumpur. The 90-hectare park, built around an artificial lake, is popular with

Weekends are the best time to visit the Lake Gardens, an oasis in the heart of the city

joggers, picnickers and local families at weekends. On weekdays it is less crowded.

Set on a hilltop, the well-landscaped Orchid Garden (Taman Orkid) displays around 800 species of orchid, while the neighbouring Hibiscus Garden (Taman Bunga Raya) boasts around 500 rare and exotic blooms set out along shaded walkways and beside cooling fountains.

Just down the hillside is the Bird Park (Taman Burung), where a large enclosure houses tropical species within a landscape of trees, flowering shrubs and miniature waterfalls. It houses many species of hornbill, and is steadily expanding.

The newest addition to the Lake Gardens is the Butterfly Park, with around 150 species of butterfly housed in an environment designed to resemble the Malaysian rain forest. There are also displays of giant frogs, stick insects, millipedes and other exotica.

Across Jalan Parlimen is the massive National Monument, sculpted by Felix de Weldon (creator of the Iwo Jima monument in Washington, DC), which commemorates the Malay and Commonwealth forces who died fighting the Communist insurgents during the 12-year Emergency.

Also within the Lake Gardens are Parliament House, an 18-storey building of no particular architectural interest, and the Memorial Tun Razak, which together house a large collection of the personal _memorabilia_ of Malaysia's second Prime Minister.

Orchid Garden and Hibiscus Garden open: daily, 9am–6pm, including Sundays and public holidays. Admission free. Bird Park open: daily, 8am–6pm. Admission charge. Butterfly Park open: weekdays, 9am–5pm; weekends and public holidays, 9am–6pm. Admission charge (extra for cameras and videos). Memorial Tun Razak open: Tuesday to Sunday and public holidays, 9am–6pm; closed Friday, noon–3pm. Admission free.

MASJID JAME

Surrounded by palm trees on a triangular spit of land at the confluence of the Klang and Gombak rivers, the Masjid Jame lies on the site where the city of Kuala Lumpur began. Built in 1909 in classic Arabian-Moorish style, this beautiful mosque has a triple-domed prayer hall and is surmounted by elegant minarets.

Entrance on Jalan Tun Perak. Open: daily, 9–11am; 2–4pm. Visitors must be suitably attired (see below).

MASJID NEGARA (NATIONAL MOSQUE)

Built in the 1960s, the National Mosque is one of the largest in Asia and can accommodate up to 8,000 worshippers at any one time. The main dome is in the form of an 18-point star, and within the grounds are a further 48 smaller domes and a towering, 73m high minaret.

Jalan Sultan Hishamuddin. Open: Saturday to Thursday, 9am–6pm; Friday 2.45–6pm. Visitors must remove their shoes and be properly clothed: men in shorts or women with short skirts will be lent robes.

MERDEKA SQUARE

Known in colonial times as the Padang, the square was formerly used as playing-fields (for tennis, rugby and, of course, cricket) by the British, who built the mock-Tudor Selangor Club on the western side. Appropriately, the Padang was the venue for the historic ceremony that took place on 30 August 1957, when Independence was proclaimed and the chapter closed on colonial rule. A round, black marble plaque commemorates the spot where the Union Jack was finally lowered and the Malaysian flag hoisted for the first time.

The national flag now flies from a 100m high flagpole at one end of the Padang. Behind it a gigantic video-screen broadcasts at all times of day and night, leading to occasional pile-ups on Jalan Raja as drivers crane round for a view of what's on.

Jalan Raja.

MUZIUM NEGARA (NATIONAL MUSEUM)

Situated between two expressways at the foot of the Lake Gardens, the National Museum was built in 1963 to replace the old Selangor Museum, destroyed during World War II. The exterior draws on various elements of traditional Malay architecture, with the entrance flanked by mosaic murals depicting Malaysian culture and history. Inside, various displays focus on the history of Kuala Lumpur, the rubber and tin-mining industries, Malay arts and crafts and the flora and fauna of Southeast Asia. Other exhibits document Orang Asli traditions, Peranakan culture, and life at the royal courts of the Malay sultanates. The presentation is rather dated and static, but it will give you a good overview of Malaysia's culture and peoples.

Jalan Damansara/Jalan Travers (located 1km from the railway station). Tel: (03) 282 6255. Open: daily, 9am–6pm. Closed Friday noon–2.30pm. Admission charge.

NATIONAL ART GALLERY

Housed in what used to be the Majestic Hotel, the art gallery is on three levels, with current exhibitions by local and international artists on the ground floor, landscape painting by Malaysian artists from the permanent collection on the second floor, and figurative work on the third floor.

Figures from Hindu mythology crowd together on the gateway of the Mahamariamman Temple

Jalan Sultan Hishamuddin (opposite the Railway Station). Tel: (03) 230 0157. Open: daily, 10am–6pm. Closed Friday, noon–3pm. Admission free.

RAILWAY STATION

Looking more like a mosque than a train terminus, the railway station is a riot of Moorish architecture with scalloped eaves, keyhole arches, minarets and cupolas. Designed in 1910 by architect A B Hubbock, it replaced the original station of 1885. The Malayan Railway Administration Building opposite the station is designed in a similar, although more restrained, style.
Jalan Sultan Hishamuddin.

SRI MAHAMARIAMMAN TEMPLE

The oldest Hindu temple in Kuala Lumpur, built in 1873, it was originally located on the site of the present railway station and moved to Chinatown in 1885. The temple has the usual decorative *gopuram* (gateway) and the interior features ornate Italian and Spanish ceramic tiles. See also **Thaipusam Festival** (pages 144–5).
Jalan Tun HS Lee.

SULTAN ABDUL SAMAD BUILDING

Facing Merdeka Square, the Sultan Abdul Samad Building with its 41m-high clock tower is one of Kuala Lumpur's most prominent and most photographed landmarks. The Moorish-style building, completed in 1897, was originally the home of the State Secretariat. It now houses the Supreme Court and the High Courts. The courts are not open to the public, although permission can be obtained by writing in advance to the judiciary department.
Jalan Raja.

PENINSULAR MALAYSIA

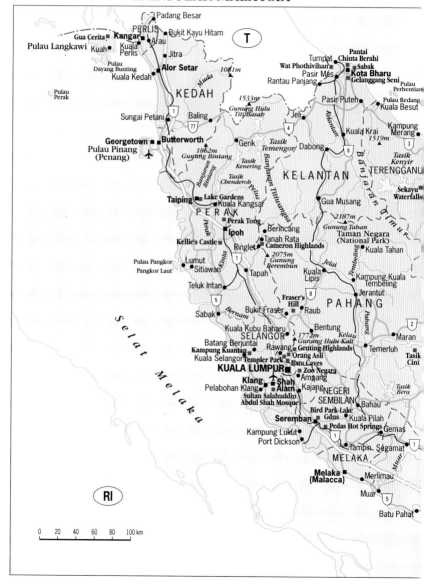

Padang Besar
PERLIS
Gua Cerita ■ Kangar ■ Bukit Kayu Hitam
Pulau Langkawi Kuah ● Kuala ● Arau
Perlis
Pulau Jitra
Dayang Bunting Alor Setar
Kuala Kedah 1081m
Pulau Perak
KEDAH
1533m
Gunung Hulu
Titi Basah
Sungai Petani Baling
77
Jeli

Pantai
Tumpat Chinta Berahi
Wat Phothivihan ■ ■ Sabak
Pasir Mas Kota Bharu
Rantau Panjang Gelanggang Seni
Pulau
Perhentian
Pasir Puteh ● Pulau Redang
Kuala Besut

Georgetown ■ ■ Butterworth
Pulau Pinang 1862m Gerik Tasik
(Penang) Gunung Bintang Temengor Dabong
Kuala Krai 1519m Kampung
Merang
3
Tasik
Kenyir
TERENGGANU

Taiping ■ ■ Lake Gardens
Kuala Kangsar KELANTAN Sekayu
Waterfalls
PERAK
Perak Tong Gua Musang
Ipoh ● Berinchang
Kellie's Castle ■ Tanah Rata 2187m
Ringlet Cameron Highlands Gunung Tahan
▲ 2075m Taman Negara
Pulau Pangkor Lumut Gunung (National Park)
Pangkor Laut ● Sitiawan Berembun Kuala Tahan
Tapah Kuala
Lipis Kampung Kuala
Teluk Intan Tembeling
5 Jerantut
Fraser's 8 PAHANG
Sabak Hill ■ Raub
Bukit Fraser 2
Kuala Kubu Baharu Bentung Maran
SELANGOR 1772m Kelau
Batang Berjuntai Gunung Hulu Kali
Kampung Kuantan Rawang Genting Highlands Temerluh
Kuala Selangor Templer Park ■ Orang Asli Tasik
KUALA LUMPUR ■ ■ Batu Caves Cini
Klang ▲ Shah Zoo Negara
Pelabohan Klang ● ■ Alam Ampang Tasik
Sultan Salahuddin Kajang NEGERI Bera
Abdul Shah Mosque SEMBILAN
Bird Park-Lake Bahau
Seremban ■ Gdns ● Kuala Pilah
Kampung Lukut ● Pedas Hot Springs Gemas
Port Dickson Tampin Segamat
MELAKA
Melaka ■ Merlimau
(Malacca)
Muar
Batu Pahat

Selat Melaka

T
RI

0 20 40 60 80 100 km

Kuala Terengganu
Pulau Kapas
Marang
Rantau Abang
Turtle Sanctuary
Tanjung
Jara
Pulau Tenggul
Dungun
14 3
Kerteh
Kampung Kemaman
Cukai
Cerating
ancing Kampung Baluk
Beserah
Kuantan
pahang Pekan
12
Nensai
3
Pulau Tioman
Rompin Kampung Tekek Kampung Juara
Endau-
Rompin Padang Endau
1036m **Pulau Rawa**
Gunung
Besar Mersing Pulau
Aur
abis Jemaluang Pulau Tinggi
Semberong Pulau
Sibu
JOHOR
Keluang 3
Ayer Hitam Johor
Kulai Kota Tinggi
1 **Kampung Johor Lama**
Pontian Johor **Istana Besar** Desaru
Kechil **Bahru**
SGP

AROUND KUALA LUMPUR

BATU CAVES

These gigantic caverns were first
discovered in 1878. The main cavern is
the vast Cathedral Cave, where shafts of
sunlight filter through holes in the
ceiling some 100m above. In 1891, the
caves became a place of pilgrimage when
the local Hindu community erected a
shrine to Lord Subramaniam inside. The
best time to visit is during the annual
Thaipusam Festival (see pages 144–5).
At the bottom of the hill, there is a small
museum dedicated to the Hindu deities
in one of the more accessible caves.
*13km north of Kuala Lumpur, on the Ipoh
Road. Open: daily, 7am–9pm. Admission
free. Minibus 11 or Len Sen bus 69 or 70
from Kuala Lumpur, 30 minutes.*

ORANG ASLI MUSEUM

Set up in 1987 in order to preserve the
cultural heritage and history of
Malaysia's Orang Asli (see pages 60–1),
this museum has exhibits ranging from
jewellery to hunting equipment.
*Kilometre 24, Jalan Pahang, Gombak (tel:
689 2122). Open: Saturday to Thursday,
9am–5pm. Closed: Friday. Check weekends
and holidays. Admission free. Bus 174.*

PAK ALI'S HOUSE

A beautiful, traditional-style house
raised on stilts, which was built in 1917
entirely from local timbers. The house
displays many typical vernacular features
of a Malay *kampung* house, including the
use of natural coloured woods, elaborate
carvings and cooling verandas.
*Jalan Gombak, Gombak. Open: daily,
9am–6pm. Bus 174. Not far from the
Orang Asli Museum, and can be
conveniently visited on the same trip.*

ORANG ASLI

Visiting Malaysia you will often be reminded that this is a multiracial society of Malays, Indians and Chinese. And yet, driving up to the Cameron Highlands or trekking in Taman Negara, you may encounter a group of people who fit none of these categories. Sitting by the roadside with the fruits of the forest spread in front of them, or quietly walking the hills with their blowpipes to hand, these are the Orang Asli, or 'original peoples'. In fact, the blanket term 'Orang Asli' is misleading, since the 83,000 people who belong to Peninsular Malaysia's indigenous minority comprise 19 different ethnic groups, each with its own language and culture.

The characteristics of Orang Asli vary greatly from tribe to tribe, as do their occupations and lifestyles. Some are easily identifiable, such as the distinctive Negrito peoples, with their dark skin and frizzy hair. They are the smallest and oldest group, and are thought to have arrived in Malaysia between 8,000 and 10,000 years ago from the Andaman Islands. They mostly live in the north of the peninsula and are one of the last tribes to lead a truly nomadic life. Other Orang Asli are not recognisable as such at all, blending into the urban Kuala Lumpur scene and doing conventional jobs. Those on the road to the Cameron Highlands are most likely to be Semai, part of the Senoi group, who traditionally lived as shifting cultivators. Others, such as the Orang Laut, Orang Seletar and Mah Meri, live near the coast and gain their livelihoods mostly by fishing.

Whatever their diverse origins, the Orang Asli have suffered from neglect, poverty and the abuse of their human rights since before colonial times. In the

The oldest indigenous people in Malaysia, many Orang Asli still lead traditional lifestyles. A park ranger (far left) talks to an Orang Asli hunter collecting poison for his blowpipe darts

no longer under their control. This is still the situation today under the Aboriginal Peoples Act, which has taken away the right to self-determination for the majority of Orang Asli communities. While there have been considerable advances in terms of health, education and agricultural development for the Orang Asli, the crucial issue of land rights is their chief cause for grievance in the 1990s.

19th century they were subject to slave-raids, and even under the British were referred to as *sakai*, or debt-slaves.

With the advent of independence, the Orang Asli found that the land they had always considered their own was

For more information on Malaysia's indigenous peoples, contact the Centre for Orang Asli Concerns, 86B, Jalan SS24/2, 47301 Petaling Jaya, Malaysia.

Melaka

*M*alaysia's oldest town, Melaka (Malacca) has witnessed the sweep of history as rival colonial powers fought for possession and occupied it, each in turn leaving their mark. This heritage has left Melaka with a legacy of historical relics and monuments unparalleled elsewhere in the country.

Melaka was founded in 1400 by a Hindu nobleman, Prince Parameswara, who came from Sumatra. In 1405 Admiral Cheng Ho came as an envoy of the Ming dynasty and offered to provide protection against the Siamese to the north. Melaka soon prospered. The Chinese brought gold, silver, porcelain and silk; Indian traders brought textiles and brassware; the Siamese brought ivory; and Arabian merchants brought perfumes, pearls, incense and opium.

Tales of this wealthy seaport reached the Portuguese, who conquered it on 25 July 1551 under Admiral Alfonso d'Albuquerque. The Portuguese were overthrown by the Dutch in 1641 after a six-month long siege. Then it was the turn of the British, who seized Melaka in 1795. In 1818 it was returned to the Dutch under treaty, but was restored to the British again in 1824. In 1826 it became a Straits Settlement and, a year later, a Crown Colony along with Pinang and Singapore. During World War II it was under Japanese occupation. With Independence in 1957, the first local Governor was appointed.

Over the centuries, successive communities brought with them their culture, religion and architecture. The result is that the streets of Melaka make up a multicultural tapestry of mosques, churches and other ancient buildings. The best way to see these is on a walking tour (see **Melaka walk**, pages 66–7); you can also get around town by trishaw.

Apart from day-time sightseeing (for which you should allow a couple of days), there isn't a great deal to do. Sound-and-light shows take place in the stadium on the Padang every evening.

Melaka has several antique shops (see **Shopping**, page 134), and is one of just a handful of places where you can try Nyonya food (see **Food and Drink**, page 162).

BABA NYONYA HERITAGE MUSEUM

The Baba Nyonya Heritage is one of two museums devoted to Peranakan or Straits Chinese culture (see **The Straits Chinese**, pages 20–1) which is in a real Peranakan house, with many of the furnishings and artefacts displayed as they would have been used (the other is the **Peranakan Showhouse Museum**, Singapore; see page 38). The interior of the house is almost palatial, extending some 30m back from the street with several interior courtyards open to the skies to admit light and air. The museum is run by the same Peranakan family whose ancestors originally built it, and it is well worth a visit.

50 Jalan Tun Tan Cheng Lock (tel: (06) 231 273). Open: daily, 10am–12.30pm and 2–4.30pm. Admission charge (includes conducted tour).

BUKIT CHINA

The history of Bukit China, the 'Chinese

Hill', can be traced back to the earliest contacts between Imperial China and the Melaka Sultanate. In 1405 the Imperial envoy, Admiral Cheng Ho, pitched his quarters here. And in 1459, when Sultan Mansur Shah married Princess Hang Li Poh, daughter of Emperor Yung Lo, he gave her the hill as a place of residence to accommodate her entourage of 500 handmaidens. Under the Portuguese, a monastery and chapel were built on top of the hill, but these were destroyed by the Archinese in 1629. Under Dutch rule, the hill was donated to the Chinese community for a burial ground, which it has remained to this day, with around 12,500 graves on its slopes – many dating back to the 17th century.
Jalan Hang Li Po.

CHENG HOON TENG TEMPLE
Melaka's oldest and most grandiose Chinese temple, Cheng Hoon Teng ('The Abode of Green Clouds') is dedicated to Kwan Yin, the Goddess of Mercy. Built between 1646 and 1704, craftsmen and materials were brought over from South China to decorate the temple: the result is a colourful fantasy of dragons and other mythical creatures on the eaves and ridges of the roof, while the interior of the main hall is resplendent with ornate wood-carvings and lacquerwork.

At the back of the main hall are the ancestral tablets of all the *Kapitans China* of Melaka, including that of Kapitan Lee Wei King, who founded the temple.
Jalan Tokong.

Mythological figures, flowers and birds embellish the roof of the Cheng Hoon Teng Temple

CHRIST CHURCH

In the heart of the town, Christ Church was built by the Dutch to commemorate the centenary of their occupation of Melaka. Started in 1741, it was completed in 1753 and the original, hand-carved wooden pews from that date are still used by worshippers today. The nave is supported by a series of 17 massive, 15m-long beams, each carved from a single tree.
Dutch Square.

MASJID KAMPUNG KLING

The Kampung Kling Mosque is an unusual structure. Instead of the usual dome, it has a pyramid-shaped roof of Sumatran design, and instead of the normal spire-type minaret it has a square-shaped pagoda. Further cross-cultural influences can be seen inside, where Corinthian columns support the carved wooden ceiling. Both British and Portuguese tiles grace the interior of the main prayer hall, while the wood-carvings on the pulpit display both Chinese and Hindu influences.
Jalan Tokong Emas. Open: daily, except at prayer times.

MAUSOLEUM OF HANG JEBAT

One of the legendary heroes of the Malay Sultanate during the mid-15th century, Hang Jebat was a loyal warrior whose life ended tragically when he was killed on the orders of the Sultan by one of his blood brothers, Hang Tuah, as a result of a convoluted series of intrigues of which they were both innocent.
Jalan Kampung Kuli.

MEMORIAL HALL

Formerly the Malacca Club, this handsome building now houses a permanent exhibition (opened in 1985) illustrating the history of Malaysia from the 15th-century Malay Sultanate up to the struggle for independence. Outside stands the battered '57 Chevy used by the first Prime Minister-elect, Tunku Abdul Rahman, to campaign across the country.
Jalan Parameswara (tel: (06) 242 231). Open: Tuesday to Sunday, 9am–6pm; Friday 9am–noon, 3–6pm. Closed: Mondays. Admission free.

MUZIUM BUDAYA (CULTURAL MUSEUM)

This magnificent wooden building is a reconstruction of the 15th-century Sultanate's *istana* (palace). Built in 1985 using entirely traditional methods of construction – there are no nails in the whole building – the design is based on sketches from the *Sejarah Melayu* (Malay Annals). It houses the Melaka Cultural Museum, with tableaux depicting life at the Sultanate's Court,

---

MELAKA RIVER

Although Melaka's harbour has long since silted up, shallow-drafted Indonesian cargo boats still unload at the quayside downtown. The cargoes (of mangrove poles and sacks of charcoal) may not be as exotic as in the past, but the magnificent wooden sea-going vessels evoke the ghosts of traders from earlier centuries. Boat trips on the river, which encompass the quay, the downtown area and a Malay *kampung* (village), leave from behind the Tourist Information Centre.
Details: Tourist Information Centre, Jalan Kota, Melaka, tel: (06) 284 6622. Open: weekdays, 8.45am–5pm; Saturday, 8am–12.45pm.

the epic duel between the warriors Hang Tuah and Hang Jebat, and an Islamic Gallery and Costume Gallery.
Jalan Istana, St Paul's Hill (tel: (06) 241 934). Open: daily, 9am–6pm. Admission charge.

PORTA DE SANTIAGO
Porta de Santiago is the last remnant of the massive stone fortress known as A Famosa, which was built by Alfonso d'Albuquerque after he conquered Melaka in 1511. When the Dutch overthrew the Portuguese A Famosa was badly damaged, but they renovated the fort and inscribed 'Anno 1670', together with the Dutch East India Company's coat-of-arms, on the gateway to mark their victory. With the arrival of the British, the order was signed to destroy the fort to prevent it falling back into Dutch hands. This task was nearly completed when Sir Stamford Raffles, visiting Melaka in 1808, persuaded them to save the gateway.
Jalan Kota.

STADTHUYS
After the take-over of Melaka by the Dutch in 1641, this was the first building they erected. The Stadthuys (Town Hall) is a massive, solid structure with thick masonry walls and heavy wooden doors, designed to protect the Governor and his staff who had their offices here. In the early 1980s it was converted into the Melaka Historical and Ethnographic Museum, which houses Dutch and Portuguese relics, Malay and Chinese wedding costumes and a variety of other displays.
St Paul's Hill (tel: (06) 220 769). Open: Saturday to Thursday, 9am–6pm; Fridays 9am–noon, 2.45–6pm. Admission charge.

The Muzium Budaya is a skilfully crafted replica of the Sultan's 15th-century Palace

ST PAUL'S CHURCH
Now in ruins, this church was originally built by the Portuguese in 1521 and was known as Our Lady of the Hill. With the arrival of the Dutch, the church was renamed St Paul's. Once they had finished building Christ Church they no longer used St Paul's for worship but simply as a burial ground, and many of the huge old tombstones can still be seen. After his death St Francis Xavier was initially buried here before his body was taken to its final resting-place in Goa.
St Paul's Hill.

TEMPLE OF ADMIRAL CHENG HO
Admiral Cheng Ho was the Imperial trade ambassador to Emperor Yung Lo during the Ming dynasty. Legend has it that on his way to visit Melaka his ship was holed, but that he was saved by a fish, known as a Sam Po, which blocked up the hole (hence the temple is also known as Sam Po Kong Temple).
Admiral Cheng Ho Road. Open: daily.

Melaka

This walk covers all of the important historic sights of Melaka north and south of the river. Owing to the town's one-way system, traffic is fast and furious, so be careful when you step off the pavement. *Allow 2–3 hours.*

Start from the Tourist Information Centre in Jalan Kota, near Dutch Square.

1 DUTCH SQUARE

Directly facing you in Dutch Square are several important historic buildings dating from the Dutch era, including Christ Church (see page 64) and the Stadthuys (see page 65). In the middle of the square is the Teng Beng Swee Clock Tower, erected by a notable Peranakan family in 1886, and the Queen Victoria Jubilee Fountain.

Walk along Jalan Kota towards St Paul's Hill. Take the steps up to St Paul's Church (see page 65), and descend the other side of the hill to the Porta de Santiago (see page 65). On your left is the Muzium Budaya (see page 64).

2 THE PADANG

In front of you is the Padang, an open space that is as significant to 20th-century history as Dutch Square is to the

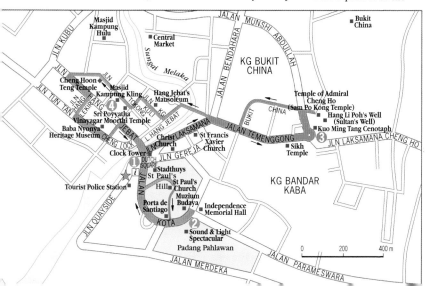

19th century. Hidden away behind the souvenir stands is an unassuming, green-coloured obelisk bearing the letter 'M' on all four sides (which stands for *merdaka*, meaning independence). It was on this spot that Independence was declared on 31 August 1957, at the same moment that an identical ceremony took place on the Padang in Kuala Lumpur. Fronting the Padang is the Memorial Hall (see page 64).

Dutch tombstones line the walls of St Paul's

Return to Dutch Square via Jalan Kota and enter Jalan Laksamana. Pass Christ Church and the twin-towered Church of St Francis Xavier, then take the second right, down Jalan Temenggong. At the roundabout, turn left and cross the road.

3 PRINCESS HANG LI POH'S WELL

Immediately in front of you is the Kuo Ming Tang Cenotaph, which commemorates some 1,000 Chinese civilians massacred during the Japanese occupation. Just past here on the right is the Temple of Admiral Cheng Ho (see page 65). Next to it is Princess Hang Li Poh's Well (also known as the Sultan's Well), which was once the main source of drinking water for the town. In 1551 the Johor forces who were besieging Melaka poisoned the well, killing around 200 Portuguese. No doubt mindful of these stories, when the Dutch took Melaka they built a fortified wall around the well – the sentries' gunports can still be seen.

Turn right out of the temple, where steps lead up to Bukit China (see pages 62–3). Cross over the road and go down Jalan Puteri, passing some magnificently restored old town houses on your left. Follow the road round and turn right into Jalan Temenggong, crossing the river at the end of the road. Take the first left, Lebuh Hang Jebat, and then the first right into Jalan Kampong Kuli (not signposted). Near the end of this road, on the right, is the Mausoleum of the 15th-century warrior, Hang Jebat.

Turn left at the end of the road and immediately right again into Jalan Tokong. Immediately on your left is the Sri Poyyatha Vinayagar Moorthi Temple and, just past it, the Masjid Kampung Kling (see page 64) on the corner with Jalan Lekiu.

4 SRI POYYATHA VINAYAGAR MOORTHI TEMPLE

This is the oldest Hindu temple in Melaka, built in 1781 and dedicated to Sri Vinayagar (Ganesh). On the central altar sits a carving made from Indian black stone of the deity, who has an elephant's head and four hands.

Cross over into Jalan Tokong (Temple Street). Further up on the left-hand side is the Cheng Hoon Teng Temple (see page 63). Follow the road round to the left, turn left on Jalan Hang Jebat and right into Jalan Hang Lekir. Turn left again on Jalan Tun Tan Cheng Lock, and you will soon find the Baba Nyonya Heritage Museum (see page 62) on your left.

When leaving the heritage museum, turn left and then left again, turning right on to Jalan Hang Jebat to reach the river bridge.

Central Highlands

*H*ill stations were an essential part of colonial life in the tropics, and it was common for the British in particular to establish residences high above sea-level where they could escape the desultory heat of their postings. In Malaysia the nearest mountains to Kuala Lumpur are in the Central Highlands, and the two main resorts here, Cameron Highlands and Bukit Fraser (Fraser's Hill), both date back to colonial times. Genting Highlands is a more recent development that holds little appeal for overseas visitors.

In the cooler climate of the highlands mist and rain swathe the hillsides where pitcher plants, mosses and ferns flourish in the damp undergrowth of the upper montane forests. The altitude lends itself to the cultivation of tea, coffee, flowers and vegetables, and cooling breezes allow visitors to play golf or go walking without suffering from heat exhaustion. For longer walking expeditions in the Central Highlands with Orang Asli guides, see **Trekking** (pages 154–5).

CAMERON HIGHLANDS

Malaysia's largest hill station, the Cameron Highlands consists of three townships at an altitude of just over 1,500m, surrounded by tea plantations, flower and vegetable nurseries and golf courses.

First discovered by a British surveyor, William Cameron, in 1885, the area was not developed as a hill station until 1926. Tourism has recently fuelled a construction boom, which environmentalists say is leading to soil erosion, siltation, landslides and flooding. The scars on the landscape are all too evident as you pass up through the townships.

The first town in the Highlands is Ringlet, an unattractive conurbation where few visitors bother to stop. Tanah Rata (13km further on) is the main town, with a wide range of facilities including banks, restaurants and hotels. The last town is Brinchang, where hotels, shops and restaurants crowd in around a sloping town square.

The towns have none of the charm of Fraser's Hill (see below), and the appeal of the Highlands lies mostly in walking in the surrounding hills (see **Cameron Highlands walk**, pages 72–3), playing golf or visiting tea plantations (see pages 70–1) and the resort's many market gardens. Other notable sights include the Sam Poh Temple near Brinchang, a butterfly garden, and the atmospheric Smokehouse Hotel.

330km north of Kuala Lumpur. From Kuala Lumpur buses and trains run to Tapah on the Kuala Lumpur-Ipoh Road, from where taxis and buses operate regular services for the last 60km. There are also long-distance, direct buses to/from Kuala Lumpur, Melaka and Butterworth. Self-drive takes around 4 hours from Kuala Lumpur, 2 hours from Ipoh.

BUKIT FRASER (FRASER'S HILL)

Set in the middle of the Central Range, Fraser's Hill is an attractive little hill resort reached after a spectacular drive up through the forest-clad mountain slopes from the Ipoh Road.

Named after a maverick Englishman,

Flowers, vegetables, tea and coffee thrive in the cooler climate of the Central Highlands

Louis James Fraser, who lived here at the turn of the century (supposedly operating an opium and gambling den), it was developed as a hill station by the British from around 1910. They built a series of neat, greystone bungalows surrounded by roses, hollyhocks and geraniums, which still characterise Fraser's Hill today. The small township, with its colourful flower gardens and well-kept roads, makes a pleasant stop-over for a day or two. At the centre of the resort is a nine-hole golf course; there are also facilities for tennis, swimming, squash, and cycling and horse-riding. Near by are the Jeriau Waterfalls (5km from the centre).

100km north of Kuala Lumpur. Regular buses run from Kuala Lumpur's Pudu Raya bus station, with a change at Kuala Kubu Baharu. Self-drive takes about 2 hours from the capital.

GENTING HIGHLANDS
A brash, modern resort with high-rise hotels, an artificial lake, golf club, miniature railway and cable-car rides, and Malaysia's only casino. It is popular at weekends and mostly patronised by residents of Kuala Lumpur, just an hour's drive away to the south.
Genting Highlands coach service from Pudu Raya bus station, Kuala Lumpur; eight services daily.

TEA PLANTATIONS

Thought to have originated somewhere in the mountainous Indo-China region, the tea plant (*Camellia sinensis*) is a hardy evergreen with fragrant white flowers. Left to grow naturally it would produce a tall, straggly bush, but this would make plucking on a commercial scale difficult, so bushes on plantations are carefully shaped and pruned for the first few years of their lives to produce a flat 'table top' to make the plucker's job easier. Once mature, the bushes are plucked every fortnight, with an experienced plucker able to harvest around 200kg of leaves in a day. If well looked after, the bushes will continue to provide good-quality tea leaves for up to 100 years.

they're ready for the teapot. Nowadays, the machinery is fully automated and computerised, rapidly subjecting the raw material to withering (to reduce the moisture content), rolling (to crush the leaf cells), fermentation (to give the tea aroma), drying (which stops further fermentation) and, finally, sorting. The last stage, packing, is something that no machine can do, but the fastest packers

Like the best wines, good-quality tea is also influenced in its flavour, bouquet and character by factors such as the climate, altitude and soil where it is grown. The rich, fertile soils, ample rain and sunshine, and cool temperatures of the Cameron Highlands provide the ideal conditions for tea-growing, and the region now accounts for 70 per cent of all the tea produced in Malaysia.

Baled up and trucked off to the factory, the natural tea leaves are put through a variety of processes before can fill up to 1,000 packets a day.

The largest tea plantation in the Cameron Highlands is the Boh Estate, established by John 'Archie' Russell, an English entrepreneur who persuaded the Government to grant him a large tract of land in 1928 to see if tea cultivation could work in Malaysia. Today, spread over three different sites, the Boh Estates are the largest producers in the country, with some 1,200 hectares of mature tea plants carpeting the rolling hillsides in emerald green.

There are several tea plantations in the Cameron Highlands, most of which operate guided tours between 9am and 4.30pm.
Blue Valley Tea Estate (tel: (05) 947 847); Boh Tea Estate (tel: (05) 948 643); Gunong Tea Estate (tel: (05) 948 634). They all close on Mondays.

Ye Olde Smokehouse, By-the-Golf Course, Cameron Highlands (tel: 941 214). Open for lunch noon–2pm, tea all afternoon, dinner 6.30–9pm.

Tea plantations were first established here in the 1920s. Tea bushes are picked about once every 15 days and experienced pickers can harvest 200kg of leaves in a day (45kg of tea)

Cameron Highlands

This walk makes use of some of the more easily accessible jungle tracks around the resort areas. The starting point is Ye Olde Smokehouse (half-way between Tanah Rata and Brinchang), climbing gradually up to the summit of Gunung Berembun at 2,075m before descending again to the Robinson Falls and then looping around through Tanah Rata, past the Parit Falls and back to the Smokehouse. It is a fairly hard walk, with some steep sections, but for most of the way the tracks are spongy underfoot and easy going. Good walking shoes are essential. *Allow 3–4 hours.*

From the Smokehouse, follow the road past the red British telephone

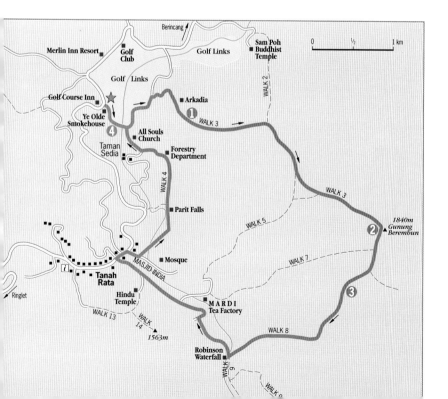

box, skirting the golf course until you see a sign to 'Arkadia' and Jungle Walk 3 on your right. At the top of the metalled track, a sign indicates the path into the forest.

1 FOREST WORLD

You soon enter a Hobbit-like world, with the track winding along between banks covered in mosses, lichens and liverworts. Gnarled and withered tree trunks and limbs twist and turn in all directions, supporting numerous ferns, flowering orchids and other epiphytes. *Continue along this track. After a further 20–25 minutes you will see a sign to the right for Walk 5: keep going up to the left.*

2 GUNUNG BEREMBUN

The path gets increasingly steep until finally you emerge among thickets of bamboo and the going is level to the summit of Gunung Berembun, a few metres further on. Due to the thick vegetation the views from the top are disappointing. *A short distance beyond the summit, Walk 7 is signed to the right: continue straight on towards Walk 8.*

3 SIAMANGS AND BUTTERFLIES

The track soon begins to descend. You may hear the booming double-note call of the siamang, a black-furred gibbon with the unusual characteristic of having two webbed toes. Even if you don't hear (or see) siamangs, it would be hard to miss the many beautiful butterflies flitting about the forest. *After descending for around an hour (the distance from the summit is 1.35km), you will reach a concrete path: on your left are the Robinson Falls. Walk back up the concrete path to the road, from where it is around 15 minutes to Tanah Rata. In*

Tanah Rata, turn right at the main road, then immediately right into Masjid India. After 200m, a sign on your left indicates the path to the Parit Falls.

Crossing the bridge over the waterfall, turn left. The track here is flat for most of the way, a pleasant, easy section that skirts the edge of towering pine and eucalyptus plantations. After 1.6km, you emerge on to the road again. Follow it to the main junction (do not take the first left turn) and turn left to return to the Smokehouse.

4 YE OLDE SMOKEHOUSE

You now deserve some refreshment, and what better place than an English country inn? As you sink into a deep leather armchair in front of a roaring log fire, tea with scones and strawberry jam is served.

Numerous walking trails criss-cross the forested hills of the Cameron Highlands

Northwest Coast

*F*rom the highlands down to the sea, the coastal plains of the northwest are dominated by endless rows of rubber and oil-palm trees undulating over the hillsides and valleys. After leaving Kuala Lumpur and passing through the state of Selangor you soon cross the border into Perak, one of the oldest states on the peninsula.

For centuries, Perak has been the centre of tin-mining in Malaysia – even the name (Perak means 'silver' in Malay) derives from the shining tin ore on which so many fortunes have been founded. Warring factions fought over the tin deposits until the British took control of the state in 1874. Mining on a large scale began in the mid-18th century, with the richest deposits being discovered towards the end of the century in the Kinta Valley, transforming the small market town of Ipoh into the tin capital of Malaysia.

Located about half-way between Kuala Lumpur and Pinang, Ipoh is the state capital of Perak. For the visitor, there are cave temples near by and a magnificent mosque at Kuala Kangsar (50km to the north), but otherwise Ipoh is largely a transit stop. To the south-west is the port of Lumut, home-base for the Malaysian Royal Navy and the main departure point for the islands of Pulau Pangkor and Pangkor Laut.

Travelling northwards 164km from Ipoh you reach Butterworth, the gateway to Pulau Pinang. The island

Traditional boat-building on Pulau Pangkor, an important anchovy-fishing centre

was first discovered by the hippy travellers of the 1960s and later became Malaysia's most well-known international resort. Previously only accessible by air or ferry, it is now linked to the mainland by the 13.5km Pinang Bridge, the third longest in the world. Beyond Pinang are the states of Kedah and Perlis, with the islands of Pulau Langkawi off shore (reached from either Kuala Perlis or Kuala Kedah) right up by the Thai border.

PULAU PANGKOR AND PANGKOR LAUT

Overlooking the Selat Melaka (Straits of Malacca), Pulau Pangkor is a popular island with some fine beaches: the smaller and more exclusive island of Pangkor Laut is tucked away off the southwest tip of the main island.

Pangkor is an important centre for anchovy fishing, the main fishing villages being on the east coast. The beaches are on the west coast, the principal resort area being Pasir Bogak. North of Pasir Bogak there are several good beaches, such as Teluk Ketapang (where turtles nest during May, June and July), Teluk Nipah (a lovely beach from where you can rent canoes and paddle out to the islet of Pulau Gian), and Coral Bay. The island is crowded at weekends and during holidays.

Pangkor is small enough to explore by bicycle (a circuit of the island takes around half a day) or motorbike, both of which can be rented. The busy boat-building yards and workshops on the east coast are worth a look, and there are also a handful of curiosities (such as a restored Dutch fort, rock inscriptions and a Chinese temple) to enliven your tour around the pot-holed coast road.

Neighbouring Pangkor Laut is a gem

Ikan bilis (dried anchovies) from Pulau Pangkor are marketed all over Malaysia

of an island, just 300 hectares covered in jungle and with only one hotel, the Pangkor Laut Resort, on the east coast. On the other side of the island from the resort – reached by a short jungle track – is Emerald Bay, which is indisputably one of the most beautiful beaches on the whole west coast of Malaysia. The horseshoe-shaped bay has clear water and a fine sandy beach surrounded by casuarinas and spiky pandanus palms. Behind the beach, magnificent hornbills swoop between the tree-tops – this is probably one of the best places in Malaysia for a guaranteed close look at these fabulous birds in the wild.

There is a regular ferry service from 6.45am to 7.30pm from Lumut directly to either island, with smaller boats making the short crossing between the two from Pasir Bogak from 10.30am to 7.30pm. There are buses between Lumut and Kuala Lumpur, Cameron Highlands, Ipoh and Butterworth (and long-distance taxis from the latter two). An airport has recently been completed at Teluk Dalam on Pulau Pangkor.

Pulau Pinang

The state of Pulau Pinang encompasses the island itself and a mainland coastal strip, Province Wellesley, with the port of Butterworth directly opposite the island. The capital of Pinang is Georgetown, a thriving port that has many sights of historic interest.

The first settlement on Pinang was founded in 1786 by Captain Francis Light, an adventurer working on behalf of the East India Company. Desperate for a station on the east side of the Indian Ocean to supply and protect their ships carrying precious cargoes of tea and opium from China, the British tricked the Sultan of Kedah by offering him protection from his enemies in return for Pinang. By the time the Sultan realised they had no intention of honouring their side of the bargain it was too late, and when he tried to retake Pinang he was easily defeated.

Light carved his capital out of the jungle and named it Georgetown in honour of King George IV. The colony soon prospered, with traders drawn from far and wide to the tax-free port. In 1826 Pinang joined together with Melaka and Singapore to form the Straits Settlements, although later it was eclipsed by Singapore as the centre of trade and commerce in the region. Pinang benefited enormously from the tin trade and, later, from the boom in rubber early in the 20th century.

Georgetown today is a prosperous, cosmopolitan city. The population of 400,000 is mostly Chinese, and although the modern, 65-storey Komtar building towers above the downtown area it is in the intriguing shop-houses and crowded streets of Chinatown that the soul of the city lies. Most of the areas of interest are within 3sq km and easily explored on foot (see **Georgetown walk**, pages 82–3). Bicycle rickshaws are also a practical way of getting around downtown. It is also well worth hiring a car for the day to explore the island (see **Pulau Pinang tour**, pages 84–5).

BATU FERINGGI BEACH

Pinang's only major beach resort is a tourist magnet with a dozen up-market hotels overlooking a 3km sandy strip on the north coast of the island. The beach offers a full range of watersports and activities such as parasailing, water ski-ing, jetskis, Hobie sailing, horse-riding, and snorkelling trips to nearby islands. Under the shade of the casuarinas, reflexology and traditional acupressure massages are also popular. Behind the beach road is an abundance of seafood restaurants, bars, market stalls, photo-processing shops, money-changers and the like.

The sea at Batu Feringgi has always been murky, a fact which has prompted many visitors to avoid it altogether and stick to the hotel swimming-pools. Their instincts were right, since a study by the Consumer's Association of Pinang found that seawater all around the Pinang coastline was heavily polluted with sewage – at Batu Feringgi, bacteria levels at one time exceeded the Malaysian Department of the Environment guidelines by a factor of 13,000! Things are gradually improving,

but it is safer to stick to the hotel pools, which have first-rate facilities.
14km from Georgetown. Bus 93, or taxi.

BOTANICAL GARDENS

The 30-hectare gardens nestle at the base of Bukit Bendera (Pinang Hill). The spacious lawns are surrounded by hardwood trees, fern rockeries, ponds, palm groves and flowering plants. If you have come for a picnic, be wary of the acquisitive common leaf monkeys that roam the grounds.
Off Waterfall Road, 8km from George-town. Open: daily. Admission free. Bus 7 or taxi.

BUKIT BENDERA (PINANG HILL)

Pinang Hill has long been the lungs of Georgetown, a cool retreat 830m above sea-level that is held in great affection by local residents, who have been coming up here by funicular railway for generations to relax and to walk the jungle paths and ridges in the hill complex. The natural vegetation of Pinang Hill is the last remnant of the rain forest that once covered the island, and is home to around 80 species of birds as well as a rich flora, including several endemic species.

The first funicular railway was built up the hillside in 1922, after which a hill resort developed with just a few bungalows, gardens and one hotel (the old Bellevue, which still exists). The only way up the hill is still by funicular, although now it is a modern, Swiss-built system. From the top, there are good views across Georgetown and towards the mainland.
The funicular runs from just near Ayer Itam, 6.30am–11.30pm, with later departures coming back down on weekends and holidays. It takes 45 minutes to reach the top (with a change of cars half-way). Bus 1 to Ayer Itam, then walk or Bus 8.

BUTTERFLY FARM

This fabulous garden houses thousands of butterflies from over 50 species, many of them rare and very beautiful. At times, the air is so thick with butterflies fluttering around your head that it is unnerving. The butterflies are at their most active early in the morning. Next to the butterfly enclosure there is an excellent Insect Museum with a well-presented collection of beautiful and bizarre moths and butterflies as well as the world's longest, heaviest and biggest insects. Even if insects give you the creepie-crawlies, this is an absorbing display.
Butterfly Farm, 830 Mk 2, Jalan Teluk Bahang (tel: (04) 885 1253). Open: weekdays, 9am–5pm; weekends and public holidays, 9am–6pm. Admission charge (extra for cameras and videos).

PENANG OR PINANG?

Pinang Island has changed names five times since it first appeared in recorded history. Centuries ago, the Malays knew it as Pulau Ka Satu, or Single Island. On early charts it became Pulau Pinang, or Betelnut Tree Island. Francis Light renamed it Prince of Wales' Island, in honour of the as-yet uncrowned George IV (hence also Georgetown). After Independence it was known as Pulau Penang, and 'Penang Island' is how it was marketed as a tourist destination from the 1970s onwards. Latterly, it has reverted to the correct Malay spelling of Pulau Pinang. Perhaps the next change will be a further step back into time, to Pulau Ka Satu?

CLAN PIERS

The clan piers are a series of wooden jetties projecting out over the harbour with houses built on stilts around them. They are unusual because the Chinese fishing families who inhabit them live on separate jetties according to their clans, of which there are seven.

Pengkalan Weld Quay. Ten minutes' walk south from the Clock Tower, Georgetown.

FORT CORNWALLIS

When Captain Francis Light landed on this spot on 17 July 1786, it was no more than a sandy beach backed by solid jungle. Legend has it that Light fired a cannon full of silver dollars into the undergrowth in order to spur his men on to clear the jungle, and thus soon established camp. The first fort was made of wood, but Light persuaded the directors of the East India Company to rebuild it in stone at the beginning of the 19th century. They were reluctant to do so, despite the escalation of Anglo-French hostilities in the region, and in the end they were proved right, since a shot has never been fired in anger from its cannons.

The fort became the central focus of the growth of Pinang, even after it fell into decay. In 1977 it was declared a National Monument, and the area inside was landscaped to include a small park, a Police Museum, and a minute but interesting Memorial Gallery housed inside one of the old powder magazines, which contains old prints, documents and photographs.

Lebuh Light,

Georgetown. Open: daily, 8.30am–7pm. Admission charge.

KAPITAN KLING MOSQUE, see page 83.

KEK LOK SI TEMPLE

Work began on this enormous and ornate temple complex, the largest Buddhist temple in Pinang, in 1890 and took 70 years to complete. Expansion is still going on today, and the complex now includes a multi-storey car park and a smart, air-conditioned vegetarian restaurant. The Great Pagoda Tower, seven storeys high, is renowned for its architectural oddity, since it has a Chinese base, a Thai middle section, and is topped off with a Burmese spiral dome tower. Above the temple on the hillside a gigantic statue of Kuan Yin presides over all.

Ayer Itam, 8km from Georgetown. Open: daily. Bus 1 from Jalan Maxwell.

KHOO KONGSI

A *kongsi* is a Chinese clan-house, the focus of the community for members of the same clan, which serves not only as a temple but as a meeting place and a venue for ceremonies. Members of the Khoo clan from Hokkien province in China started to build this clan-house in the 1890s. It took them eight years to complete, but soon afterwards it was gutted by a mysterious fire. Taking this as a sign that the opulence of the clan-house had offended the deities, they rebuilt it on a lesser scale. The original

A Buddha at Kek Lok Si: the long earlobes symbolise princely rank

The huge Kek Lok Si Temple complex

building must have been amazing because even its replacement is magnificent, covered in a profusion of colourful carvings representing scenes from Chinese legends. A separate hall contains the clan's ancestral tablets and in the large courtyard is a stage for opera.

Cannon Square, Jalan Acheh, Georgetown. Open: weekdays, 9am–5pm; Saturday, 9am–1pm. Admission free.

KUAN YIN TENG TEMPLE, see
page 82–3.

The enormous reclining Buddha at Wat Chayamangkalaram

PINANG MUSEUM AND ART GALLERY
The ground floor of the museum holds an unusual collection of curiosities, memorabilia, maps and photographs. As well as a mock-up of an ornate Chinese bridal chamber, there are displays of jewel-encrusted *kris* (the traditional Malay dagger), magnificent opium beds inlaid with mother-of-pearl, and early rickshaws. There is an art gallery on the first floor.
Lebuh Farquhar. Tel: (04) 613 144. Open: Saturday to Thursday, 9am–5pm. Closed Fridays. Admission free.

SNAKE TEMPLE, see page 85.

SRI MARIAMMAN TEMPLE, see page 83.

WAT CHAYAMANGKALARAM
The enormous, 32m-long reclining Buddha inside the temple was built during the celebrations to mark the 25th centenary of the birth of Buddha in 1958. Across the road is the equally interesting Dhammikarama Burmese Temple.
Jalan Burmah. Open: daily, 8.30am–6pm.

PULAU LANGKAWI
The northernmost resort island on Malaysia's west coast, Pulau Langkawi is the main one of 104 islands that make up the Langkawi group, most of which are uninhabited. The approach by ferry is sublime, as the hazy silhouettes of the islands gradually resolve themselves into a series of wooded hillsides and cliffs separated by a maze of inlets and bays, with hardly a building in sight. As the ferry enters Kuah harbour, the large number of yachts at anchor bears testimony to the delights of cruising in the archipelago.

Langkawi has always been considered 'an island apart', relatively unspoiled and traditional in outlook. The majority of the 50,000 population are Malays, and fishing and rice-farming are still the mainstays of the economy. The island has recently been targeted for tourist development and although there has been an increase in the number of hotels under construction, much of it remains untouched, with wonderful landscapes of emerald-green *padi*-fields on the flatlands leading off to forest-clad mountain peaks swirling with cloud.

The main town of Kuah is a duty-free port, with plenty of shops and seafood restaurants. Most of the island's beach accommodation is at Pantai Cenang, with some facilities also available at Pantai Kok. The island does not have a vast number of tourist sights, but it makes up for this in the richness of the myths and legends that surround those it does have. All the places of interest can easily be seen on a day tour (see **Pulau Langkawi tour**, pages 86–7). Island-hopping excursions are popular (particularly to Pulau Dayang Bunting, the Island of the Pregnant Maiden, and the wildlife sanctuary on Pulau Singa Besar), and

CLAN-HOUSES (GEORGETOWN, PINANG)

The resplendent Khoo Kongsi is one of several 'clan-houses' in Pinang. Clan-houses were built by Chinese immigrants who belonged to clan associations. A common feature among Chinese immigrant groups in the 19th century, as they provided mutual support between people who spoke the same dialect or came from nearby villages.

The clan associations, governed by a body of elders, not only helped to welcome newcomers and settle disputes between members, but also provided important benefits in case of sickness and death. However poor they are, clan members could rest assured that they would have a proper ceremonial burial, without which, according to Chinese belief, the spirits of the dead cannot rest in peace.

The *kongsi,* or clan-house, was the focal point of the community, housing not only the all-important ancestral table but also a hall of fame honouring clansmen who had risen to positions of prominence. Although not as important as they used to be, the *kongsi* today are still active in ancestor-worship ceremonies and gatherings to celebrate achievements by clan members.

scuba-diving trips to the Pulau Payar Marine Park can also be arranged (see **Scuba-diving**, page 122).
MAS operates direct daily flights from Kuala Lumpur, Singapore and Pinang.

Regular ferries run from either Kuala Perlis (45 minutes) or Kuala Kedah (1 hour). There are also express ferry services to Pinang (daily) and Satun in Thailand (Mondays and Wednesdays).

Fishing boats await the tide on the shoreline at Kuah, Pulau Langkawi

Georgetown

This walk criss-crosses through the heart of Georgetown, taking in some of the most interesting buildings as well as the sights and sounds of Chinatown. The walk starts and finishes at the Clock Tower next to Fort Cornwallis. *Allow 2–3 hours.*

From the Clock Tower, walk back down Lebuh Light, past Fort Cornwallis (see page 78) and take the third turning on the left, Jalan Masjid Kapitan Kling. At the junction with Lebuh Farquhar, St George's church is on your right.

1 ST GEORGE'S CHURCH

The splendid, classically proportioned church was built in 1818 by convict labour and is one of the oldest landmarks in Pinang. In 1941 it was bombed by the Japanese, and stood unused without a roof until it was finally rebuilt in 1948. The small pavilion in front of the church is a memorial to Captain Francis Light.

Further down Jalan Masjid Kapitan Kling is the Kuan Yin Temple.

2 KUAN YIN TEMPLE

While it may not be the most ornate temple in Pinang, the

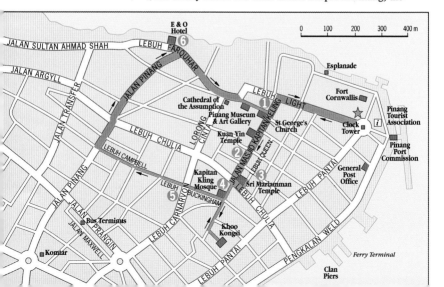

Kuan Yin (Goddess of Mercy) Temple is certainly one of the most popular, with a constant stream of devout people paying their respects to Kuan Yin. Thought to have been built around 1800, it is the oldest Chinese temple in Pinang.

Continue down Jalan Masjid Kapitan Kling, then turn left into Lebuh Chulia and left again into Lebuh Queen to reach the front entrance of the Sri Mariamman Temple.

3 SRI MARIAMMAN TEMPLE

The Sri Mariamman is the earliest Hindu temple on the island. Built in 1883, the architecture is traditional Dravidian. The interior holds the statues of several deities, among them that of the richly decorated Lord Subramaniam, which leads the chariot procession during the **Thaipusam Festival** (see pages 144–5).

Retrace your steps to the Jalan Masjid Kapitan Kling junction and cross over to explore the Kapitan Kling Mosque.

4 KAPITAN KLING MOSQUE

Completing this quartet of Pinang's oldest places of worship, the Kapitan Kling Mosque is named after the headman (the 'Kapitan') of the South Indian Kling community, who first arrived in Pulau Pinang as *sepoys* (Indian mercenaries) with Captain Francis Light. Rebuilt in 1916, the mosque is a typical example of Moorish design with strong Indian influences.

Continue down Jalan Masjid Kapitan Kling until the road begins to narrow. Halfway down the row of neat houses on your left a sign reads 'Leong San Tong Khoo Kongsi', which is the entrance to the courtyard of the ornately decorated Khoo Kongsi (see page 78). Retrace your steps and turn left down Lebuh Buckingham.

5 LEBUH BUCKINGHAM

Wander down Lebuh Buckingham and the neighbouring streets to savour the hustle and bustle of Malaysia's largest Chinese community. Bicycle repair shops, sign-makers, and fabric and shoe shops vie for space with restaurants advertising 'Famous Hainan Chicken Rice' and street-stalls with piles of salted duck eggs and other exotica. In the air-conditioned calm of the many goldsmiths' shops, phalanxes of sales assistants sit aloof from the clamour out in the surrounding streets, poised behind their glittering display cases. In traditional Chinese funerary shops, the needs of the departed are carefully catered for by providing paper replicas of their worldly goods so that they may enjoy a comfortable existence in the afterlife.

Turn right on Jalan Pinang and continue straight on, crossing Jalan Sultan Ahmad Shah, until you come to the E & O Hotel on Lebuh Farquhar.

6 E & O HOTEL

Founded by the Sarkie Brothers before they went on to build Raffles in Singapore, the E & O (Eastern & Oriental) is an old colonial landmark in the city and still retains a delightful atmosphere. Dance parties in the Ballroom and Curry Tiffin on Sunday afternoons echo the bygone days, when it was advertised as 'The Premier Hotel East of Suez'.

Turn left out of the E & O, follow Lebuh Farquhar, and cross the road near the Cathedral of the Assumption on your right. Shortly thereafter is the Pinang Museum and Art Gallery (see page 80). Turn right out of the museum, left again on Jalan Masjid Kapitan Kling and right on Lebuh Light to regain the Clock Tower.

Pulau Pinang

This 70km, circular route covers most of the sights outside of Georgetown. Driving on Pinang presents few problems, although Sundays should be avoided since most of the places of interest and the roads are packed with local residents on family outings. If you are staying at Batu Feringgi you can avoid driving into Georgetown. The tour can also be done in part by public transport with several changes of bus. *Allow most of the day.*

From Georgetown follow the signs to Batu Feringgi, which is 14km along the winding, northern coast road. From the beach, continue westwards to the fishing village of Teluk Bahang, where the road

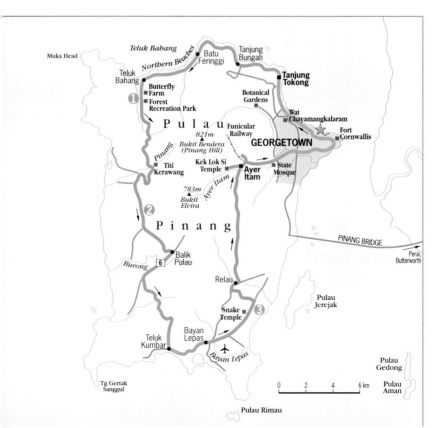

leaves the coast and heads inland. Turn left at the roundabout and after 1km you will come to the Butterfly Farm (see page 77) and, just next to it, the Forest Recreation Park.

1 FOREST RECREATION PARK

The park covers 10 hectares, with some pleasant walks through its wooded slopes. A museum displays traditional uses of forest products (such as musical instruments and rattan craftwork) as well as modern industries such as plywood and furniture manufacture.

Turn left out of the Forest Park. The road winds uphill for 11km, passing the Titi Kerawang waterfall just after the summit.

2 TRADITIONAL KAMPUNGS

As the road drops down the other side of the hill there are extensive views of the rice paddies stretching across to the western coast of the island. Once down on the plains, you pass through small _kampungs_ where the pace of life has changed little, with traditional Malay houses elevated on stilts to keep the damp and insects at bay.

Follow the signs to the town of Balik Pulau, and from here to Bayan Lepas (airport). Approximately 2km after the airport is the Snake Temple, but, set back from the road with no signpost, it is easily missed.

3 SNAKE TEMPLE

As you enter the Snake Temple, a sign requests mediums not to fall into a trance in the temple, 'to avoid causing inconvenience to worshippers and visitors'. Whether this is because they are hypnotised by the snakes or vice versa is not clear, but the snakes themselves – coiled around the altars and lounging in trees in the courtyard – exert a magnetic fascination. Around 50

or so pit vipers have taken up residence here, and their numbers are said to increase around the birthday of Chor Soo Kong, to whom the temple is dedicated. Some have been de-fanged for tourist photographs. The rest should not be approached.

Continue down the dual carriageway and take the first left exit, signed Bukit Bendera or Ayer Itam. On entering the town of Ayer Itam, follow the one-way system to the left of the market and take the first left to Kek Lok Si Temple (see page 78). Now follow signs to the left for Bukit Bendera (Pinang Hill, see page 77). Heading back towards Georgetown, follow the signs for either Batu Feringgi or the downtown area.

Forest Recreation Park: open daily, 7am–7pm. Admission free.
Museum: open Tuesday to Saturday, 9am–5pm; Fridays, 9am–noon and 2.45–5pm; closed Mondays. Admission charge.
Snake Temple: open daily, 7am–7pm. Admission free.

Pit vipers drape themselves around the Snake Temple

Pulau Langkawi

Starting at Pantai Cenang, this tour encompasses all the sights of interest and the best beaches on the island. There are excellent, well-signposted roads on the island and very little traffic. Scooters are readily available and some resorts also have jeeps for hire. *Allow 3–5 hours.*

Take the road that skirts the end of the airport runway and just after the village of Kuala Teriang turn left towards Pantai Kok.

1 PANTAI KOK

The road winds around the unspoiled forested headland of Tanjung Belikit down to Pantai Kok, one of the better swimming beaches on the island. This beautiful bay is framed to the north by the jagged limestone peaks at Tanjung Belua. *Continue to the end of the bay and turn right down a dirt track at the end of the beach, signposted Telaga Tujuh (Seven Wells). Continue for 1.5km until you reach a car-park and refreshment stalls, then continue on foot up to the falls.*

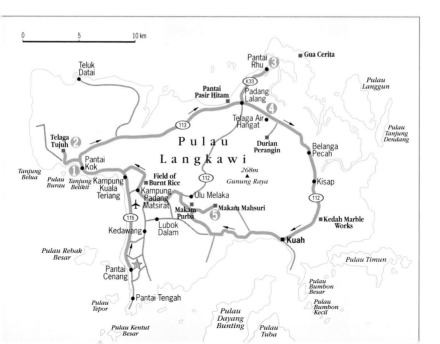

2 TELAGA TUJUH

Cascading down a massive rock face, the first waterfall and the rock-pools beneath it are reached via a short track off to the left. It is well worth continuing up to the top (a steep, 10-minute hike), where you can cool off in more rock-pools, with a fabulous view back across the headland and down to the beach.
Retrace your route and turn left at Pantai Kok. Continue past Pasir Hitam to the roundabout and turn left to Pantai Rhu.

3 PANTAI RHU

This is a peaceful beach in a superb setting, overlooking the thickly wooded crags of Langkawi's northernmost promontory. The islets in the bay (Pulau Kelam Baya and Pulau Cabang) can be reached on foot at low tide, or by canoe (which you can rent on the beach). From here there are boat trips which go round the cape to Gua Cerita, the Cave of Legends, whose walls have been inscribed with Koranic texts.
Drive back to the roundabout and turn left, shortly after which you will come to Telaga Air Hangat.

4 TELAGA AIR HANGAT

Legend has it that two powerful families fell out over the marriage proposed between their offspring. In the ensuing fracas, pots and pans were flung about, with the gravy dish landing at Kuah (which means gravy), a pot landing at Belanga Pecah (broken pot) and the pans of boiling water landing here, at Telaga Air Panas (hot-water springs).

The three original hot springs, previously a rather uninspiring attraction, have now been transformed into the centre-piece of Telaga Air Hangat, an excellent cultural centre. The springs themselves now well up

through a three-tiered fountain and flow through the gardens to a 6m long, free-standing mural depicting the story of the feuding families. The centre hosts a wide range of activities, including Malay folk and classical dances, snake shows, and demonstrations of *silat* (Malay martial arts) and arts and crafts.
Continue down the same road for 16km to Kuah. Turn right and follow the signs for Makam Mahsuri (Mahsuri's Tomb).

5 MAKAM MAHSURI

Mahsuri's marble tomb is set in a white-walled garden against a backdrop of flowering frangipani trees. The subject of one of Langkawi's most enduring

Boat trips run regularly from Pantai Rhu around the headland to Gua Cerita

legends, Mahsuri was a beautiful princess who was wrongly accused of adultery with a weary traveller to whom she had given help. A soldier was ordered to kill her by plunging a *kris* (Malay dagger) into her heart, and as he did so her innocence was proven by the white blood that flowed from the wound. As she lay dying, Mahsuri laid a curse on the island that it would not prosper for seven generations.
Return back down the road and turn right at the junction, following the signs for the Field of Burnt Rice and then on back to Pantai Cenang.

East Coast

*I*n contrast to the energetic, crowded cities and busy highways and towns on the west coast, the east coast has a more relaxed, easy-going atmosphere. Here, the enduring image is of crescent-shaped fishing boats hauled up on the beach, in front of quiet *kampungs* (villages) hidden away among the coconut groves. The reason the east coast has managed to retain its traditional character is because until recently it was relatively inaccessible. The impenetrable jungles of the central mountains effectively cut off the east from the west.

Although the life-style has remained practically unchanged, there are now good transport links to the rest of the country. The east-coast highway runs for 730km from north to south, and the central highway links Kuantan with Kuala Lumpur, crossing the middle of the peninsula. The east–west highway carves its way through the mountains near the Thai border, linking Kota Bharu with the west coast.

The northernmost state on this coast is Kelantan, the heartland of Malay culture. The state capital, Kota Bharu, is just a few kilometres from the Thai border. Further south, the state of Terengganu has miles of sandy beaches along the coastline, with the islands in the Perhentian group off shore to the

Fishermen unload their catch into carts pulled by water-buffalo at Beserah

north and the famous turtle-nesting beaches at Rantau Abang to the south of the capital, Kuala Terengganu. Beyond here is Pahang, with well-known resorts such as Cerating and Teluk Cempedak (Kuantan) on the coast. Inland, jungle encompasses the peninsula's biggest National Park, Taman Negara (see **Getting Away From it All**, page 120), and there are the mysterious lakes at Tasik Cini. Finally, there is Johor, jumping-off point for popular islands such as Pulau Tioman.

Most destinations on this coast are linked by an express bus network; driving down the coast is also an option (see **Driving**, page 182).

BESERAH

This small fishing village north of Kuantan is a major centre for *ikan bilis* (anchovy) fishing. Its main appeal for tourists is in watching the catch being landed at midday, since fishermen here use the rather unusual method of hauling it up the beach using water-buffalo carts. Beserah is also well known for batik and other cottage handicrafts. *10km from Kuantan.*

CERATING

The home of Asia's first Club Med (which covers three of the best beaches along here), Cerating is also a popular beach centre for overland travellers, with a wide range of budget chalets at Pantai Cerating, 2km north of the main village. Cerating is a centre for handicrafts (batik courses are available) and there are cultural performances in season. *47km north of Kuantan.*

KOTA BHARU

The capital of Kelantan, this congenial town, set on the banks of the Kelantan River, is one of the foremost centres in Malaysia for traditional arts and crafts. Most of the historic sights are located around Merdeka Square. At the eastern end of the square is the old royal palace, the Istana Balai Besar (Palace with the Large Audience Hall); built in 1844, it houses some beautiful wood-carvings (entry requires special permission). Beside it stands a smaller palace, the lovely Istana Jahar: completed in 1889, it is now the Museum of Royal Traditions and Customs. Just past here is the State Mosque and the State Religious Council Building. Also found in Merdeka Square is the Handicraft Village and Craft Museum.

A short walk from Merdeka Square is the cavernous, three-storey Central Market where a profusion of tropical produce is displayed over the vast central floor. Stalls on the other two floors specialise in spices, dried foods, batik and basketware. There is also an excellent *pasar malam* (night market) with a wide range of tasty Malay foods.

The main attraction in Kota Bharu, however, is the cultural performances at the Gelanggang Seni (Kelantan Cultural Centre). Between February and October performances take place daily featuring traditional games, arts and sports.

Other sights in the vicinity include a massive, 40m-long reclining Buddha at

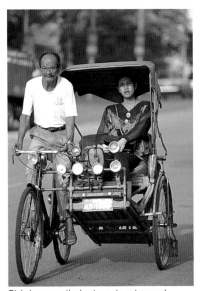

Rickshaws are the best way to get around

Wat Phothivihan (15km to the north) and Pantai Cahaya Bulan (the Beach of the Shining Moon) 10km to the north. The beach is by no means as enticing as the name suggests, but there are a number of batik, songket-weaving and kite-making workshops on the road leading to it (see **Shopping,** pages 134–5).

MAS flies to Kota Bharu from Kuala Lumpur, Pinang and Alor Setar. Express buses link Kota Bharu with the west coast, Kuala Lumpur, most towns on the east coast and Thailand.

Royal Museum: open Saturday to Wednesday, 9.30am–12.30pm; 2–5pm; Thursday 9.30–noon. For performances at the Gelanggang Seni, check with the Tourist Information Centre on Jalan Sultan Ibrahim (tel: 748 5534).

KUALA TERENGGANU

Situated at the mouth of the Terengganu River, Kuala Terengganu has been transformed by oil revenues into a busy modern town that holds little of interest for visitors. Stroll down Jalan Bandar, a narrow, curving thoroughfare lined with old Chinese shop-houses.
MAS has flights to Pinang and Kuala Lumpur. Buses connect north and south along the coast.

KUANTAN

State capital of Pahang, Kuantan is a modern city and an important transport hub. Most people head through on the way to the beach at Teluk Cempedak (see page 93).
MAS has flights to Kuala Lumpur and Singapore. Buses connect Kuantan to Singapore, Kuala Lumpur and coastal resorts.

MARANG

A picturesque fishing village on the mouth of the Marang River with a laid-back atmosphere that appeals to travellers stopping here on their way out to Pulau Kapas (see below). Guest-houses near the beach cater for people waiting for a ride to the island.
15km south of Terengganu, 45 minutes by bus.

PULAU KAPAS

One of the most easily accessible islands, just ½ hour by speedboat from Marang, Pulau Kapas has good, unspoilt beaches and reefs. There are huts and chalets on the main beach (camping is possible).
6km off shore from Marang.

PULAU PERHENTIAN

The fishing port of Kuala Besut is the jumping-off point for the islands in the Perhentian group, notably Pulau Perhentian Besar and Pulau Perhentian Kecil. The islands have long been a stop-over point for migratory birds as well as fishermen (hence the name, Perhentian, meaning 'stop'). The larger of the two is Perhentian Besar, which is separated from its smaller sister island by a narrow channel. Most of the accommodation is on Perhentian Besar, but small boats ply between the two. Both islands are delightfully unspoilt with excellent beaches, shallow reefs, and (on Perhentian Besar) jungle trails.
20km off shore from Kuala Besut (1½–2 hours by boat).

PULAU RAWA

The best-known resort island off shore from Mersing after Pulau Tioman, Pulau Rawa is tiny by comparison and has just one chalet resort hidden away behind the coco-palms on the beach. It has good beaches, though the coral is badly damaged, but tends to be crowded at weekends owing to its proximity to Mersing. Facilities available include fishing, snorkelling and scuba-diving.
16km from Mersing, 1½ hours by boat. Rawa Island Safaris Resort, Tourist Centre, Jalan Abu Bakar, Mersing. Tel: 799 1204.

PULAU REDANG

One of the more remote east-coast islands, Pulau Redang has long been popular with scuba-divers thanks to the excellent condition of the reefs and the abundant marine life that surrounds it. It was gazetted as a marine park in 1985. The Bejaya Redang Golf and County Resort has changed the island's character somewhat.
45km from Kuala Terengganu, 3–4 hours by boat.

PULAU TENGGUL

The small rocky island of Pulau Tenggul is famous for its beautiful reefs, rocky cliffs, caves and a lovely white-sand beach on the western side. A small resort with just 20 Malay-style chalets, the Tenggul Aqua Resort, has opened, offering scuba diving and watersports facilities.

For bookings at the Tenggul Aqua Resort (tel: 986 1807).

PULAU TIOMAN

The largest island on the east coast, Tioman is also one of the most popular. It is an intriguing island in more than one respect. Owing to its isolation from the mainland it has developed several sub-species of flora and fauna: as much as 25 per cent of the plant life is thought to be unique to the island and separate sub-species of squirrels, butterflies, insects and small cats have evolved here. There are relatively large populations of mouse deer and lizards, as well as bats. The island's single primate, the long-tailed macaque, can be seen roaming the forest fringes near the sea.

Tioman's rich natural history is complemented by an equally absorbing maritime history. Thanks to abundant fresh water supplies and its two 1,000m high peaks – easily visible to seafarers – Tioman became an important trading post and storm shelter for ships engaged in the spice trade. It was first mentioned in *Tales from China and India* (an early Arabic book upon which the *Tales of Sinbad* was based). In the 1950s Tioman achieved fame as the setting for the Hollywood musical *South Pacific*.

The island's main village is Kampung Tekek. Over the headland to the south there is a long beach occupied by the Bejaya Tioman Beach Resort, the most exclusive place to stay on Pulau Tioman; to the north there are several beaches with accommodation.

In addition to snorkelling or lazing on the beach, a popular activity is to trek across the central ridge to Juara Bay on the other coast, which will take about three hours. If you don't want to walk back you can get a lift on the round-island Sea Bus service (in season only).

Tioman's airport has been upgraded, and has direct flights to Kuala Lumpur and Singapore. From Mersing, boats range from slow fishing boats (3–4 hours) to express launches (2 hours). A new ferry service now links Tioman and Singapore (4½-hour journey, daily except Wednesday). Buses connect Mersing with Johor Bahru, Singapore and Kuala Lumpur.

A beach barbecue gets under way, Pulau Tioman

RANTAU ABANG

Although it is by no means the only place in Malaysia where turtles nest, Rantau Abang is by far the most famous, and for this reason has drawn thousands of visitors over the years to watch this compelling sight. Seven different species of turtle nest along this section of coast, but for most people the star attraction is the giant leatherback, the largest of all sea turtles, and Rantau Abang is one of their prime nesting locations.

In the past, considerable disturbance has been caused to the turtles on this beach, with people riding on them after they had nested and having beach parties – with bonfires and radios – during the nesting season. Thankfully, all these activities have now been stopped, and visitors' conduct during turtle nesting is more closely controlled. The beach is divided up into sanctuary areas and those areas where access is allowed. No lights, fires, noise or egg collecting is permitted, and the turtles must have started laying before you can approach them.

The season usually runs from June to September, with the peak during August. The optimum viewing time is at high tides or on a full moon – at night, of course.

There are numerous small chalets and huts where you can stay, and you will generally be called out if turtles are seen starting up the beach to lay. The Turtle Information Centre is well worth a visit beforehand.

58km south of Kuala Terengganu, 160km north of Kuantan. Rantau Abang Turtle Information Centre, tel: (09) 844 1533. Open: Saturday to Thursday 9am–11pm; Friday 9am–noon, 3–11pm (shorter times out of season). Buses run to Dungun hourly, from where there are services to Kuantan, Mersing and Kuala Lumpur.

TASIK CINI (THE LOTUS LAKE)

Malaysia's second-largest natural lake, Tasik Cini is hidden away in the wilds of Pahang, 100km west of Kuantan. During the flowering season from June to September the surfaces of a dozen interconnecting lakes are carpeted in the pink and white blossoms of the lotus flower from which Tasik Cini gets its name.

Getting to Lake Cini is half the adventure, and there are two ways of

---

LEATHERBACK TURTLES

The leatherback is the largest turtle in the world, and individuals can weigh up to 900kg. Unlike other marine turtles, it does not have a hard shell but a leathery carapace with seven long ridges. Its upper jaws are deeply notched to help it catch its favourite food – jellyfish. Leatherbacks regularly dive down to 400m or more, the maximum recorded dive being an astonishing 1,200m.

Like all marine turtles, leatherbacks only ever come ashore to lay eggs, which they may do between four and six times during the season. After laboriously dragging herself up the beach, the female excavates an egg chamber with her flippers, into which she deposits between 50 to 200 white, soft-shelled eggs. After covering up the hole, she lumbers back down the beach. Two months later, the young hatchlings emerge and make their way down to the sea to begin their perilous lives, with the chances of survival to adulthood being only one in 10,000.

Beach bar at Teluk Cempedak: this boat originally carried Vietnamese 'boat people' to the East Coast

doing this. The classic approach is by boat, in which case you turn off the Kuantan–Kuala Lumpur highway towards Kampung Belembing and hire a motorised longboat at the jetty. After crossing the fast-flowing Pahang River, the boat enters the jungle up the Sungai Cini (Cini River). This is a beautiful journey, as the boat follows the tributary to the lake: kingfishers, butterflies and dragonflies scoot over the water, while monkeys leap from tree-top to tree-top above. Twisted and gnarled lianas hang in great loops over the water and tree branches are blanketed with enormous and luxuriant bird's-nest ferns.

The other means of reaching the lake is to drive down the Kuantan–Segamat highway, following the signs from the Cini village junction: the last part of the journey is along a bumpy track through oil-palm plantations, until finally the Lake Cini Resort appears among the trees.

In front of the resort there is a jetty where boats can be hired for trips around the lakes. Chalet, dormitory and camping accommodation are provided in a pleasantly low-key resort which organises numerous jungle activities.

Lake Cini Resort, c/o Lembaga Kemajuan Pahang Tenggara, Wisma Sultan Ahmad Shah, 26700 Muadzam Shah, Pahang, Darul Makmur (tel: (09) 408 6308 or fax: (09) 452 110). Or: Malaysian Overland Adventures, Lot 1.23, 1st floor, Bangunan Angkasaraya, Jalan Ampang, 50450 Kuala Lumpur (tel: (03) 241 3569 or fax: (03) 241 4030.

TELUK CEMPEDAK (KUANTAN)

Five kilometres outside Kuantan, Teluk Cempedak is a sizeable beach with good swimming and a wide range of accommodation and watersports facilities. Some development is taking place, but a few minutes walk around the headland to the north will bring you to an untouched, natural beach where eagles ride the thermals above the headland and monkeys from the jungle behind roam the sands. Teluk Cempedak has a good selection of seafood restaurants and food stalls on the beachfront.

MAS has flights to Kuala Lumpur and Singapore. Buses connect Kuantan to Singapore, Kuala Lumpur and coastal resorts. From Kuantan, Teluk Cempedak is reached by bus or taxi.

CORAL REEFS

A thriving coral reef is a glorious sight, a magical kaleidoscope of beautiful fish and colourful life-forms. Second only to rain forests in the number of animals and plants that they support, it is little wonder that reefs captivate the imagination of divers and snorkellers, compelling them to return again and again to experience this dazzling and intricate environment.

Coral reefs have existed for around 450 million years in one form or another, making them probably the oldest ecosystems on the planet. Although corals look like plants, coral reefs are in fact built by a tiny animal, the coral polyp. This remarkable creature is responsible for building the largest structures made by life on earth. This ability is even more extraordinary in that it is achieved in shallow, tropical waters where the nutrients essential for growth are virtually non-existent. The polyp is able to do this thanks to the symbiotic relationship it has with tiny plants called zooxanthellae that live within its tissues. The zooxanthellae convert carbon dioxide by photosynthesis into oxygen and carbohydrates, which the polyp uses to build its stony, limestone

skeleton – which in turn builds up to form a reef.

Anyone seeing a coral reef for the first time is likely to find it a bewildering and mysterious place, teeming with life of every description in what seems to be a random explosion of exuberance and colour. But beneath the apparent chaos there are complex patterns of behaviour that allow the vast array of reef creatures to share this habitat and thrive. Some fish, such as cardinalfish,

A diver surrounded by a flurry of butterfly fish

squirrelfish and soldierfish, only feed at night. As they disappear into nooks and crannies at daylight, others emerge to take over the niches they have vacated. The gaudy parrotfish (which spends the night wrapped in a protective layer of mucus which renders it undetectible to predators) emerges to nibble away on corals; damselfish take up their places

on patches of seaweed, which they 'farm', chasing away other herbivores; other fish – such as fusiliers or the glittering members of the Chromis family – feed on passing plankton while others, like triggerfish and pufferfish, specialise in eating sea-urchins. As the day dawns, the main reef predators like sharks and barracuda cruise in from the open ocean, sweeping in to hunt on the reef walls and channels.

Since the dawn of time, reefs have provided coastal communities in the tropics with a bountiful harvest of food as well as products such as jewellery, medicines and building materials. Until recently coral reefs were able to withstand this harvest, but they are now under threat from a wider range of human activities – coastal development, over-fishing, sewage pollution and damage by tourists. The need to protect this fabulous and fragile ecosystem has never been greater.

The reefs of Malaysia are home to a teeming array of iridescent fish and colourful corals

East Malaysia

SARAWAK

Sarawak is the largest state in Malaysia, stretching about 700km along the northwest coast of Borneo and flanked by Sabah, Brunei and the Indonesian province of Kalimantan. The economy is mostly dependent on natural resources such as oil, gas, pepper and, of course, timber.

Around 300,000 people visit Sarawak every year, most of them drawn by the forests, national parks, caves and the fascinating diversity of peoples and tribal culture. While oil and timber wealth may have transformed a few boom towns, many of the tribes still follow their traditional life-styles (with the exception, naturally, of head-hunting) and live in longhouses, with the entire community under one roof. For many visitors, an overnight stay in a longhouse is the highlight of their trip.

There are few good roads in Sarawak so transport is mostly by river-boat or aeroplane: internal MAS flights (and flights to Sabah) are good value and save days of arduous travelling.

KUCHING

When James Brooke became Rajah of Sarawak in 1841, he chose Kuching as his base. Located on the banks of the Sarawak River 32km inland from the sea, it is a delightful city and the main springboard for adventures in Sarawak. It has several first-class hotels, a handful of interesting sights, and is one of the best places to buy tribal arts and crafts (see **Shopping**, pages 135).

SARAWAK

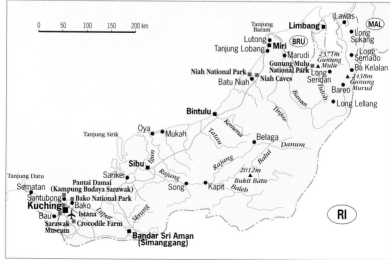

Astana

Charles Brooke, nephew of James, built this palace when he became Rajah in 1870. Brooding on the opposite side of the river from the Kuching, it is not open to the public, but you can jump on one of the small *tambangs* or river-taxis, which ply backwards and forwards to the other bank, for a closer look.

Fort Margherita

Built by Charles Brooke and named after his wife, it was designed to protect Kuching from pirates. It is now a Police Museum.
Downstream from the Astana, accessible by tambang. Open: 10am–6pm, except Monday and holidays. Admission free.

Pasar Minggu (Sunday Market)

This is an incredible market with an amazing variety of edible roots, berries, plants and fruits harvested from the forests by the Bidayuh people (Land Dyaks). They come in with their produce on Friday nights and sleep by their stalls for the weekend, trimming up neat, symmetrical displays of curious roots and fruits as well as more familiar items such as whole honeycombs or small, very fierce chillies.

Other Bidayuh whittle away at bamboo hearts or sell whole bamboos for cooking rice in (known as *pulut*, it is served sliced into sections). The busiest day is Sunday (hence it is known as the Sunday market, although it is open on Saturday night as well).
Jalan Satok (from the town centre, walk down Jala P Ramlee and turn right at the roundabout).

Sarawak Museum

Well worth a visit for the extensive ethnographic sections in both the older

A Bidayuh woman displays jungle fruits and roots in the Pasar Minggu, Kuching

half (founded in 1891) and the new section (opened in 1983). Other displays focus on the animals and birds of the Borneo jungle, the marine life, and the cats – in deference to the name of the capital of Sarawak (*Kuching* means cat in Malay).
Jalan Tun Haji Openg. Five minutes' walk from the town centre. Open: Saturday to Thursday 9am–6pm. Admission free.

Iban children peer out from the door of their longhouse on the banks of the Katibas River

BAKO NATIONAL PARK

Covering the entire northern section of the jagged Muara Tebas peninsula, Bako National Park is just two hours away from Kuching and is one of the most easily accessible wilderness areas in Sarawak. The country's oldest national park, it was chosen because of the enormous variety of flora and bird life found here: the diversity of plant life is unique, with many different types of vegetation and habitat. In addition, the coastline is spectacular, with small bays, beaches and coves backed by tall sandstone cliffs, and sea arches weathered into honeycomb patterns.

The park headquarters and visitors' accommodation is behind the beach at Telok Assam, where there is a well laid-out Interpretative Centre. Within the park grounds are long-tailed macaques, silver-leaf monkeys and the strange bearded pig that saunters around the compound. Throughout the park there are over 30km of well-maintained trails, divided into 16 different routes (see **Bako National Park walk**, pages 102–3). Perhaps not the most spectacular of Sarawak's parks it is,

however, well managed and easily accessible, containing much that can be quietly enjoyed and appreciated.

37km from Kuching. Permits must be obtained in advance from the Sarawak National Parks Booking Office, Tourist Information Centre, Main Bazaar, Kuching 93000 (tel: 248 088/410 944). Bus 6 from the market-place operates to Kampung Bako, from where you have to catch a boat. Accommodation in the park ranges from camping to hostel beds, rooms or rest-houses.

GUNUNG MULU NATIONAL PARK

Sarawak's largest national park, covering 529sq km of mixed peat swamp and dipterocarp and montane forests. It is rich in plant and bird life (including eight species of hornbill), but the most compelling attractions are the massive caves, notably the Deer Cave (which is said to have the largest cave passage in the world), Clearwater Cave (which is criss-crossed with underground rivers), Wind Cave and Lang Cave.

Further caverns are being explored and opened to the public. On the other side of Gunung Mulu (a three-day trek around the mountain) are the spectacular, 45m-high limestone pinnacles. *Permits for Gunung Mulu must be obtained in advance (and accommodation booked at the same time) from the National Parks Office, Petra Jaya, Wisma Sum ber Alam, Kuching (tel: (082) 442 180), or Old Forestry Building, Jalan Ankasa, Miri (tel: (085) 436 637). Flights from Miri land just outside the park.*

IBAN LONGHOUSES

Each tribe has its own variation on the longhouse (several variations can be seen at the **Sarawak Cultural Village**, see page 100), but essentially they all embody the same principle, which is of several families living under one roof with their individual rooms leading off from a communal, enclosed veranda.

The most accessible longhouses to visit are those of the Iban, since they nearly always settle on the banks of navigable rivers. From the boat jetty, steps lead up the river bank to a central garden with strips of land allocated to each family. Corn, beans and pumpkins share garden space with fishing nets hung out to dry, boats under repair, and foraging chickens and pigs. Around the garden are the longhouses themselves, raised off the ground on stilts.

Longhouse visits on the Skrang River can be organised through travel agents in Kuching. There are fewer organised tours on the Rajang River, so you will either have to go it alone or try to hire a freelance tour guide. The latter is the best option, since unless you speak Iban you will need a guide to translate, as well as to advise you on how to behave with your hosts and to make arrangements for hiring a boat and organising food and gifts to take with you.

Once at the longhouse, you will stay in the family room of the *Tuai Rumah* (chief) and, after eating, the whole community will gather on the veranda for singing and dancing with plenty of *tuak* (rice wine) to make the party go. This is not a goldfish-bowl show for your benefit, since you will be expected to participate actively – usually with the result of much hilarity all round. In this respect, the larger group you travel with the better, since the Iban will be disappointed if performances fizzle out early because your talents (musical or otherwise) have been exhausted.

Although many longhouses now have tin roofs and electricity, there may not be any toilet facilities and you will have to wash in the river, as they do, so you should be prepared to rough it.

Tattooing is common among the Sarawak tribes

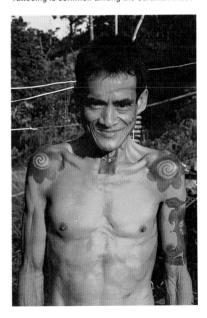

KAMPUNG BUDAYA SARAWAK (SARAWAK CULTURAL VILLAGE)

Designed as a 'living museum' of Sarawak's rich cultural heritage, this award-winning project is set in 7 hectares of landscaped grounds at the foot of Gunung Santubong, behind Damai Beach. Scattered around an artificial lake are seven different ethnic dwellings, with typical longhouses of the Bidayuh, Iban and Orang-Ulu, a Melanau 'Rumah Tinggi' (a massive communal house on stilts), Penan huts, a Malay home and a Chinese farmhouse.

Upon entering, guides welcome you and cheerfully chat about the lifestyles and customs of their various tribes. There is something going on in each one, whether it be a handicraft demonstration, preparing ethnic foods, blow-pipe making, drumming or traditional games. Twice daily there is a highly entertaining dance show.

It sounds contrived and the entrance price is steep, but it is extremely informative and well organised, and there is plenty to occupy at least half a day. There is a restaurant and handicraft shop (see **Shopping**, page 135). *Kampung Budaya Sarawak, Pantai Damai, P O Box 2632, 93752 Sarawak (tel: (082) 422 411). Open: daily, 9am–5.15pm. Admission charge. A shuttle bus from the Holiday Inn and Riverside Majestic, Kuching, stops at the gates.*

An Iban warrior performs the Ngajat Lesong, a dance requiring agility and strength

MIRI

A boom oil town near the border with Brunei, Miri is a useful transit point for permits for the Niah Caves or Gunung Mulu from the National Parks Office. Dull in the daytime, it is enlivened by numerous seedy bars – and some excellent seafood restaurants – in the evenings (Bruneians cross the border for R & R).
Frequent MAS flights to Kuching, Kota Kinabalu and other East Malaysia destinations, with connections through to Kuala Lumpur.

NIAH CAVES

'The cave deposits of this part of Borneo are wholly without interest except to local naturalists' wrote the explorer A Hart Everett in 1879. He was mistaken, but it was not until nearly 80 years later that it became clear just how spectacularly wrong Everett had been, when excavations at Niah revolutionised prevailing theories on the distribution of early humankind across the globe. In 1957 the Curator of Sarawak Museum,

Tom Harrisson, discovered a skull and other artefacts dating back to 37,500 BC, drawing worldwide attention to the caves and conclusively disproving the idea that early *Homo sapiens* had originated in Europe. Some of these finds are on display in the Sarawak Museum in Kuching. The famous skull can be seen at the Niah Park Headquarters.

The cave system lies underneath the limestone massif of Gunung Subis, in the centre of what is now the Niah National Park. The crucial evidence was unearthed in the west mouth of the Great Cave (where the archaeological workings can still be seen), an awesome natural cathedral over 60m high and around 245m wide which is among the largest caves in the world. The magnitude of the cave, heightened by the sense of scale given to it by a handful of old buildings at its entrance, is overwhelming.

The caves are also still one of the major centres in Sarawak for a trade that is itself centuries old, the collecting of swifts' nests to make the highly prized bird's-nest soup.

The park headquarters is at Pangkalan Lubang, which is reached by a short boat ride from Batu Niah village. Buses or shared taxis run from Miri and Bintulu to Batu Niah. Accommodation at the park must be booked in advance at the National Parks Office, Jalan Angkasa, Miri (tel: (085) 436 637). The caves are 4km away along a plankwalk from the park HQ.

PANTAI DAMAI (DAMAI BEACH)

The nearest coastal resort to Kuching, Damai has a reasonable beach, good views of Gunung Santubong (Mount Santubong) and a comfortable hotel. *35km north of Kuching. Holiday Inn Damai Beach Resort, P O Box 2870,*

Song and dance are woven into the fabric of daily life for the people of Sarawak

93756 Kuching (tel: (082) 846 999). Shuttle bus from the Holiday Inn Kuching all day.

SIBU

The second town of Sarawak and the main port on the Rajang river, Sibu is 60km from the coast. You can travel from here further upstream to Song or Kapit and then branch off into tributaries of the Rajang to visit Iban longhouses. From the top of the Chinese temple on the waterfront in Sibu there is a bird's-eye view of river traffic, including the log barges being towed downstream to the sawmills. Directly beneath the temple is the quay where the passenger boats berth. These extraordinary, fuselage-shaped speedboats that churn up and down the river from jetty to jetty all day are the chief means of transport on the river.

Bako National Park

This relatively easy walk mostly follows the Lintang Trail, which loops around behind the park headquarters and encompasses most of the different types of habitat to be seen at Bako. If you leave in the early afternoon you will arrive at Telok Delima, near the end of the walk, at the right time of day to try and see proboscis monkeys. *Allow 3–4 hours.*

Starting from the park headquarters, cross the boardwalk through the mangroves and ascend the hill to the plateau. After a 10-minute climb you will come out in the Kerangas scrub.

ANT-PLANTS

Kerangas is an Iban word meaning 'land where rice cannot be grown'; because of the poor soil conditions there are few large trees and many plants have adapted ingenious mechanisms in order to make the most of the harsh environment. One such is the extraordinary ant-plant, of which there are four common species on the plateau, immediately noticeable all around you as bulbous growths clinging to the trees. The ants and the plants co-exist in a symbiotic (mutually beneficial) relationship: the ants live inside the plant, thereby gaining a home, and the debris they deposit is digested by the plant, which gains nutrients that are in short supply in the soil. The two most easily identifiable ant-plants are *Myrmecodia tuberosa* and *Hydnophytum formicarium* (the former has a wrinkly, spiny tuber with just one stem growing from it, while the latter is smoother and may have several stems sprouting out). *At the junction with the Tajor Trail, turn right. Shortly afterwards, the track slopes gently up through typical kerang pole forest.*

Ant-plants are easily visible on the plateau

KERANGAS POLE FOREST

Such forest is characterised by dense strands of saplings and enormous Nibong bamboos, with sunlight dappling the spreading leaves of wild sago palms and cicadas trilling incessantly in the background as you wander along the cool, shady track.
Follow the signpost on your left to the Bukit Tambi look-out.

An ingenious adaptation, the symbiotic ant-plant makes the most of its harsh environment

BUKIT TAMBI LOOK-OUT

From this vantage point there are magnificent views of Mount Santubong in front and Pulau Lekei at the northernmost extremity of the park. To the left, some of Kuching's buildings can be seen rising from the plains in the distance.
Continue along the Lintang Trail, following the red way-marks through the root-entangled path until you come to the junction with the Ulu Serait path. Turn left down here for a short way.

CARNIVOROUS PLANTS

This section of track is a good place to look for some of the rarer species of the pitcher plant, another of nature's creative adaptions to nutrient-poor soils. The leaves on these carnivorous plants have been modified to form a hollow tube containing a liquid into which insects fall. It is from this liquid that they are then digested. Species commonly seen are *Nepenthes ampullaria* (which has a distinctive, pot-shaped pitcher), *Nepenthes rafflesiana* (easily recognised by the red-and-white stripes around the bowl), and *Nepenthes gracilis* (extremely abundant, clinging to branches by its tendrils and often decorating trees in large numbers). Other carnivorous plants are harder to spot. They include bladderworts (whose

underground leaves trap insects) and sundews (which appear as clusters of minute red flowers on the forest floor).
Continue back down the Lintang Trail. Eventually you will emerge at a look-out point above Telok Delima, from where the track descends more steeply, with wooden steps skirting huge, lichen-covered boulders.

PROBOSCIS MONKEYS

Telok Delima is one of the best place to see the park's extraordinary-looking proboscis monkeys. As you descend, you will hear them hooting in the tree-tops. The males, with their huge, pendulous noses and large pot-bellies, look insanely human. Females have a shorter, stubbier nose. The proboscis is an extemely shy species. Found only in Borneo and two small islands off its northeast coast, it is restricted to mangroves and the river-bank and peat-swamp forests of the central lowlands. Habitat destruction is the greatest threat to their survival, and of the tiny population of 1,000 still extant, around 150 live here in Bako National Park.
Continue on past Telok Delima to return to the park headquarters.

RAIN FORESTS

Most people tend to think of tropical rain forest simply as 'jungle', a steamy, impenetrable mass of vegetation containing enormous trees that somehow play a role in reducing the greenhouse effect. In fact, there are several kinds of rain forest, each with its own plant and animal communities, each recognisable as a distinct ecosystem shaped by variations in soil, rainfall, altitude and human impacts.

Lowland rain forest is one of the most productive and biologically diverse habitats on the planet, home to more than half of all species in existence. Several hundred tree species may co-exist within a space the size of a soccer pitch; the most abundant trees are the

LOGGING

Malaysia is the biggest exporter of tropical hardwoods in the world. In many parts of the country you will witness the destruction that has caused such an outcry in the west. In the Cameron Highlands, trucks loaded with logs roar down the mountain roads at night; on the rivers of Sarawak, streams of barges loaded with tree-trunks are hauled by tugs down to the sawmills. In 1991 the International Tropical Timber Organisation claimed that if logging rates were not reduced, Sarawak would be 'logged out' within a decade.

One of the problems with forestry management in Malaysia is enforcement of the laws, with insufficient resources to police the vast areas of forest. Another is corruption, with politicians able to amass vast fortunes by awarding lucrative logging licences.

In 1992, Sarawak pledged to reduce logging from 15 million cubic metres a year to 9 million, and in 1994 a total ban on raw log exports was imposed; local revenue and employment has been adversely affected. Whether such measures will be sufficient to save Sarawak's rain forests remains to be seen, since timber exports still form the mainstay of the economy.

The rain forests of Malaysia are home to hundreds of magnificent species of trees, plants and flowers, all crowded together in this dynamic ecosystem

dipterocarps, pushing through the canopy to heights of 50–80m with huge trunks up to 2m in diameter supported by enormous buttress roots. Beneath the canopy, lianas cling to the vertical trunks and epiphytes (plants such

as ferns that grow on trees) abound. At ground level the vegetation is less dense, making it relatively easy to move around in the forest. The largest remaining tract of lowland rain forest in Malaysia is in the Taman Negara National Park.

At higher altitudes the rain forest changes character, with completely different communities of animals and plants. Up to 750m above sea level it is known as lower montane (from 'mountain') forest, above 1,500m as upper montane forest. The forest giants are less common at higher altitudes, with few trees reaching above 10m. Temperate species such as oaks and

heather predominate, and mosses and lichens thrive in the moist, cool air. These types of rain forest (sometimes also called 'cloud forests') can be found in the Central Highlands on the peninsula and on the slopes of Gunung Kinabalu in Sabah.

Where the virgin rain forest has been cleared by logging or for agriculture, a host of secondary species spring up to fill the vacant niches. Fishtail palms, resam ferns and other light-dependent species coat the forest floor. In the short term, animals and birds are driven out, but as the original plant communities regenerate some wildlife gradually returns.

Sabah

Sabah is the second-largest state in Malaysia after Sarawak and occupies the northeast sector of the island of Borneo. Whereas Sarawak is dominated by rivers, Sabah is synonymous with mountains – in particular, the towering massif of Gunung (Mount) Kinabalu, which at 4,101m is the highest mountain between Papua New Guinea and the Himalayas. The surrounding national park is a treasure-house of plant and animal communities, an oasis of biological splendour in one of the largest remaining tracts of rain forest left in the country. Other popular attractions include the world's largest orang-utan sanctuary at Sepilok, colourful *tamus* or tribal markets, and offshore islands ringed with coral reefs such as those in the Tunku Abdul Rahman National Park and Pulau Sipadan in the Celebes Sea – the jewel in Malaysia's crown for scuba-divers.

During the 17th and 18th centuries when the European powers fought over the great seaports of Peninsular Malaysia, the island of Borneo remained relatively isolated. Most trading ships avoided this mysterious land, from whence came tales of rapacious pirates and head-hunting tribes lurking in the impenetrable jungle. Most of the land was nominally under the control of the Sultan of Brunei.

In the late 19th century an Englishman called Alfred Dent signed a lease with the Sultan of Brunei and the Sultan of Sulu (who ruled in the northeast of the country) and gained control of North Borneo. In 1881 Dent formed the British North Borneo Company, but they were not as successful as the white rajahs in neighbouring Sarawak at governing the populace. In 1895 the introduction of new taxes led to the famous Mat Salleh Rebellion, led by the charismatic figure of Mat Salleh, who was believed to be in possession of supernatural powers. The rebellion was not put down until 1905, although Mat Salleh himself was killed in 1900. Today, he is one of Sabah's most well-known national heroes.

After World War II both Sabah and Sarawak were handed over to the British government and became Crown Colonies. In 1963 they were merged into the Federation of Malaysia.

As you will find elsewhere in Malaysia, Sabah is a melting-pot of people and cultures, of immigrant and indigenous groups. The population of just over 1.5 million encompasses over 30 different tribes and races speaking some 100 different dialects, all with their own unique traditions, customs, festivals and culture.

The largest indigenous group are the Kadazan/Dusuns, who comprise around 30 per cent of the population and live mostly on the west coast. Traditionally they were the main rice producers in the country, although many now work outside agriculture. The second-largest group are the Bajau, who were once fearless sailors and wanderers. Now, most Bajau are settled on the land and renowned for their skills in horsemanship as well as in rearing livestock. Many Bajau Laut ('Sea Bajau', also called Sea Gypsies) still live on or near the water, in stilt villages or in boats known as *lipa-lipa*. The third main group are the Murut, who are mostly from the southwest and the interior. Their livelihood traditionally depended on hunting and shifting cultivation.

Travelling around Sabah presents few problems, with frequent and reliable minibuses linking towns and cities. Although some roads are still pot-holed and bumpy, many have been upgraded. If you want to save time, MAS operates a network of regular flights which are good value for money.

The peaks of Gunung Kinabalu dominate the landscape of northwest Sabah

SABAH

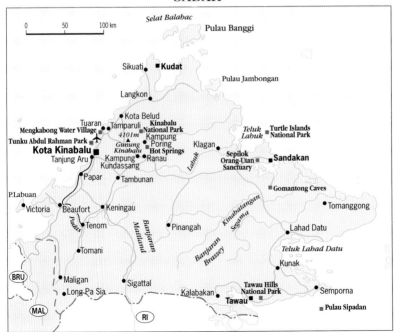

GOMANTONG CAVES

These huge limestone caves, 32km from Sandakan, are home to around a million swiftlets. Locals collect the nests using the same, centuries-old techniques as they do at the Niah Caves in Sarawak (see page 100). The trip to the caves involves a boat-ride across the bay from Sandakan and then 16km by four-wheel drive through the forest.

Two-day expeditions to the Gomantong Caves and wildlife watching on the Kinabatangan River are organised by Wildlife Expeditions, Room 903, 9th floor, Wisma Khoo Siak Chiew, Sandakan (tel: (089) 219616).

KINABALU NATIONAL PARK

The Kinabalu National Park is one of Sabah's major attractions. Climbers are drawn to the towering peaks of Gunung Kinabalu (Mount Kinabalu), but there is more to Kinabalu than simply the challenge of climbing the mountain,

Hibiscus flower on Gunung Kinabalu

since within the huge expanse of the park (which covers over 750sq km) a great variety of habitats can be found.

Within this protected environment a rich and diverse flora flourishes. One of the most famous species for which Kinabalu is known is the parasitic *Rafflesia*, the world's largest flower with red blooms that can measure 1m wide. Over 1,000 species of orchid can be found within the park, as well as over 20 varieties of rhododendron and a dozen different kinds of carnivorous pitcher plants (*Nepenthes*). Over half the plants growing above 900m are found nowhere else in the world.

Despite claims that Kinabalu is an 'easy climb', the ascent to the summit takes two days and is a demanding haul even for those who are fit. If you intend to make the ascent, a comprehensive booklet, *Guide to the Summit Trail*, is available at the park shop. If you don't have the time to reach the summit there are well-marked trails around the park headquarters (see **Kinabalu National Park walk**, pages 114–15).

Within the park there is a wide range of accommodation, two canteens and a shop selling necessities.

Overnight accommodation must be booked in advance through the Sabah Parks Office, Block K, Sinsuran Complex, PO Box 10626, Kota Kinabalu (tel: (088) 211585/211652). Park headquarters is 60km from Kota Kinabalu, 2 hours by bus.

KOTA BELUD

This small town to the northeast of Kota Kinabalu is well worth visiting on Sunday mornings for the weekly *tamu* (market), where tribal peoples bring their produce to sell and Bajau 'cowboys' auction their horses and buffalo. Although colourful enough on a

Bajau women sell their brightly patterned basketware at the Kota Belud *tamu*

normal Sunday, the best time to visit Kota Belud is at the annual Tamu Besar (see **Festivals**, page 147).

Minibuses from Kota Kinabalu take 1½ hours. The tamu is a short distance outside Kota Belud.

KOTA KINABALU

The state capital of Sabah is a relatively new city – the town was almost totally destroyed in World War II – and although its tree-lined avenues are pleasant enough it has none of the historical resonances of Kuching. Apart from the State Mosque, whose gold dome glistens against a backdrop of jungle-clad hills, the main tourist attraction is the Sabah State Museum, which houses ceramics and craftwork from Bajau, Murut, Kadazan/Dusun and Rungus peoples. The mock-ups of tribal longhouses in the museum grounds are also well worth a look.

For most people Kota Kinabalu is a transit stop before heading out to explore points north and east. Day trips from here can be made to the Tunku Abdul Rahman National Park (see page 112) and Kota Belud (see opposite). *Sabah State Museum, Jalan Mat Salleh (tel: (088) 53199). Open: Monday to Thursday, 10am–6pm; weekends and holidays, 9am–6pm. Closed Fridays. Admission free.*

PORING HOT SPRINGS

Part of the Kinabalu National Park, the hot springs are an hour or so away from park headquarters. The sulphurous water steams into a series of old-fashioned tubs where you can soothe your aching muscles after climbing the mountain.

A short walk further up the hill there is a terrific Canopy Tree Walk that sways between the tree-tops and provides a great view of the forest at canopy level. Despite the fact that it is netted and quite safe, the 200m long walkway can still induce vertigo as you look down to the forest floor some 50m below ('scary but great fun' was a typical comment in the visitors' book at the last tree).

19km north of Ranau, reached by minibus or taxi. Open: daily, 7am–6pm. Admission charge. Canopy Tree Walk open 10.30am–4pm. Admission charge. There are hostels and chalets for overnight stays – book through the Sabah Parks Office (see page 108).

PULAU SIPADAN

As the boat from Semporna approaches Pulau Sipadan across the Celebes Sea, it looks no different from any other tropical island – a small blob in the ocean surrounded by white coral-sand beaches and topped off by jungle vegetation. Sipadan, however, is not just any old island. It is the only deep-water oceanic island in Malaysia and sits on top of a massive limestone sea-mountain that extends some 600m down to the sea-bed. A magnificent reef ecosystem has developed on the sheer walls of this sea-mountain, and it is a magnet for divers from all over the world.

Accommodation on the island is basic, as befits a resort where the majority of visitors are inclined to spend most of the day underwater. There are three dive lodges on the island, the longest-established of which is the Sipadan Dive Lodge operated by Borneo Divers. For non-diving partners the 12-hectare island has a few, short jungle

Visitors and ranger watch a turtle laying her eggs on the beach at Pulau Sipadan

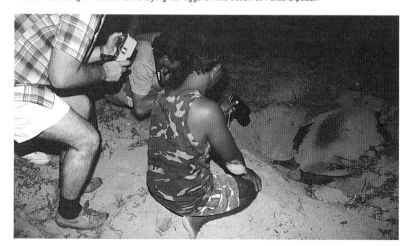

Dive lodge on Pulau Sipadan, whose pristine reefs draw divers from all over the world

trails to explore (the island is also an important bird-nesting site), but apart from that there is nothing to do except relax.

The diving is exceptional. Just a stone's throw from the beach bar, the pale aquamarine waters over the sandy sea-bed change abruptly to hues of deep blue, indicating the beginning of the massive coral drop-off. Underwater, the reef is a profusion of sea-fans, black coral, soft corals and iridescent hard corals inhabited by shoals of fusiliers, parrotfish, grouper, sweetlips and other colourful fish.

Because of its position in mid-ocean, Sipadan also has large numbers of pelagic (open-water) species cruising the reefs, with schools of manta rays, barracuda and hammerhead sharks frequently seen in currents on the reef headlands. There are so many turtles here (hundreds, possibly thousands, live around Sipadan) that once underwater you can hardly turn around without seeing them snoozing under reef ledges, scooting off into the deep blue, feeding on the reef or floundering around on the surface as they mate.

Turtles nest on the beach all year round (the peak season is from August to October) and most nights there is a guided walk with a ranger to watch them (walking on your own at night around the island is prohibited).

Pulau Sipadan is 1½ hours by speedboat from Semporna. Dive packages are available, usually for five days, typically including transfers from Kota Kinabalu, accommodation, food, three boat-dives per day and unlimited beach diving. Borneo Divers, Rooms 401–404, 4th floor, Wisma Sabah, Kota Kinabalu (tel: (088) 2222226). Sipadan Dive Centre, A1026, 10th Floor, Wisma Merdaka, Jalan Tun Razak, Kota Kinabalu (tel: (088) 240584); and Pulau Sipadan Resort, 484 Bandar Sabindo, Block P, PO Box 290, Tawau (tel: (089) 765200).

SANDAKAN

Sandakan was the capital of Sabah from 1884 until it was demolished by Allied bombing at the end of World War II, after which the capital was transferred to Kota Kinabalu. This compact, modern city holds few attractions, but is the main gateway in eastern Sabah for nearby attractions, such as the Sepilok Orang-Utan Sanctuary, the Gomantong Caves and the Turtle Islands National Park.

Frequent MAS flights link Sandakan with Kota Kinabalu (40 minutes). Long-distance minibuses take around 8 hours to cover the 386km to the capital.

SEMPORNA

This small town on the southeastern tip of Sabah is the departure point for Sipadan Island. It has a lively waterfront market, and boats can be hired to visit the nearby stilt village of the Bajau Laut, Sabah's renowned 'sea gypsies'. Tourist facilities are virtually non-exisitent, and excursions are costly.

MAS flies to Sandakan and there are frequent minibuses to Tawau. The comfortable Dragon Inn stands on stilts over the water.

SEPILOK ORANG-UTAN SANCTUARY

The Sepilok Orang-Utan Sanctuary was established in 1964 to re-train young orang-utans that had been captured illegally for the wildlife trade to fend for themselves and re-adapt to natural ways. The sanctuary now primarily handles orphaned orang-utans brought in from logging camps. The young apes have to be taught survival skills by the wildlife rangers before being taken to the forest where their new life begins, but they are still fed twice daily while learning to forage for themselves.

Feeding times (10am and 2.30pm daily at Platform A) are the high point of the day and are a great magnet for tourists and photographers.

Further into the forest (half-an-hour's walk from Platform A) is the second feeding station, Platform B, where some orang-utans still turn up for a supplementary feed. Rangers leave the Education Centre at 11am for this trek.

The sanctuary is just a small part of the 4,000-hectare Sepilok Forest Reserve, which is home to a wide range of wildlife including Bornean gibbons, proboscis monkeys, Malaysian sun bears, barking deer and pangolins.

24km from Sandakan, 11km from Sandakan airport. Open: daily, 8am–noon, 2–4pm. Further details from Sabah Parks Office (see page 108). Admission charge. Buses (marked 'Sepilok Batu 14') depart Sandakan at 9.20am, 11.20am, 1pm and 3pm; journey time 45 minutes. The timing for watching the feeding is inconvenient, and it is better to take a shared taxi if possible. It is feasible to visit Sepilok for the day from Kota Kinabalu, using an MAS return flight.

TUNKU ABDUL RAHMAN PARK

The five islands in the Tunku Abdul Rahman Park are easily reached from Kota Kinabalu for day trips or overnight stays. The islands have good beaches, coral reefs for snorkelling and diving, and unpolluted water.

The largest island is Pulau Gaya, covering 1,500 hectares, with one of the best beaches at Bulijong Bay (also known as Police Bay). The island has 20km of walking trails through the forests and mangroves, and is home to monkeys, pangolins and bearded pigs.

Screw-pine fruit on Pulau Manukan in the Tunku Abdul Rahman Park

Outside the park boundaries, there is a huge stilt village.

The second-largest island is Pulau Manukan, the location of the park headquarters, which has been redeveloped with chalets, a swimming-pool, restaurant and bar. Watersports available include water skiing, windsurfing and dinghy-sailing.

The most heavily visited of the islands is Pulau Sapi, off the southwest tip of Pulau Gaya. There are camping and picnic facilities. Pulau Mamutik is the smallest island in the park, and is also popular with day-trippers on weekends and holidays. Pulau Sulug, the most remote of the islands, is the least visited and as yet has no facilities.

For details on snorkelling and diving, see **Marine Parks**, pages 122–4.
Boats to the islands leave from the quay behind the Hyatt Hotel in Kota Kinabalu. Accommodation or camping must be booked in advance through the Sabah Parks Office, Lot 3, Sinsuran Kompleks, Kota Kinabalu (tel: (088) 211585).

TURTLE ISLANDS NATIONAL PARK

These islands are an important turtle-nesting location and have been a marine park since 1977. The main islands are Pulau Selingan, Pulau Gulisan and Pulau Bakungan Kecil; green turtles predominantly nest on Pulau Selingan, while hawksbills are more common on Pulau Gulisan. The main nesting season is August to October, and you can stay in the Sabah Parks Chalets on Pulau Selingan to watch the turtles at night.
40km from Sandakan, three hours by boat. Permits and accommodation bookings through the Sabah Parks Office, 9th floor, Wisma Khoo, PO Box 768, Sandakan (tel: (089) 273453).

Free bananas at Feeding Platform A for orang-utans at the Sepilok sanctuary

Mount Kinabalu National Park

This walk links up the Kiau View Trail with parts of the Silau-Silau and Mempening trails to make a circuit around the central park area. It is an easy walk, and the starting point is the reception area at the park entrance. *Allow 2½ hours.*

Pass underneath the entrance archway and take the track on the right marked Kiau View Trail.

1 KIAU VIEW TRAIL

The trail climbs fairly steeply beside a moss and fern-covered bank for the first 10 minutes before levelling off near the first shelter. As you walk along the ridge, the dense woodland on either side displays a glorious profusion of mosses, ferns and

bamboo. Since this is one of the least-used trails; there is a good chance of seeing birdlife, such as the gorgeously coloured scarlet sunbird. Even if you don't catch sight of the birds themselves, you will hear their rich, melodious warblings and liquid-sounding mating calls in the stillness of the forest canopy above. Other birds seen along these trails include grey drongos, noisy flocks of laughing thrushes, and the awkward Malaysian treepies.

The trail winds gently up the eastern end of the ridge until you reach the second shelter, after which it is more or less level going.

2 ORCHIDS

Along the track, cobwebs by the hundred festoon the wayside plants. Hidden away on the forest floor are ground-dwelling orchids such as the yellow-flowered *spathoglottis*, the small,

The unmistakable *Heliconia rostrata*, whose leaves resemble a curved bird's beak spiralling *spiranthes* and the bamboo orchid, *Arundin*. From ground level up, almost every tree trunk and branch has its share of orchids and other epiphytic plants. Whatever the time of year, several species will be in flower, creating bright splashes of colour against the misty backdrop of the forest.

After about 1 hour, you will reach the last look-out point, and immediately afterwards the track descends to the metalled Power Station Road. Turn left and then immediately right again on to the Silau-Silau Trail.

3 SILAU-SILAU TRAIL

The path follows the course of the Dewan Kinabalu, crossing several smaller tributaries on the way. Look out for frogs along the riverbanks (some 45 species inhabit Kinabalu), or the bizarre Borneo sucker-fish (*Gastromyzon borneensis*), which has developed a means of clinging to rocks in fast-moving streams so that it can graze on the algae found there. There are also thousands of species of insects in the park; one of the easiest to spot is the black and orange trilobite beetle, which chews its way slowly over decaying logs.

Elsewhere on the forest floor you might be able to spot the lovely emerald-green jewel beetle, or the fierce-looking rhinoceros beetle.

Turn left at the next junction and follow the signs up to Bukit Tupai shelter, turning right on the Mempening Trail until you reach the look-out point.

4 MEMPENING TRAIL

On a clear day there are spectacular views of the summit of Mount Kinabalu from here. In this, the lower montane zone, temperate species such as oaks proliferate, with ferns such as the broad-

The parrot's plantain (*Heliconia psittacorum*) is abundant around the park headquarters

leaved dipteris covering the ground beneath them. One unusual tree that is common here is *tristania*, easily identified by its peeling, orange-coloured bark; it is thought that the tree's bark peels off to avoid creepers clinging to it.

Continue on past the shelter until you reach Bukit Burung shelter, and then descend from here. Once you reach the stream turn right, then left across the wooden bridge, and right at the road. Follow the road up past the Sports Centre until you reach the Mountain Garden.

5 MOUNTAIN GARDEN

This very beautiful and well-kept little garden, fenced off from the forest which surrounds it, is a good introduction to the plant life of Kinabalu. Within it there are over 3,000 orchids (representing some 500 species) and 4,000 other plants (from around 350 species) laid out in a natural-looking environment around the garden walkways.

In front of the Mountain Garden is the administration building, with a road leading back to the park entrance.

Mountain Garden open: weekdays, 7.30am–4.30pm; Saturdays, 8am–5pm; Sundays and public holidays, 9am–4pm.

NIGHT MARKETS

The *pasar malam*, or night market, is an integral part of rural and urban life in Malaysia and you are bound to come across several in your travels through the country. Whether held in a narrow sidestreet or in the town square, shortly after dusk it will be busy with people out for a stroll, browsing among the stalls, maybe stopping for a snack here and there, or simply chatting to friends.

It is a great place to try local specialities. You might find anything from delicious cinnamon rolls to sugar-cane juice or *won ton* (Chinese dumplings). Elsewhere, Malaysian satay, steamed corn-on-the cob, or *murabak pisang* (banana cakes) tempt the palate.

While some markets only sell food, in others you can find anything from cheap clothes to Asian pop cassettes or Chinese herbal medicines. For people working late, they are the only alternative once restaurants have closed, with many of the stalls staying open up until 1am. When the shops have closed, locals can pop down for their necessities. It is, if you like, the Malaysian equivalent of the late-night supermarket and fast-food joint, all rolled into one.

Once the sun goes down *pasar malam* (night markets) spring to life, with stalls selling everything from watches to woks and hot chestnuts to hot curry powder

GETTING AWAY FROM IT ALL

'The Malaysian countryside
is rather like a rich feast,
with a little too much of
everything good.'
GEORGE WOODCOCK,
Gods and Cities (1966)

Getting Away From it All

Despite the destruction of large tracts of wilderness areas, Malaysia does have a network of protected areas, national parks and marine parks. The national parks are generally well managed, with dedicated rangers and staff who are knowledgeable about their domains and conscious of the need to preserve them.

Usually, a national park has a compound containing the headquarters building (sometimes with an interpretative centre) and a range of accommodation for all budgets from VIP chalets to student hostels, most of which have facilities for self-catering. Often there is a café (or canteen) on site providing basic meals (national parks are one of the few places in Malaysia where you may have to do without the usual gourmet range of foods). Most have marked walking trails, some better maintained than others. There is almost nowhere in the country that you need worry about personal safety when off the beaten track, except from the point of view of weather conditions. Check the monsoon seasons (see **Climate**, page 180), and make sure you are suitably equipped for heavy rainfall if you are travelling during this time.

NATIONAL PARKS AND NATURE PARKS

BAKO NATIONAL PARK, see page 98.

ENDAU-ROMPIN

One of the last remaining areas of protected lowland forest in Peninsular Malaysia, Endau-Rompin straddles the boundary between Pahang and Johor. This relatively undisturbed and lush region covers an area of 870sq km and contains a wealth of endemic plants as well as hornbills, tigers, elephants, wild boar and tapirs. It is the last refuge on the peninsula for the rare Sumatran rhinoceros. Waterfalls, palm forests, highland swamps and visits to Orang Asli villages are all part of the Endau-Rompin experience.

The entry point for the park is Padang Endau, around 40km north of Mersing on the east coast. Boats can be chartered from here to go upriver; facilities for visitors are *very limited. Permits must be obtained in advance from the Johor State Security Council, 2nd floor, Bangunan Sultan Ibrahim, Bukit Timbalan, Johor Bahru (tel: (07) 231033). Day trips and longer treks are organised by Wilderness Experience, 6B, Jalan SS21/39, Damansara Utama, Petaling Jaya (tel: (03) 7178221).*

GUNUNG MULU NATIONAL PARK, see page 98.

KAMPUNG KUANTAN FIREFLIES

Although not a protected area, Kampung Kuantan has recently become a popular place to visit since the discovery that the riverbanks near the village are home to an unusual species of firefly that flashes in synchronised groups. Thousands of people have since descended on the village to take a night-time boat-trip down the river to witness this beautiful, magical sight as the whole riverbank is lit up with millions of fireflies twinkling in the vegetation. The creatures in question are folded-wing fireflies (*Pteroptyx malaccae*), the only fireflies that have developed this striking synchronised flashing. Sometimes only a dozen will flash at once, sometimes whole tree-loads, numbering thousands, light up the riverbank. Sometimes, tree-loads that are close together may flash in time with each other. The fireflies only choose trees with open foliage so their lights can be seen.

Flashing usually begins around an hour after sunset, and is at its height for the next two to four hours, diminishing towards dawn. The *kelip-kelip* (firefly) tours start from around 8pm through to midnight and last about 30–40 minutes. A jetty has been built with the help of

River transport is the only way to reach the heart of Taman Negara, the largest protected area of rain forest in peninsular Malaysia

nature groups and now, as the hand-out says 'This blinking trees of Kampung Kuantan are well known among the worldwide'.

Kampung Kuantan is 20 minutes from Kuala Selangor. Driving west from Kuala Lumpur, turn right after 56km at Bukit Rotan and right again to Kampung Kuantan. The booking office is in a row of shops in the village; contact Mr Jalaludin, Kampung Kuantan, Batang Berjuntai, Selangor (tel: (03) 8892294). Be warned that this boom has brought a certain degree of chaos, with over 30 boat trips per night going out, and reservations are not always honoured. The trip is not recommended on rainy nights or when there is a full moon.

KINABALU NATIONAL PARK,
see page 108.

NIAH CAVES NATIONAL PARK,
see page 100.

A quiet backwater in Taman Negara, where many walking trails lead to seldom-visited spots

TAMAN ALAM/KUALA SELANGOR NATURE PARK

On the west coast of the Peninsula, the Taman Alam/Kuala Selangor park covers 26sq km of mangroves and wetlands. It is one of the most accessible places to see typical mangrove inhabitants such as the mangrove blue flycatcher, mangrove whistler, pied fantail and the elusive mangrove pitta. You are also likely to spot kingfishers, bee-eaters, kites, white-bellied sea eagles and grey herons.

At the entrance to the park there are chalets and an information centre, with short trails leading off to an artificial lake with purpose-built hides. Along the trails you will probably come across troupes of silver-leaf monkeys, an experience that is unlikely to be repeated elsewhere: silver-leaf monkeys usually live high up in the forest canopy, making them hard to spot, but those at Kuala Selangor have become used to people and are approachable.

65km from Kuala Lumpur, 1 hour by shared taxi or bus to Kuala Selangor Town. Open 9am–5pm. Reservations for *accommodation: Malayan Nature Society (Persatuan Pencinta Alam), Taman Alam, Kuala Selangor (tel: (03) 8892294).*

TAMAN NEGARA NATIONAL PARK

Malaysia's first national park, Taman Negara covers 4,343sq km spread over three different states (Pahang, Kelantan and Terengganu). It is the largest single area of protected tropical rain forest in the Peninsula.

The park is home to some 250 species of birds and is rich in animal life, including elephants, Malayan tapirs, sambar and barking deer, tigers, otters and several species of primates. The typically dense rain forest foliage means that wildlife-spotting requires a great deal of patience, but there are numerous salt licks, some with observation hides, where you may have a better chance of seeing something.

The park headquarters at Kuala Tahan can only be reached by boat from Kampung Kuala Tembeling near Jerantut, from where it is a 2- to 4-hour journey up the Tembeling river. At the headquarters there are chalets and hostels for up to 200 people, and restaurant facilities. Camping and hiking equipment can be hired, and there are well-marked trails leading off into the jungle around the headquarters. Boat-trips further upriver and longer treks (for instance, to the summit of Gunung Tahan, which is a 9-day round trip) can also be arranged.

The park is closed during the monsoon (November to January). The gateway to the park is Jerantut, from where there are taxi and bus connections to Kota Bharu and Kuala Lumpur (change at Temerluh). From Jerantut, buses leave every 2 hours for the boat jetty at Kampung Kuala

Tembeling; the park headquarters is a further 59km upstream. Advance bookings for transport to the park and accommodation are compulsory: the easiest place to do this is at the National Parks desk in the Malaysia Tourist Information Complex at 109 Jalan Ampang, Kuala Lumpur (tel: (03) 2434929).

TAWAU HILLS PARK

The rugged volcanic terrain of the Tawau Hills Park lies north of Tawau in Sabah. Wildlife that you might spot here includes red-leaf monkeys, giant tree squirrels, macaques and hornbills. The park is also reputed to be home to clouded leopards. Vegetation ranges from dipterocarp forest in the lowlands to mossy forests on the upper reaches of Bombalai Hill (530m). From the top of the hill there are views across the rolling plantations of cocoa, palm oil and rubber trees on the coastal plains. The park is popular for weekend picnics, but you need a four-wheel drive vehicle to reach it.

24km north of Tawau. No permits needed, but for further information contact either: Rangers Office, Tawau Hills Park, WDT 118, Tawau (tel: (01) 810 676) or: Sabah Parks, 9th floor, PO Box 768, Wisma Khoo, Sandakan (tel: (089) 273453).

TUNKU ABDUL RAHMAN PARK,
see page 112.

TURTLE ISLANDS NATIONAL PARK, see page 113.

De-husking cocoa in one of the many cocoa plantations which surround the Tawau Hills

MARINE PARKS

As well as the national parks, Malaysia also has a network of marine parks to protect the country's marine resources for the enjoyment of present and future generations. For most visitors, it is the mystery and beauty of coral reefs that provide the most compelling reason to explore the underwater world (see **Coral Reefs**, pages 94–5).

With a mask and snorkel in your luggage, you will find plenty of opportunities to float in this watery realm and watch vividly coloured fish going their strange ways among the corals and seagrasses. Snorkelling has many advantages over scuba-diving: it requires almost no training; it's free; you can jump in when and where you please; and a great deal of the life and colour on a reef is found within the top few metres of the water anyway.

If curiosity impels you to explore beyond the limitations of mask and snorkel, a scuba-training course is the answer. Scuba-diving courses are available in most resorts near reef areas, with generally high standards of rental equipment and training. Before leaving home get a medical check-up, and take the certificate with you. A good mask and snorkel are a sound investment if you plan to take a course, but you can always hire them if necessary. Qualified divers will need to bring proof of diver training from a recognised agency, and preferably also their log books.

In Peninsular Malaysia the best reefs are on the east coast, most of them being patch or fringing reefs around the offshore islands. Owing to the turbidity of the water, reefs on the west coast are not so well developed except near Pulau Langkawi in the north.

Sarawak has virtually no reefs, since coral does not grow well where there is fresh-water run-off from rain forests. In Sabah, fringing reefs occur around offshore islands on the north and northeast coasts. The best reefs in Sabah are those around the oceanic island of Sipadan off the coast near Semporna.

Coral reefs are fragile ecosystems, easily damaged by human activities. Like reefs elsewhere in the world, those in Malaysia have been subjected to destruction from pollution, coral mining and dynamite fishing. Within the marine parks they are generally in good condition, although not of the same calibre as more pristine reefs elsewhere in the Indo-Pacific region. The only exception to this is Pulau Sipadan, which is a world-class dive site and attracts serious sport-divers from every continent.

The best season for diving on the west coast is from December through to April/May, on the east coast from February/March through to September/October. The seasons in Sabah are similar to the east coast, the best diving being from February/March through to September/October, with top visibility from May/June onwards.

NORTHWEST COAST

Off the Kedah coast, the Pulau Payar Marine Park encompasses a cluster of islands, foremost among them Pulau Payar itself. The other islands include Pulau Segantang, Pulau Kala and Pulau Lembu. The diverse and colourful reefs are known for a prolific variety of lionfish, feather stars, sea anemones and other creatures. The best diving is around the southwest tip of Pulau Paya and the north and northeast sides of Pulau Kala.

There is no accommodation on the islands

Snorkelling off the beach at Pulau Manukan in the Tunku Abdul Rahman Park, Sabah

although camping is allowed. Permits must be obtained from either: Fisheries Department, Wisma Tani Jalan Sultan Salahuddin, Kuala Lumpur (tel: (03) 2982011); or Fisheries Dept, Wisma Persekutuan, Jalan Kampung Baru, Alor Setar (tel: (04) 725573). The islands are accessible from Pulau Pinang, although Pulau Langkawi is closer (1 hour by boat). Day trips are organised by Langkawi Adventures (tel: 911533) and Pelangi Cruises (tel: 916535).

NORTHEAST COAST

Off the shores of Terengganu, the Pulau Redang Marine Park includes Pulau Perhentian, Pulau Redang, Pulau Kapas, Pulau Tenggul and Pulau Lang Tengah. Reefs extend to around 20m deep, with the best-developed corals on the north and east sides of the islands. *For accommodation and access details, see separate entries for Pulau Perhentian, Pulau Kapas, Pulau Redang and Pulau Tenggul.*

Setting off for a night dive on Pulau Sipadan. As dusk falls the reef comes alive with corals stretching out their tentacles to feed and nocturnal fish emerging from day-time hiding places

SOUTHEAST COAST

The islands of the southeast coast form two marine parks: Pulau Tioman and its neighbouring islands (off Pahang), and the Pulau Sibu Archipelago (off Johor), which includes Rawa, Sibu, Besar, Tinggi and Tengah. On many of these islands the north and east sides have rocky cliffs dropping straight into deep water, with no reefs, but the more sheltered south and west sides have well-developed fringing reefs. The reefs are generally no more than 15m deep and in variable condition, some good, some badly damaged. Pulau Tioman has a good selection of dive sites around the coast and offshore islands such as Pulau Labas, Pulau Tulai and Pulau Chebeh; an artificial reef of concrete pyramids recently built by the Fisheries Dept is now home to groupers, yellowtails, trevallys, batfish and moray eels.

See separate entries for Pulau Rawa and Pulau Tioman for access and accommodation. There are PADI Dive Centres at the Berjaya Tioman Beach Resort, Lalang (tel: (07) 414 5445) and at Ben's Diving Centre, Salang Beach, Pulau Tioman.

SABAH

PULAU SIPADAN, see page 110.

TUNKU ABDUL RAHMAN PARK

Reefs around the five islands extend to depths of around 17m, with good diving and snorkelling around the southern tip of Pulau Gaya, the northeast tip of Pulau Mamutik (where there are extensive colonies of staghorn and plate corals), the east and west sides of Pulau Manukan and the southern side of Pulau Sulug (which has some of the best reefs in the park).

The islands of this marine park can be visited all year round, but between May and October storms may materialise in minutes, so care should be taken with boating arrangements. The heaviest rain falls during November to January; the driest months are February to May.

Diving trips can be booked through Paradise Divers, Pulau Manukan, Kota Kinabalu (tel: (011) 814393). Day trips from Kota Kinabalu can be booked through Borneo Divers 4th floor, Wisma Sabah, Kota Kinabalu (tel: (088) 222226).

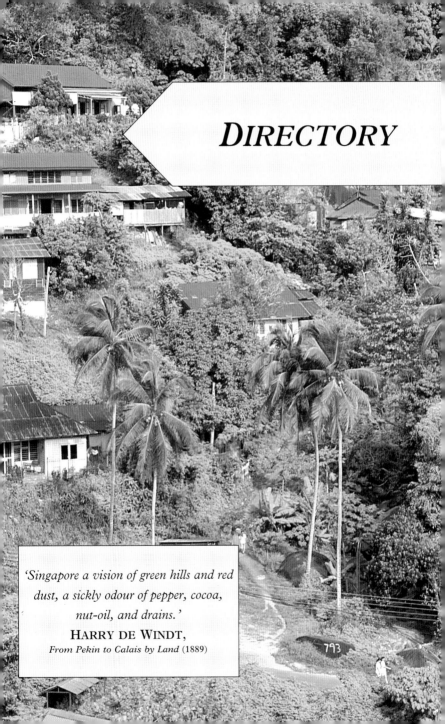

DIRECTORY

'Singapore a vision of green hills and red dust, a sickly odour of pepper, cocoa, nut-oil, and drains.'

HARRY DE WINDT,
From Pekin to Calais by Land (1889)

Shopping

SINGAPORE

Shopping has always been one of the major attractions of Singapore – no wonder, considering the enormous variety of things to buy in thousands of outlets ranging from small street-stalls to huge, air-conditioned shopping plazas. Shopping here is not just a necessity, it is a way of life. Shops are open at all hours – as much for the convenience of Singaporeans (who rate shopping as one of their favourite pastimes) as for tourists.

From Turkish carpets to Toshiba computers, there is very little that can't be found here: the variety of goods is enormous, ranging from the latest electronic gadgets, stereos and cameras to Asian handicrafts and jewellery, European designer clothes or American sportswear.

Ethnic arts and crafts are widely available

Value for money

Singapore claims to offer some of the best buys in the world at affordable prices. However, to make sure of getting your money's worth, some groundwork helps.

When you arrive, head for the department stores, where prices are fixed, to get an overview of what's available and roughly what the standard price might be. After that, browse around the big shopping malls to compare prices. This is an easy task, since most will have several shops of the same kind under one roof.

Bargaining is expected almost everywhere except in the department stores. Start off by asking the retailer for their 'best price' and then make an offer. It's difficult to say how much lower this should be than the initial price (it could be anywhere between 10 and 50 per cent), but be realistic. When bargaining, always ensure you specify the method of payment, since you will get a better price for cash or travellers' cheques than with a credit card.

Make sure you are comparing prices for exactly the same brand and model of photographic or electronic goods, since this will vary according to which is the most up-to-date version.

Consumer protection

Singapore has stringent laws to protect consumers, but this doesn't mean that all rip-offs have been eliminated. Check all guarantees and warranties issued with the product. Insist on a worldwide warranty: 'local guarantees' are useless outside the country of issue.

Make sure that you get an itemised receipt with the shop's stamp on it, which you may need for insurance, customs inspection, or if you need to obtain a refund. Always check that your purchases are in working order before leaving the shop, and it is best to watch them being packed in case something is 'mistakenly' missed out. For very expensive items, consider paying by credit card if your card company offers some form of consumer protection.

Silk clothes are one of the best buys

Check the voltages on electrical and electronic goods to make sure they are the same as back home (UK, Hong Kong, New Zealand and Australia: 220–240 volts, 50 cycles; USA, Canada and Japan: 110–120 volts, 60 cycles).

Ignore the touts who will undoubtedly approach you in shopping malls. Touting is illegal and you will only end up paying their commission on top of the purchase price. Counterfeit goods are less common than previously, but there are still plenty of 'Rolex' and other copy watches on the streets: if you insist on buying a fake, bargain hard and don't expect it to last too long.

Most retailers are reliable and honest, but if in doubt shop with members of the Good Retailers Scheme; these shops display a white Merlion logo on a red background. If you have a complaint, you can either contact the Consumer's Association of Singapore, CASE (tel: 270 5433) or take action through a special Small Claims Tribunal.

Credit cards
Major credit cards such as Diners, Carte Blanche, American Express, MasterCard and Visa are widely accepted in most shops.

Shopping hours
Most shops open daily from around 10am through until 9–10pm at night. On Sundays some department stores and smaller shops are closed.

The bright lights of Singapore's shops beckon

WHERE TO SHOP

The long, tree-lined boulevard of Orchard Road is Singapore's 'Golden Mile', lined with major department stores and multi-storey plazas selling goods from every corner of the globe. Shopping here is simply a matter of hopping from one air-conditioned complex to the next. Just off Orchard Road is Scotts Road, which has another batch of big shopping malls.

Although it has the largest concentration of shops in the city, shopping doesn't stop beyond Orchard Road. To the south, there are plenty of opportunities for browsing in large malls such as Marina Square and Raffles City, as well as the up-market Raffles Arcade.

Many shopping malls have department stores occupying one or two floors. Locally owned stores such as Tangs, DFS and Metro (all of which have several branches) are good places to look for Singapore-made goods, particularly fashions. Japanese goods are available in stores such as Isetan, Yaohan and Sogo, quality French products are available at Galeries Lafayette, and European imports at the Robinson's department store.

Don't neglect the ethnic areas such as Chinatown, Little India and Arab Street, where you can often pick up some unusual bargains as well as imported crafts, jewellery and textiles.

To help you find your way around free shopping maps are available in hotel lobbies. The American Express Map of Singapore is very clearly laid out and one of the most popular.

SHOPPING MALLS
Orchard Road and Tanglin Road
Delfi Orchard
Fashions, jewellery, Waterford crystal,
Wedgwood, rattan furniture; Meitetsu department store.
402 Orchard Road.

Far East Shopping Centre
Tailors, jewellers, computers; antiques at Kwok Gallery.
545 Orchard Road.

Lucky Plaza
Sporting goods, leather; Metro department store.
304 Orchard Road.

Orchard Towers
Jewellery, antiques, Thai silk, leather; gems at Larry Jewellery.
400 Orchard Road.

Plaza Singapura
Fashions, lighting, furniture, audio and video equipment; Yaohan department store.
68 Orchard Road.

Specialists Shopping Centre
Sportswear, fashions; John Little department store.
277 Orchard Road.

Tanglin Shopping Centre
Oriental carpets at Hassan's; antique maps and prints at Antiques of the Orient; pearls at C T Hoo.
19 Tanglin Road.

The Paragon
Quality fashions are available at Intermezzo, Dunhill, Gucci, Karl Lagerfield, Lanvin, Offenbach; Metro department store.
290 Orchard Road.

The Promenade
Jewellery, lingerie, contemporary furniture; Charles Jourdan, Ralph Lauren.
300 Orchard Road.

Wisma Atria
Fashion boutiques, shoes; regional curios at Legaspi; Filippino leatherwork at Cora Jacobs. Isetan department store.
435 Orchard Road.

Scotts Road
Far East Plaza
Electronics, sportswear, watches; fashion
accessories at Coco; Metro department
store.
14 Scotts Road.
Scotts Shopping Centre
Quality fashions at China Silk House,
Tangs Studio, Bylines, Chomel, Mondi
Boutique.
6 Scotts Road.
Shaw Centre
Curios at Ming Blue and Singapore
Woodcraft.
1 Scotts Road.

Off Orchard Road
Funan Centre
Computers and electronics.
109 North Bridge Road.
Holland Park Shopping Centre
Arts and crafts, batik, antiques.
211 Holland Avenue.
Marina Square
Fashion at Tokyu, Export Shop and
Stockmarket; sportswear; China Silk
House; Habitat.
6 Raffles Boulevard.
People's Park Complex
Gold and electronics.
101 Upper Cross Street.
Raffles Arcade
Exclusive boutiques including Kenzo,
Hugo Boss, Mulberry, Loius Vuitton,
Lowe, Aquascutum, Tiffany.
North Bridge Road.
Raffles City
Antiques, handicrafts, fashions,
sportswear, watches; Sogo department
store.
250 North Bridge Road.
Sim Lim Square
Electronics, stereos, televisions, videos,
telephones.
1 Rochor Canal Road.

Gleaming shopping malls, Singapore's hallmark

DEPARTMENT STORES
DFS
2 Tanglin Road (tel: 734 4522); 100
Orchard Road (tel: 235 7900); 22 Scotts
Road (tel: 737 7411).
Galeries Lafayette
541 Orchard Road, Liat Towers (tel:
732 9177); 1 Raffles Place, OUB Centre
(tel: 535 7069).
Isetan Orchard
435 Orchard Road, Wisma Atria (tel:
733 7777).
Isetan Havelock
405 Havelock Road (tel: 733 1111).
Metro Far East
14 Scotts Road, Far East Plaza (tel: 733
3322).
Metro Grand
304 Orchard Road, Lucky Plaza (tel:
737 6033).
Metro Marina
6 Raffles Boulevard (tel: 337 2868).
Robinsons
176 Orchard Road, Centrepoint (tel:
733 0888).
Sogo
250 North Bridge Road (tel: 339 1100).
Tangs
320 Orchard Road (tel: 737 5500); 6
Scotts Road (tel: 737 0033).
Yaohan Orchard
68 Orchard Road (tel: 337 4061).
Yaohan Thomson
301 Upper Thomson Road (tel: 454
6511).

WHAT TO BUY
Antiques, arts and crafts

Singapore offers a wide selection of antiques and curios from all over the Asia-Pacific region. As well as Chinese porcelain, snuff bottles, jade and silverware, you can find Thai buddha images, Burmese lacquerware, Indonesian masks and woodcarvings, and tribal art from the South Pacific.

Genuine antiques should be over 100 years old, and you should insist on a certificate of antiquity as well as a receipt.

One of the best places to start looking is the Tanglin Shopping Centre, where you may also find Nyonya antiques such as handcrafted silver ornaments or beadwork slippers. The

Check shipping costs before buying that pot!

Holland Road Shopping Centre in Holland Village has numerous little shops selling everything from brass Dutch lamps to old coins and jewellery. Other areas for general curios include Smith Street and Temple Street in Chinatown.

On the second floor of Marina Square there are several shops specialising in handicrafts and daily demonstrations are given of old trades such as painting Chinese opera masks and carving marble seals (known as *chop*).

For basketware, caneware, rattan and camelskin and leather bags and sandals one of the best places is Arab Street.

Electronic goods

The range of high-technology goods available is mind-boggling: as with cameras, it's a good plan to get a rough idea of what you want before leaving home. Prices are extremely competitive, but make sure TV/video systems and electrical supplies are compatible with your own.

Electronics shops are found almost everywhere, but two places in particular that are worth checking out are Plaza Singapura and Sim Lim Square. The latter has one of the largest concentrations of shops for stereos, VCRs, televisions and cassette and CD players in town.

Computer peripherals and accessories are good buys, and all the big-name computer brands – Apple, Epson, IBM, etc – are available. Try Ultimate Lap Top Shop and others in the Funan Centre.

Fashions and clothing

Singapore has a huge range of fashion, clothing, shoe and sportswear shops.

International designers such as Ralph Lauren, Gucci, Gianni Versace, Louis Feraud and Issey Miyake are well represented, and as well as these Singapore now has a home-grown industry of local designers. Look for Esther Tay, Celia Loh, Dick Lee, Arthur Yen, David Wang and others in Tangs, Metro and other department stores.

Tailoring and dressmaking services are widely available, and you will find most textile stores have a make-up service with good-quality workmanship. Be specific about design, cut and detailing and insist on fittings. Try any hotel arcade or Mode O Day in the Tanglin Shopping Centre, Couples in Far East Plaza, or Vanda Ladies & Gents Tailoring, Holland Road Shopping Centre.

For accessories, check out department stores such as Robinsons, Tangs and Isetan, or the Raffles Arcade. For bags, belts and leather goods from India and Indonesia head for Arab Street.

Countless shoe stores can be found in Far East Plaza.

Curios in a backstreet shop

Jewellery

The oriental love of ornamentation and fascination with precious gems, gold and pearls has not been swept away in Singapore, where there is a huge range of traditional and contemporary designs for all kinds of jewellery. Gold jewellery is sold according to weight, and is principally either 22K or 24K. Gold shops are found almost everywhere, with ethnic designs available in Serangoon Road in Little India and Arab Street; the People's Park Complex is another good place to look. Cultured and freshwater pearls, precious stones and jade can also be found in shops specialising in imported jewellery along Orchard Road.

Photographic goods

If you're looking for cameras and other photographic goods, find out which model you want before leaving home and check out the price in discount stores, since European and North American prices often match those in the Far East. Camera stores are found all over Singapore, so shop around. Try Cost Plus at Scotts Shopping Centre, Albert Photo in Orchard Towers and Tanglin Shopping Centre, or A & P Photo at Lucky Plaza. Film processing is good quality and good value; for transparencies a reliable lab is Albert Photo (see above).

MALAYSIA

Malaysia is trying hard to catch up with its neighbour to the south by promoting itself as a shopper's paradise. While it can never compete with Singapore in terms of convenience and the vast range of shops found there, it does have advantages if you're looking for handicrafts and other locally produced goods.

Malaysia is well known for its batik fabrics, pewterware, silverware, ceramics and rattan work. There are plenty of opportunities to buy direct from craftspeople and to visit factories or handicraft centres to see how things are made. Sports equipment is a good buy, and there are many bargains to be had in leatherwork belts and bags.

In the major cities and towns there are air-conditioned department stores and shopping malls (known as *kompleks*) where prices are fixed, but outside of these you are more likely to be buying from roadside stalls or in markets where bargaining is normal. The islands of Langkawi and Labuan (off the coast of Sabah) are duty-free ports where you can find items such as cameras, watches, perfumes, electronic goods, liquor and tobacco at competitive prices. Most shops accept major credit cards.

WHERE TO SHOP
KUALA LUMPUR
Antiques, arts and handicrafts
Artiquarium

Housed in an unusual old mansion, this is more of a gallery than a shop, with a good selection of antiques (both colonial and Chinese), contemporary Malaysian art and tribal artefacts.
273A Jalan Medan Tuanku (tel: (03) 2921 1222).

Central Market

A focal point for Kuala Lumpur's craftspeople, with numerous stalls selling hand-painted T-shirts, leatherwork, jewellery, batik, traditional Malaysian kites (*wau*), pewterware and silverware and a good selection of basketware and rattan. Several stalls specialise in tribal arts from the Asia-Pacific region.
Central Market, Jalan Hang Kasturi (tel: (03) 274 6542).

Infokraf Centre

Infokraf is the promotional arm of the Ministry of Rural Development (MRD), who have a team of talented artisans designing items of high quality for the export market. Changing displays showcase the very best in contemporary fabrics and rattan and cane furnishings as well as more traditional crafts. A shop on the premises sells fabrics, ceramics and jewellery.
Jalan Hishmuddin (tel: (03) 293 4929).

Karyaneka Handicraft Centre

A good place to get an idea of the range of handicrafts available from the different regions of Malaysia. Inside a series of individual houses, representing the various states, you can see craftsmen at work and there is a showroom where the finished products can be bought.
Jalan Raja Chulan (tel: (03) 242 7466).

Royal Selangor Pewter

Pewter is one of the best buys in Malaysia. Established in 1885, Royal Selangor Pewter is the country's biggest manufacturer and has a huge range of traditional and contemporary designs. Many out-of-town tours visit the factory where you can see the processes involved.
Main showroom: 231 Jalan Tunku Abdul Rahman (tel: (03) 298 6244).

Shopping complexes

Kuala Lumpur has a number of air-conditioned shopping complexes scattered over the city filled with small boutiques, department stores, eating stalls and food shops. Some are fairly ordinary, catering more to local needs, while others house branches of chic designer-name boutiques. Among the major shopping centres are:

The Weld
One of the smaller shopping centres, with a good range of locally made clothing as well as foreign shops such as Benetton and Lacoste. The Weld also has a Times Bookshop, two art galleries and the Guardian department store. *Jalan Raja Chulan.*

KL Plaza
Centrally located, with a good selection of jewellery shops and menswear (Christian Dior, Givenchy and Polo Ralph Lauren as well as the local tailoring chain, Jim's Shop). *Jalan Bukit Bintang.*

The Mall
This five-storey mall is the second largest in Kuala Lumpur, and is popular with tourists. There is a wide variety of shops selling everything from carpets to cosmetics, as well as the Yaohan department store and a historical-looking hawker's centre, the Medan Hang Tuah. *Jalan Putra (opposite the Pan Pacific Hotel and Putra World Trade Centre).*

Yow Chuan Plaza and Ampang Park
The Yow Chuan Plaza is an up-market mall catering for a sophisticated crowd, with *haute couture*, jewellery, wicker furniture, oriental carpets, silks and handicrafts. Ampang Park, the city's oldest mall, is connected to it by a footbridge. *Jalan Ampang.*

Sungei Wang Plaza
Kuala Lumpur's largest shopping

A convenient kerb-side shop

complex, with 550 shops, two cinemas, department stores and food centres under one roof. It is connected to the next-door Bukit Bintang Plaza on Jalan Bukit Bintang which has a similar mix of shops. *Jalan Sultan Ismail.*

Night markets
Kuala Lumpur's biggest and most colourful *pasar malam* (night market) takes place in the heart of Chinatown every evening, when Jalan Petaling and surrounding streets are closed off to traffic. Dozens of stalls spring up to create a noisy, crowded, brightly lit bazaar popular with locals out bargain-hunting. Alongside the stalls selling Chinese and Malay food you can find anything from cheap sunglasses to calculators, shoes, Chinese groceries, radios, jeans, copy watches and fake Armani shirts as well as luggage, shoes and other leathergoods. In the often congested lanes between the stalls, keep a tight hold of your bags.

Kuala Lumpur's other main *pasar malam* is held on Jalan Tunku Abdul Rahman every Saturday night from 7pm to midnight, when the road is closed to traffic.

Kota Bharu's Central Market is one of the largest and most colourful in the country

PULAU PINANG

George Town on Pulau Pinang is the second major shopping centre after Kuala Lumpur and, while it doesn't have the same range of shops, it is much more compact and easier to get around. As well as the usual electronic and photographic goods, it is a good place for local handicrafts, T-shirts, antiques and sports equipment. Handicrafts from Thailand are also popular.

The main shopping malls are the Komtar and the Super Komtar, which are both in the massive Komtar Tower on the corner of Magazine Road and Pinang Road. There are three department stores within the tower, as well as the usual array of fast-food outlets and shops.

Most of the other shops in Pinang are concentrated along Jalan Pinang and Jalan Campbell. Within one block on Jalan Pinang are found most of the antique and curio shops, with a range of Chinese, Malay and Indonesian artefacts. Also on Pinang Road, the Piccadilly Bazaar and Chowrasta Market sell a wide range of goods.

Pinang's *pasar malam* is a movable feast, changing locations every two weeks (call the Pinang Tourist Association to find out where it is currently being held). It is not always worth the effort since it can be a fair distance from the town centre, and is anyway mostly geared to local needs, supplying essentials such as household goods.

MELAKA

Melaka is acknowledged as the main centre in Malaysia for antiques, which are to be found principally in the shops that line Jalan Hang Jebat. You are unlikely to find real treasures at bargain prices (collectors have long since scoured the shops), but many shops are piled high with fascinating curios of one sort or another, ranging from old tiffin boxes to pre-World War II electric fans, clocks, coins, lamps and Chinese lacquered furniture. With a dwindling supply of antiques, a lot of shops now stock handicrafts as well, and a few have workshops at the back where 'antiques' are manufactured.

KOTA BHARU

The best selection of traditional arts and crafts on the east coast is in and around Kota Bharu, state capital of Kelantan. Kelantan is renowned for pottery, silver, textiles (batik and songket), bamboo and rattan work, as well as traditional kites (*wau*) and shadow puppets (*wayang kulit*). Owing to its proximity to the Thai border, you will also find handicrafts and clothes from Thailand.

A good starting point is the Kampong Kraftangan (Handicraft Village) which has a good selection of batik paintings, woodcarvings, songket, silver and pottery.

Also worth a look is the second floor of the Central Market, where a number of stalls sell clothes, brassware, songket and batik. The most interesting area is a 5km stretch of road on the way out to the Pantai Cinta Berahi, where you can visit numerous small workshops and watch songket-weaving or batik being made. The textile workshops are mostly clustered around Kampung Penambang, while further on you will find silversmiths, woodcarvers and several master kite-makers who proudly display their colourful wares.

EAST MALAYSIA

The best place for tribal arts and crafts is Kuching, the capital of Sarawak. An enormous variety of artefacts can be found here, ranging from colourful carvings to war shields, beadwork, baskets, charm sticks, spears and poison-dart holders. Look out particularly for Penan mats, Iban blankets (*pua*) and Bidayuh baskets and jewellery. Most of the tribal arts shops are concentrated along the Main Bazaar near Jalan Wayang. Be prepared to dig deep in your pocket if you want a genuine artefact rather than a tourist souvenir.

Good-quality handicrafts at reasonable prices can be found at the Kampung Budaya Sarawak (Sarawak Cultural Village, see page 100).

KELANTANESE CRAFTS

Many of the traditional arts and crafts for which Kelantan is famous were originally produced by craftsmen working for Malay royalty, and the relative isolation of the state from cultural influences that changed the pattern of life elsewhere in Malaysia ensured that many of the designs used remained unchanged for centuries.

Woodcarvers were employed in large numbers to decorate the magnificent wooden palaces of the nobility, creating ingenious decorative panels above the windows and doors with holes in the patterning to let in light and air. Many traditional Malay houses also display beautiful carved wooden panels in their interiors or on window-shutters.

Songket-weaving is another skill that was largely fostered by royalty, who used the elaborately woven cloth for special occasions and weddings. Songket uses a specially-dyed yarn of silk or cotton, into which gold and silver threads are woven in intricate patterns. The more threads used and the more intricate the design, the more expensive will be the songket. Traditional ceremonial costumes can use up to 9m of this laboriously worked and richly coloured material.

Silverwork also owes its current prominence to royal commissions, with silversmiths in the past living and working inside the royal courtyards, producing exquisite items such as pendants, brooches and jewellery boxes. Silversmithing is still very much alive in Kelantan, with most of the work being produced by individual craftsmen using traditional methods.

Entertainment

SINGAPORE

Much of Singapore's nightlife centres around Orchard Road, where there is a host of bars, hotel cocktail lounges, discos and karaoke lounges. Many of the best entertainments are street parades, open-air Chinese opera and other performances associated with Singapore's many festivals (see pages 142–3).

Both the *Straits Times* and the tabloid *New Paper* carry weekend supplements listing pubs, bars and lounges with live performances or other attractions. The free magazine *Singapore This Week* also has a good round-up of music, theatre, exhibitions and festivals.

Singapore has none of the raunchy nightlife of cities like Bangkok, although there are plenty of 'health centres' and

Live music can be found in many bars and cafés

escort services for the single male. The city's most notorious spot used to be Bugis Street, where flamboyant drag queens and transvestites paraded after dark around the cafés. The old Bugis Street was demolished to make way for the MRT and has been rebuilt on a new site across the road, complete with air-conditioned restaurants and a theatre-cabaret venue. However, since the transvestites have moved on elsewhere it is a shadow of its former self and no different from any other outdoor eating area with a small night market.

BARS AND PUBS

Prices for alcohol in Singapore are relatively high due to import duties on beers, wines and spirits; many bars have Happy Hours, with two drinks for the price of one, between around 5–7pm. Most open around noon and stay open until around 1am, extending to 2–3am on weekends. A lot of bars have live music, ranging from jazz to rock music, and the following is just a selection.

Anywhere

Rock and pop venue with a friendly, lively atmosphere and a long-standing resident band, Tania; standing room only at weekends.
04-08/09 Tanglin Shopping Centre, 19 Tanglin Road (tel: 734 8233).

Brannigan's

A popular meeting place for the smart set, the nearest thing in Singapore to a single's bar. Live bands every night (mostly pop or jazz fusion), bar food at lunchtimes and early evenings.
Hyatt Regency Hotel, 10–12 Scott's Road (tel: 738 1234).

Cheers

Amusing bar where the waiters alternate with the live bands in providing entertainment and singing.
Novotel Orchid Inn, Dunearn Road (tel: 250 3322).

Compass Rose

The highest bar in the city (with correspondingly high prices), on the 72nd floor of the world's tallest hotel. Fabulous views through the floor-to-ceiling windows. Dress code.
Westin Stamford Hotel, 2 Stamford Road (tel: 338 8585).

Duxton's Chicago Bar & Grill

Two resident bands belt out jazz and blues, friendly atmosphere, good chilli and chicken wings in the adjoining Grill.
6 Duxton Hill Road (tel: 222 9556).

JD's Pub and Bistroteque

Smart atmosphere (popular with ex-pats and airline crews), huge video screen, live music and dancing.
180 Orchard Road (tel: 732 6966).

Saxophone Bar

Very popular and long-standing jazz venue, with a bar, bistro and outside tables. Amiable atmosphere and excellent sounds from both local and international musicians.
23 Cuppage Road (tel: 235 8385).

CINEMAS

All the major international English-language movies reach Singapore, although they may be censored. Check the daily papers for listings. Cinemas are air-conditioned and clean. More serious art films are screened at the Jade Classics (Shaw Towers) or the Picturehouse (Cathay Building).

CLASSICAL MUSIC

When in session, the Singapore Sympony Orchestra holds concerts most

An open-air jazz concert in Singapore harbour

Friday and Saturday nights at the Victoria Concert Hall, Empress Place. Details are advertised in the local press or call the Victoria Theatre Central Booking Office (tel: 338 1230).

CULTURAL SHOWS

'Instant Asia' revues, featuring combinations of Chinese acrobats, lion dances, Indian and Malay dances and other performance arts of Southeast Asia provide an entertaining and colourful introduction to the region's cultural heritage. Dinner is usually at 7pm, with the show at 8pm.

Cockpit Hotel

Lion City Revue with lion dances and other local performances.
Cockpit Hotel, 6–7 Oxley Rise (tel: 737 9111).

Hyatt Regency

Malam Singapura (Singapore Night) at the poolside, with traditional music and dance from Singapore's main ethnic groups.
10–12 Scotts Road (tel: 738 1234).

Mandarin Hotel

ASEAN Night, featuring music, song and dance from Singapore, Thailand, Malaysia, Indonesia and the Philippines.
333 Orchard Road (tel: 737 4411).

DANCE

Singapore's professional ballet group, the Singapore Dance Theatre, usually holds a season in June; performances are held at either the Kallang Theatre, Stadium Walk, or at the Victoria Theatre, Empress Place.
Kallang Theatre Booking Office (tel: 345 8488); Victoria Theatre Central Booking Office (tel: 338 1230).

DRAMA

Amateur productions by local drama groups are usually staged at the Drama Centre, Canning Rise, or at the Victoria Theatre, Empress Place. Watch out for innovative and experimental performances by Theatreworks at the Black Box, Canning Fort or The Substation, 45 Armenian Street.

DISCOS

Singapore has a young population and discos are hugely popular, with plenty to choose from. Dress codes are usually 'smart casual' (no jeans, T-shirts and sneakers). Outrageous dress is not part of the scene here, nor is overtly affect-ionate behaviour. Entry charges are high, although they include the first two drinks.

Caesar's

Live bands interspersed with DJs; 'ancient Roman' décor with toga-clad waitresses, said to be a good singles bar.
02–46 Orchard Towers, 400 Orchard Road (tel: 737 7665).

Chinoiserie

Smart venue for the slightly older set, oriental décor, small dance floor.
Hyatt Regency Hotel, 10–12 Scotts Road (tel: 730 7110).

Fire

The trendiest teenage disco in Singapore, huge dance floor, spectacular futuristic lighting.

04–19 Orchard Plaza, 150 Orchard Road (tel: 235 0155).

The Reading Room

Recently re-vamped in black and chrome décor; smart but somewhat staid clientele.
Marina Mandarin Hotel, 6 Raffles Boulevard (tel: 338 3388).

Top Ten

Live bands alternate with the DJs in this perennially popular spot located in a converted cinema decorated with a mural of the Manhattan skyline.
04–35 Orchard Towers, 400 Orchard Road (tel: 732 3077).

The Warehouse

Located in a converted warehouse with high ceilings and one of the biggest dance floors in Singapore (with a second, smaller dance floor upstairs), this is one of the hottest discos in town.
332 Havelock Road (tel: 732 9922).

Zanzibar

Sophisticated, hi-tech disco with 'dance boxes' above the dance floor for extroverts. Lively young crowd, mostly Euro-disco music.
Le Meridien Singapore, 100 Orchard Road (tel: 733 8855).

Xanadu

Impressive laser, video and lighting system, with an up-market, slightly older clientele.
Shangri-La Hotel, 22 Orange Grove Road (tel: 737 3644).

Zouk

Another of Singapore's trendiest venues, the Zouk complex incorporates not only a disco but also a pub, wine bar, café and restaurant. *Zouk* is a French-Caribbean word meaning 'village party', and the sounds are predominantly house and world music.
17–21 Jiak Kim Street, off Kim Seng Road (tel: 738 2988).

Anyone can have a go at karaoke, a recent craze in Singapore

KARAOKE LOUNGES

As popular in Singapore as it now is all over the rest of Asia, karaoke is not everybody's idea of fun, but if you want to sing along to popular songs (with the lyrics often displayed over a video of the original singer), then there are plenty of places where you can have a go. The KJ (the karaoke equivalent of a DJ) will line up the tapes from a menu of songs in English, Mandarin or Japanese. Singapore has dozens of karaoke lounges and you should have no trouble finding one (or see the weekend listings in the daily press).

THEATRE-RESTAURANTS

Theatre-restaurants are largely respectable nightclubs for the Chinese, featuring lavish banquets in plush surroundings with attentive Chinese hostesses, followed by a cabaret or show featuring top 'song birds' and entertainers from Hong Kong and Taiwan. They are expensive but could be fun for a night out with a difference.

Lido Palace
Cantonese cuisine, local and international acts.
Concorde Hotel Shopping Centre, 317 Outram Road (tel: 732 8855).
Neptune Theatre Restaurant
The largest in town, with excellent Cantonese food and a really glitzy cabaret.
OUB Shopping Centre, 50 Collyer Quay (tel: 224 3922).

Karaoke lounges abound in Singapore

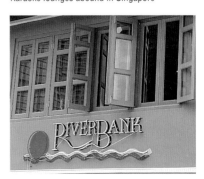

MALAYSIA

Entertainment and nightlife in Malaysia tends to be fairly low key compared to neighbouring countries such as Thailand. Even Singapore has a huge choice of live music and discos by comparison. However, there are still a fair number of bars and nightclubs in major centres such as Kuala Lumpur and Pinang. The ubiquitous karaoke lounges are found in almost every town.

Cinemas in main cities and towns screen English-language movies as well as the Hindi, Malay and Cantonese films that predominate in smaller urban centres. Kuala Lumpur cinemas screen five shows daily, starting from around midday, with the last show around 9pm. Often the best evening's entertainment is simply to wander around the *pasar malam* (night markets – see page 116). See also **Festivals** (pages 146–7). *Kuala Lumpur This Month*, available free from tourist offices, lists events and shows currently on in the capital.

KUALA LUMPUR
Bars and pubs
Aviary Bar
Piano bar. *Kuala Lumpur Hilton, Jalan Sultan Ismail (tel: 242 2122).*
Barn Thai
Excellent jazz, Thai-style. *370B Jalan Tun Razak (tel: 244 6699).*
Blue Moon
Nostalgic oldies from the 1950s and 1960s. *Hotel Equatorial, Jalan Sultan Ismail (tel: 261 7777).*
Riverbank
Café-terrace on the riverside. *Central Market (tel: 274 6651).*

Cultural shows
Central Market
The amphitheatre outside Central Market is one of the city's liveliest

---

TRADITIONAL MALAY DANCES

Among the many traditional dances that you will see performed at cultural shows or other venues, some of the more colourful include the Kuda Kepang, which originally came from the southern state of Johor. The dance re-enacts the story of the men who spread the Islamic faith, with performers riding two-dimensional 'horses' to dramatise the legends of battles waged and won. A popular dance is the Tarian Endang, which portrays villagers cleaning up at the riverbank after a hard day's work in the rice-fields and symbolises the virtues of community life. Also connected to the rice harvest, Tarian Cangging is usually performed during the harvesting season in the state of Perlis. Rice-planting and harvesting are likewise celebrated in the Jong Jong Inai, a joyous dance performed to celebrate a good season. Tarian Cinta Sayang (meaning 'the loved ones' dance) is a romantic and lively folk dance from the state of Kedah, often performed as a gesture of bidding good luck to fisherfolk as they set off to sea.

From Sabah in East Malaysia, the Sumazu is a rhythmic and graceful dance where the hands and limbs flap and flail in likeness of the flight of birds. A popular east-coast dance is the Tarian Wau Bulan (moon-kite dance), which depicts the carefree spirit of the kite-flyer as he sends his *wau bulan* aloft.

The Malaysian *gambus*, or lute, is used to accompany traditional folk dances

venues for a variety of performances ranging from Malay traditional dance to *silat* (martial arts) demonstrations, Indian drama, poetry readings, Balinese dance, and fringe theatre shows and street acts. A monthly calendar of events is available from the information desk.
Central Market, Jalan Hang Kasturi. Information counter open 10am–10pm (tel: 274 9966). Admission free.

Auditorium DBKL
Revue show of musical performances and traditional dances at 8.30pm every Saturday night. Admission free.
Jalan Raja Laut (tel: 291 6011).

Malaysia Tourist Information Complex
Cultural performances in the mini-auditorium at 3.30pm daily.
Jalan Ampang (tel: 264 3929).

Discos
Betelnut, *Jalan Pinang (tel: 241 6455).*
Club Oz, *Shangri-La Hotel, Jalan Sultan Ismail (tel: 232 2388).*
Copperfield, *Pan Pacific Hotel, Jalan Putra (tel: 442 5555).*

Legends, *1 Jalan Kia Peng (tel: 241 4929).*
Modesto's, *1d Lorong Perak (tel: 985 0385).*
Phase 2, *370 Jalan Tun Razak (tel: 248 2063).*
Renaissance, *Yow Chuan Plaza (tel: 242 0540).*
The Turf, *10 Jalan Kia Peng (tel: 242 4319).*
Tin Mine, *Hilton Hotel, Jalan Sultan Ismail (tel: 248 2322).*

PULAU PINANG
George Town has several cinemas, karaoke lounges and bars, but the main form of entertainment in the evenings is browsing and sampling from the food-stalls on Lebuh Chuliah, the Esplanade or Gurney Drive. Discos and clubs are mostly centred around the Batu Feringgi beach resorts, and include the following:
Borsalino, *Park Royal Hotel (tel: 881 1133).*
Fun Club, *Golden Sands Hotel (tel: 881 1911).*
Ozone, *Mar Vista Resort (tel: 890 3388).*

Festivals

SINGAPORE

Given the diversity of ethnic and religious groups that make up the population of Singapore it is not surprising that there is a constant stream of festivals throughout the year. Some of these are on fixed dates, but many events celebrated by the Chinese, Hindu and Malay communities are calculated according to the lunar calendar, which changes from year to year, and it is difficult therefore to give exact dates. The most reliable source of information on specific dates and locations is the annual *Calendar of Festivals & Events* produced by the Singapore Tourist Promotion Board.

Ponggal (mid-January): see page 146. In Singapore, the best place to watch the festivities is the Sri Perumal Temple on Serangoon Road.

Chinese New Year (January/February): the start of the lunar year is the most important festival of the calendar for the Chinese. Preparations begin a week beforehand, with houses spring-cleaned and redecorated for a fresh start to the year. As the festivities get underway, houses and shops are decorated with lights and banners (particularly along New Bridge Road and Eu Tong Sen Street) and stores are busy selling mandarin and plum trees, both of which are considered lucky. Children receive *hong bao*, gifts of money wrapped in red and gold packets, and many businesses still follow the old custom of clearing their debts before the year end.

Traditionally, Chinese New Year is as noisy as possible, with masses of explosive firecrackers being set off to frighten away evil spirits. Due to the number of houses that were burned down by stray fireworks, this practice has now been banned by the government. However, plenty of noisy drum- and gong-bashing accompanies the dragon and lion dances.

Chingay Procession (February): this spectacular procession marks the end of the Chinese New Year festivities and is held on the first or the second Sunday after Chinese New Year's Day. The word *chingay* refers to the Chinese-style decorated floats that are paraded along the length of Orchard Road, alongside lion and dragon dancers, stiltwalkers and acrobats.

Thaipusam Festival (January/February): one of the most intensely dramatic Hindu festivals (see pages 144–5). The procession starts at the Sri Perumal Temple in Serangoon Road and ends up at the Chettiar Temple in Tank Road. Procession times and route maps are published in the daily papers.

Monkey God Festival (March and September): the birthday of the Monkey God is celebrated twice a year at the Monkey God Temple in Seng Poh Road (opposite Tiong Bahru market). Mediums carry sedan-chairs shoulder high, which rock and jerk if possessed by the spirit of the Monkey God. They then go into a trance and pierce their cheeks and tongues, using the blood to write special charms, which are distributed to devotees.

Ramadan (March/April): see page 146.

Qing Ming (March/April): on this day, Chinese traditionally visit the graves of their ancestors to make offerings.

Hari Raya Puasa (April): see page 146. In Singapore the best place to experience Hari Raya Pusa is in and around Geylang Serai (MRT: Paya Lebar), where the streets are draped in festive lights for several days.

Chinese festivities often include the Lion Dance

Vesak Day (May): Celebration of Lord Buddha's birth, enlightenment and death, with chanting and prayers in the temples, the release of caged birds (to symbolise the freeing of the soul), and candelit processions to mark the end of the day. The festival is celebrated in every Buddhist temple.

Dragon Boat Festival (June): see page 147. In Singapore the event attracts top teams from all over the world.

Singapore Festival of the Arts (June): Southeast Asia's biggest arts festival, held biennially, with performances of drama, music, arts and dance by participants from all over the world. At the same time there is a fringe festival featuring international and local talent. See the daily newspapers for details.

Festival of Hungry Ghosts (July/August): Chinese festival marked by performances of *wayangs* (Chinese operas) and processions of floats.

Navarathiri Festival (September/October): Hindu festival of the 'Nine Nights' dedicated to the goddesses Dhurga, Laksmi and Saraswathi. Set in three cycles, the festival honours each goddess in turn, finishing up with a procession at the Chettiar Temple in Tank Road. Nightly performances of traditional dance and music take place at the Sri Mariamman Temple (South Bridge Road) and the Chettiar Temple (Tank Road).

Thimithi Festival (September/October): annual fire-walking ceremony held in honour of the Hindu goddess Draupadi at the Sri Mariamman Temple.

Deepavali (October/November): the 'festival of lights', during which small oil lamps are lit in temples and homes to symbolise the triumph of good over evil. Temples and streets in Little India are festooned with lights and garlands.

Festival of the Nine Emperor Gods (October/November): nine days of ceremonies and performances of Chinese opera to honour the nine Sons of the Queen of Heaven.

Christmas (25 December): the lighting up of Orchard Road for Christmas begins in November, when department stores and hotels compete for the most glittering and spectacular displays on the front of their buildings.

THAIPUSAM FESTIVAL

Shivering from fear as much as from the early morning cold, a young boy in thin yellow robes slides into a trance as a Hindu priest fans incense smoke across his face. The chanting in the temple changes to a higher pitch and the ringing of bells in the background becomes more insistent. The boy's body arches backwards as the trance takes hold, his eyes are tightly shut. A helper chants loudly into one ear while another steps forward and thrusts the *vel*, a 6in-long steel needle, through one cheek near the corner of his mouth, and then out through the other. The boy pushes his tongue underneath the silver rod, and another is stuck through his tongue vertically.

With the chanting, the incense, the bells, the crowds, the brief cries as metal enters flesh or the sharp intake of breath as another hook goes in, the atmosphere in the temple is highly charged. It is a spell-binding and very intense experience for the onlookers; tourists' popping flashlights are totally ignored among the general mayhem.

Outside the temple the sky is still dark: it is 6am on the second morning of the annual Thaipusam festival. All through the first day of the festival a huge silver chariot containing the image of Lord Subramanya, drawn by white bullocks, parades through the streets. Thousands of coconuts are smashed in its path so that the wheels may pass over rivers of coconut milk, 'the purest water in the world'.

On the second day hundreds of devout Hindus undergo ordeals such as piercing their cheeks with the *vel*, or slinging hooks into the skin of their backs and chests, hanging silver or gold chains or fresh limes from the hooks to weigh them down. Others opt to carry the *kavadi*, a heavy metal frame decorated with flowers and peacock feathers.

Hindu legend says that Lord Shiva gave Lord Mariamman the *vel*, the steel rod that pierces the flesh, in order that he might have knowledge. The devotees who take part are fulfilling a vow they

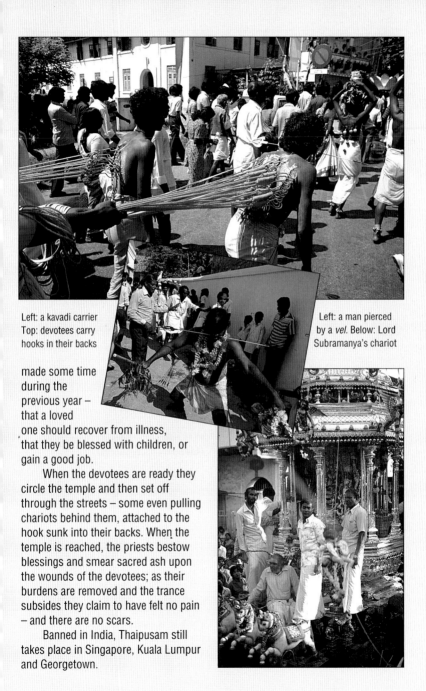

Left: a kavadi carrier
Top: devotees carry
hooks in their backs

Left: a man pierced
by a *vel*. Below: Lord
Subramanya's chariot

made some time
during the
previous year –
that a loved
one should recover from illness,
that they be blessed with children, or
gain a good job.

When the devotees are ready they
circle the temple and then set off
through the streets – some even pulling
chariots behind them, attached to the
hook sunk into their backs. When the
temple is reached, the priests bestow
blessings and smear sacred ash upon
the wounds of the devotees; as their
burdens are removed and the trance
subsides they claim to have felt no pain
– and there are no scars.

Banned in India, Thaipusam still
takes place in Singapore, Kuala Lumpur
and Georgetown.

MALAYSIA

Like Singapore, Malaysia celebrates a large number of festivals, which reflect its multiracial population, and the Hindu, Chinese and Muslim events similarly change dates according to the lunar calendar.

Ponggal (mid-January): celebrated by southern Indians, this is a spring harvest festival marking the end of the monsoon season in India. In the early morning, a dish of *ponggal* (newly harvested rice with milk, nuts, peas and raisins) is cooked in a new pot and allowed to boil over, symbolising plenty and prosperity. This part takes place in people's homes, but later on rice, vegetables, sugar-cane and spices are offered to the gods to the accompaniment of prayers and music in Hindu temples.

Chinese New Year (January/February): the start of the Chinese lunar New Year is celebrated with colourful processions and lion dances. Unlike Singapore, fire-crackers are not banned in Malaysia so you can expect it to be particularly noisy. The best places to watch all the festivities that take place are the Chinatowns of Kuala Lumpur and Pulau Pinang.

Thaipusam (January/February): see pages 144–5. In Kuala Lumpur, the procession culminates in spectacular fashion at the Batu Caves (13km north of Kuala Lumpur), where devotees scale the 272 steps to the temple with their *kavadis*. Special trains and buses are laid on at this time. In Pinang, the procession starts at the Sri Mariamman Temple (entrance on Lebuh Queen) and finishes at the Nattukotai Temple on Waterfall Road.

Monkey God Festival (March and September): see page 142.

Ramadan (March/April): the ninth month of the Islamic calendar is marked by strict fasting by Muslims from sunrise to sunset. Street-stalls selling Malay cakes and other delicacies are set up outside mosques ready for the breaking of the fast at nightfall.

Hari Raya Puasa (April): this festival heralds the end of the fasting month of Ramadan. For several days in advance, homes are decorated and special cakes and sweetmeats prepared. On the day itself, Muslims put on their best finery and visit relatives and friends.

Easter (April): most notably celebrated in Melaka, with a candlelit procession to St Peter's Church.

Wesak Day (May): a one-day celebration of Lord Buddha's birth, enlightenment and death, best seen in Buddhist temples in Pinang and Melaka.

Kadazan Harvest Festival (May): a thanksgiving festival at the end of the rice harvest celebrated by Kadazan farmers in Sabah, with feasting, buffalo races and other events.

Malaysia International Kite Festival (May): local and international competitors take part in this championship with their colourful *wau* (kites) at Tumpat, near Kota Bharu.

Gawai Festival (May/June): traditional Dyak celebrations to mark the rice harvest in Sarawak. Dances, cockfights, blow-pipe competitions and much feasting and rice-wine drinking.

Dragon Boat Festival (May/June): commemorates the death of a Chinese poet and statesman, Qu Yuan, who committed suicide by throwing himself into the river as a protest against political corruption in his day. Legend has it that fishermen tried to save him by thrashing the water with their paddles and beating drums and gongs to prevent the fish from eating his body.

The event is now celebrated with longboat races, with the oarsmen urged on by drummers sitting in the bows. Longboats adorned with dragon's heads race through the waters around Pulau Pinang.

Kelantan International Drum Festival (June/July): another rice-harvest festival, here celebrated with percussion competitions on the giant Kelanatan drums, *rebana ubi*. *Kota Bharu, Kelantan.*

Birthday of HM The Yang Di Pertuan Agong (June): cultural shows and traditional games in Kuala Lumpur mark the birthday of the reigning Sultan.

National Day Celebrations (August/September): public holiday with parades, entertainments and stage shows to mark the gaining of Independence in 1957. Kuala Lumpur hosts the most events.

Sungai Sarawak Regatta (September): longboats and dragon boats compete on the river amid various celebrations. *Sarawak River, Sarawak.*

Deepavali (October/November): a national holiday to celebrate the Hindu Festival of Lights. For more information see page 143.

Kota Belud Tamu Besar (November/December): annual market festival at Kota Belud in Sabah (see pages 108–9). Held at the end of November, it attracts around 10,000 people who come to watch the buffalo races and competitions of horsemanship by the famed Bajau horsemen. There are also dances and cultural shows by ethnic groups (in ceremonial costumes) from all over Sabah including the Irranuns, Dusun and Tindal from the south, the Tempasuk Dusun, the Dusun Tabiluing from the north, and Bajaus and Ubians.

Pesta Pulau Pinang (December): annual event on Pulau Pinang featuring carnivals, trade fairs and cultural and sporting activities.

Christmas (25 December): Public holiday in Malaysia.

Kites are a tradition on the East Coast

Children

SINGAPORE

Singapore is a great destination for families, with plenty of fun activities to amuse and entertain adults and children together, particularly since many purpose-built facilities (such as theme parks) are geared towards local families and designed with this in mind. They will also enjoy the many colourful street festivals.

Singapore's clean and green environment poses few health risks, so apart from protection from the heat and the sun few precautions are necessary.

Eating out with children is never a problem (except in the most sophisticated establishments), and Singaporeans often dine out with several generations seated at the table. Some of the spicier foods may not be suitable for young palates, but there is nearly always something acceptable on the menu and fast-food outlets such as McDonalds, Burger King and Pizza Hut can be found all over the city.

With so many toy shops children will probably need vast amounts of pocket money, and admission costs to attractions can also add up considerably, although some places (such as the Jurong Bird Park) do have family packages that offer some reductions.

Guinness World of Records: (see page 34).

Haw Par Villa: children will particularly enjoy the flume rides, audio-visual shows and participation in story-telling (see page 35).

Jurong Bird Park: (see page 36).

Sentosa Island: numerous attractions including roller-skating, Underwater World and the Dragon Trail with life-size dragons and skeletons (see page 48).

Singapore Science Centre: hands-on displays specifically aimed at youngsters, plus 'Crazy Rooms' where they can fling themselves around in a weightless environment (see page 39).

Tang Dynasty Village: Hollywood-style stunt displays, movie studios, flying swordsmen and acrobats (see page 40).

Tropical jungle: older children may enjoy an easy walk among tropical jungle foliage at either the Botanic Gardens (see page 28) or Bukit Timah Nature Reserve (see page 30).

Zoological Gardens: a top favourite, due particularly to the 'open zoo' concept and lack of cages. Animal shows and underwater viewing areas will also appeal. Children's World is a new mini-zoo with a farmyard, llamas, miniature horses, pony rides, a 'space walk', pet's corner and a 1km miniature train ride (see page 41).

GETTING WET

Most hotels have swimming-pools, but when children want to cool off and splash around to their heart's content without diluting a poolside gin-and-tonic try:

CN West Leisure Park: pools and waterslides.
9 Japanese Garden Road (tel: 261 4771). Open: Tuesday to Friday, noon–6pm; weekends, 9.30am–6pm.

Sentosa Island: on Siloso Beach there are pedal-cats, aquabikes, fun bugs, canoes and surf boards for hire (see page 48).

The Big Splash: on the East Coast Parkway, the Big Splash has several pools (with lifeguards) and water slides. *East Coast Parkway (tel: 3451211). Open: Monday to Friday, noon–6pm; weekends and public holidays, 9am–6pm; school holidays, 10am–6pm.*

MALAYSIA

Malaysians love children and will probably fuss over and pamper yours as much as their own. They are welcome everywhere and will probably have great fun. Although not as squeaky-clean as Singapore, Malaysia is less of a hygiene risk than many other Asian countries. Make sure they have all the necessary jabs and are sufficiently protected from the heat and sun.

The gateway to dragon legends, on Sentosa

Like Singapore, children are welcome in almost any eating place and it is very unusual to find a restaurant that doesn't have a high chair at the ready. They will probably love *satay*, and in larger towns and resorts you can nearly always find local or international fast-food chains.

One of the most popular family destinations in Malaysia is Pulau Pinang, where, in addition to the beach, there are attractions such as the Butterfly Farm, funicular rides up Pinang Hill, parks and gardens (see pages 77). Older children will appreciate the chance to observe wildlife, watching turtles nest at Rantau Abang (see page 92) and the Sepilok Orang-Utan Rehabilitation Centre in Sabah (see page 112).

In Kuala Lumpur the best place to take them is the Lake Gardens (see page 54), which not only has a boating lake but also a Butterfly Park and Bird Park.

Near Kuala Lumpur the two major attractions specifically designed for familes are:

Mimaland: a 120-hectare amusement park with boating lake, small zoo, dinosaur models, waterslides and the largest swimming-pool in the country. *Batu 11, Jalan Gombak, Selangor (tel: (03) 689 2133). Open: daily 8am–midnight. Admission charge. 18km from the city centre. Bus 168 (marked 'Mimaland') from Jalan Ampang.*

Sunway Lagoon: a massive theme park with waterslides and other attractions. *3 Jalan PJS 11/11, Bandar Sunway, Petaling Jaya (tel: (03) 735 6000). Bus 252B or 51 from Klang bus station, Kuala Lumpur. Open: weekdays, noon–8.30pm; weekends and holidays, 10am–8pm. Admisssion charge.*

MALAY PASTIMES

Many of the games and pastimes enjoyed by Malaysians originated on the east coast, particularly in the state of Kelantan, where old traditions are cherished in what has always been the Malay

Spinning competition with *gasing* (tops)

heartland. Although they have now caught on elsewhere in Malaysia, they are still most widely practised on the east coast. Most of the traditional games are normally held after harvests and on important state festivals, but regular events also take place at the Gelanggang Seni (Cultural Centre) in Kota Bharu (see page 89 for details).

TOP-SPINNING

With Kelantan tops weighing anything up to 5.5kg, top-spinning is an adult sport requiring considerable manual dexterity and strength. Neighbouring villages often challenge each other to a test of skill with the *gasing* (tops), sometimes with up to 500 people taking part. There are two types of contest, the striking match and the spinning competition. In the former, each team tries to topple the opposition's tops, while in the latter the winner is the one whose top spins the longest – experts claim to be able to set them going for two hours or more.

KITE-FLYING

Kelantanese kites (*wau*) come in all shapes and sizes, with the largest (measuring some 2m across) being capable of soaring to great heights. Again, inter-village competitions are often held, with matches for the kite that flies the highest, the kite that sustains the best musical hum, the best-decorated kite, and the most skilful kite-flyer. One of the most popular designs is the *wau bulan* or moon kite, which has a long, elaborate tail.

SILAT

The Malay art of self-defence is characterised by highly stylised, graceful and disciplined movements. Now it is rarely used as a martial art, and demonstrations are more often given as part of dance performances, at ceremonies and at weddings to the rhythmical accompaniment of gongs and drums.

Main picture: preparing for lift-off with a highly decorated *wau* (kite)
Inset above: a drumming display at the Kota Bharu Cultural Centre
Left: practising *silat* in a Kuala Lumpur park

WAYANG KULIT

Malaysian shadow-puppet plays, similar to those found in neighbouring Asian countries. Puppets crafted from cowhide and mounted on rattan sticks are manipulated from behind a white screen by the *Tok Dalang* (Father of the Mysteries), who relates tales from the Indian classics of *Ramayana* and *Mahabharata*. Backed by a traditional orchestra, the performance may go on for several hours.

REBANA (GIANT DRUM) COMPETITIONS

Found only in Kelantan, the *rebana* is an enormous drum weighing over 100kg that can be heard several miles away. Teams comprising 12 men, with six drums between them, compete in the village fields from February to October; see the Kelantan International Drum Festival (page 147).

Sport

SINGAPORE

From computerised bowling alleys to a remarkable number of golf courses, Singapore has a wide range of sports facilities to complement the swimming-pools and fitness clubs found in most major hotels. For details on matches, fixtures or sports not listed here, contact the Singapore Sports Council (tel: 345 7111).

BOWLING

Tenpin bowling is very popular, with a large number of bowling alleys in the city.

Jackie's Bowl, *542B East Coast Road (tel: 241 6519)*.

Kallang Bowl, *5 Stadium Walk (tel: 345 0545)*.

Orchard Bowl, *8 Grange Road (tel: 737 4744)*.

Plaza Bowl, *Jalan Sultan (tel: 292 4821)*.

Superbowl Marina South, *15 Marina Grove, Marina South (tel: 221 1010)*.

Singapore Tenpin Bowling Congress, *400 Balestier Road, 01–01 Balestier Plaza (tel: 297 3841)*.

CANOEING

The swimming lagoons of Sentosa Island and the inshore waters along the East Coast Parkway (the hire centre is near the Laguna Food Centre) both offer safe canoeing. See also Pulau Ubin (page 50).

CRICKET

Matches are held on the Padang on weekends between March and October, Saturdays from 1.30pm, Sundays from 10.30am. Contact the Singapore Cricket Club (tel: 338 9367) for details of fixtures.

GOLF

Singapore has a dozen courses, but visitors are usually restricted to playing on week-days. There are also several driving ranges.

Changi Golf Club: 9-hole, par-68 course. *Netheravon Road (tel: 545 5133)*.

Keppel Club: 18-hole, par-72 course. *Bukit Chermin (tel: 273 5522)*.

Marina Bay Golf & Country Club: three-level driving range, 150 bays. *6 Marina Green (tel: 221 2811)*.

Parkland Golf Driving Range: 60 bays. *East Coast Parkway (tel: 440 6726)*.

Raffles Country Club: two 18-hole, par-71 and -69 courses. *Jalan Ahmad Ibrahim (tel: 861 7655)*.

Sembawang Country Club: 18-hole, par-70 course. *Sembawang Road (tel: 257 0642)*.

Sentosa Golf Course: 18-hole, par-72 course. *Sentosa Island (tel: 275 0022)*.

Singapore Island Country Club: two 18-hole, par-72 courses. *180 Island Club Road (tel: 459 2222)*.

Warren Golf Course: 9-hole, par-70 course. *Folkstone Road (tel: 777 6533)*.

HORSE RACING

Set in a beautifully landscaped park, the Bukit Turf Club offers a year-round racing calendar. Races are keenly followed by locals, who gamble heavily on the outcome. When there is no live action, races from Malaysia are broadcast live on a giant, 16m-high video screen. Visitors can join special tours of an afternoon at the races, which

includes lunch and access to the members' enclosure (contact your hotel tour desk for details).
Bukit Turf Club, *Bukit Timah Racecourse (tel: 469 3611).*

POLO
Played regularly between February to October.
Singapore Polo Club, *80 Mount Pleasant Road (tel: 256 4530).*

SCUBA-DIVING
Several of the islands to the south of Sentosa have fringing reefs, although coral diversity is poor. Some of the best reefs are around Pulau Salu; Pulau Hantu and the Sisters' Islands are also popular with divers.
Asia Aquatic, *7 Circular Road (tel: 536 8116).*
Great Blue Dive Shop, *211 Holland Avenue, 03–05 Holland Road Shopping Centre (tel: 467 0767).*
Leeway Sub-Aquatic Paradise, *Blk 115, 01–51 Aljunied Avenue 2 (tel: 743 1208).*
Sentosa Water Sports Centre, *01–06 World Trade Centre, 1 Maritime Square (tel: 274 5612).*

SNOOKER
Several snooker halls cater for this rapidly growing sport. Most impose a dress code (long trousers and shoes). For more information, contact the Singapore Billiards and Snooker Council (tel: 440 5155).
Academy of Snooker, *Albert Complex, Albert Street (tel: 286 2879).*
King's Snookerium, *Amara Hotel Shopping Centre (tel: 224 6424).*

WATER-SKIING
Boat hire, driver and equipment is

costed at an hourly rate.
William Water Sports, *35 Ponggol 24th Avenue (tel: 282 6879).*

WINDSURFING
The East Coast Sailing Centre hires out boards and offers two-day beginner's courses. Laser-class dinghies are also available.
East Coast Sailing Centre, *East Coast Parkway (tel: 449 5118).*

Enjoying a *chukka* at the Singapore Polo Club

MALAYSIA

Malaysians are enthusiastic sports lovers and the country has a wide range of sporting opportunities for visitors. Soccer, badminton, tennis, squash and cricket are all popular sports. In addition, there are plenty of ways in which to experience the country's magnificent natural surroundings, such as white-water rafting, trekking or scuba-diving.

GOLF

Golf is extremely popular. Since British planters introduced golf to Malaysia

There are plenty of excellent opportunities for golfing enthusiasts

over 100 years ago, golf courses have mushroomed and there are now more than 100, with many more planned. A detailed brochure, *Golfing in Malaysia*, is available from the Tourist Office. Some of the more outstanding courses include:

Ayer Keroh Country Club: a challenging course in a scenic position near Melaka, host to many major tournaments. *Jalan Ayer Keroh, Melaka (tel: (06) 232 0822)*.

Royal Selangor Golf Club: less than 1km from Kuala Lumpur city centre, with the highest number of holes in the country. Venue for the prestigious Malaysian Open and other tournaments. *PO Box 11051, Kuala Lumpur (tel: (03) 984 8433)*.

Saujana Golf Club: another prestigious club, noted for its challenging course and excellent service. *Near Subang International Airport, Kuala Lumpur. Batu 3, Jalan Lapangan Terbang, Subang, Selangor (tel: (03) 746 1466)*.

SCUBA-DIVING, see pages 122–4.

TREKKING

Malaysia's national parks offer some excellent opportunities for short treks, particularly in Taman Negara (see page 120), and the Kinabalu National Park in Sabah (see page 108).

More adventurous backpackers might like to consider tackling sections of the Roof of Malaya Mountain Trail (RMMT), which runs for 250km along the Titiwangsa Range, linking six of the highest mountains in the peninsula (all of which are above 2,500m). The RMMT consists of two parts: the east–west section runs from Tanjung Rambutan in Perak for 33km to the Blue Valley in the Cameron Highlands.

The north–south corridor is being charted.

Treks with knowledgeable guides in some of the most beautiful areas of Malaysia are run by the country's leading ecotourism operator, Wilderness Experience. They offer small group trips to Endau-Rompin on the peninsula, Kinabalu National Park and Mount Trusmadi (Sabah), Bako National Park, Gunung Mulu National Park and Batu Lawi and Murud (Sarawak).

Treks in the Central Highlands with Orang Asli as guides are organised by the Koperasi Kijang Mas Berhad (Gold Deer Co-operative). Two treks are available: a five-day trek, staying in Orang Asli long-houses (with traditional feasts and dancing in the evenings) with an average of three to four hours walking per day; and a seven day trek, which is similar but also involves longer walks (up to seven or eight hours per day), as well as demonstrations on making bamboo rafts and a day's rafting on the Sungai Ulu Jelai.

Association of Backpackers Malaysia: *c/o Dr Wong (President), 21, SS3/46 University Garden, Selangor (tel: (03) 775 6249).*
Wilderness Experience, *6B, Jalan SS21.39, Damansara Utara, 47400 Petaling Jaya (tel: (03) 717 8221, fax: (03) 7198 090).*
Koperasi Kijang Mas Berhad (Golden Deer Cooperative): *Kilometre 24, Gombak Utara, 53100 Kuala Lumpur (tel: (03) 689 3544).*

WATERSPORTS
Resorts on the islands of Langkawi, Pangkor, Tioman and Pinang and beach resorts at Kuantan, Cerating and Tanjung Aru (Sabah) have facilities for

Canoeing off the beach, Pulau Kapas

windsurfing, sailing, water-skiing and other watersports.

WHITE-WATER RAFTING
In Peninsular Malaysia, white-water rafting and canoeing principally take place on the Tembeling River in the Taman Negara National Park, in the Endau-Rompin National Park, on tributaries of the Kelantan River, stretches of the Pahang River, and on the Sungai Muda in Kedah. Canoeing expeditions lasting up to a week are occasionally organised by the Kuala Lumpur Canoeing Association.

In East Malaysia, the principal rafting location is the Padas River in Sabah, with day tours organised by Borneo Expeditions in Kota Kinabalu. Participants travel by train to Tenom, after which the 9km ride back down the rapids takes around 2 hours.

Kuala Lumpur Canoeing Association, *Lot F 44–46, 1st floor, Yow Chuan Plaza, Jalan Tun Abdul Razak, Kuala Lumpur (tel: (03) 241 7416).*
Borneo Expeditions, *Unit 306, 3rd floor, Wisma Sabah, Jalan Tun Razak, Kota Kinabalu, Sabah (tel: (088) 222 721).*

Food and Drink

*T*he passion for food in Singapore and Malaysia is reflected in the vast number of cafés, restaurants and market-stalls serving a wide range of flavoursome local dishes as well as tempting feasts from the provinces of China, the islands of Indonesia, the Indian sub-continent and other Far Eastern countries. This is especially true of Singapore, where eating out is probably the principal national obsession after shopping.

Visiting either country, it is almost impossible not to indulge to the full and find yourself among what the Hokkien call *yau kui* – those who love to eat.

The variety of eating establishments is almost as great as the range of foods, ranging from smart hotel restaurants to Chinese coffee-houses, from Malaysian *kedai makan* (eating houses) to Indian curry houses where your food comes served on a banana leaf. Roadside stalls or markets are a great place to try hawker food, which covers almost everything from *satay* cooked on charcoal to spicy fried noodles.

One of the most practical ways of sampling as many of these culinary delights as possible is to eat out in a group, so you can all share and taste different dishes. This is usually the best way to take advantage of the huge menus in Chinese restaurants and it is also a good way of tackling the unfamiliarities of hawker centres, where you can order any number of dishes from different stalls.

Although you can pay top dollar to eat in the smarter restaurants or hotels, everyday food is incredibly good value and won't put a large dent in your

Herbs, roots and fungi contribute to the right balance of *yin* and *yang* in Chinese herbal cooking

budget. In Singapore there are fast-food outlets and hawker centres within easy reach of the deluxe hotels, and in Malaysia likewise you only have to walk a few metres from the smartest hotel to find a cheap meal.

Tempting though it may be to rush out and try everything in sight, a few sensible precautions are necessary to make sure your trip isn't spoiled by tummy upsets or other health problems (see **Health**, page 183).

CHINESE FOOD

Cantonese

Regarded by many as one of the finest of Chinese regional styles, Cantonese food is enormously popular in Malaysia and Singapore. Food is usually prepared by stir-frying, roasting or steaming and is characterised by light, delicate flavours and subtle seasonings (normally with oyster sauce or soy sauce). Imaginatively cooked seafood is a Cantonese favourite. Other classics include roast suckling pig, crisp deep-fried chicken, deep-fried prawn balls and shark's fin soup. Another speciality is *dim sum*, which covers a whole range of steamed or deep-fried snacks served in bamboo containers or small bowls; popular for breakfast or lunch, *dim sum* are brought around the tables on trolleys or trays as fresh batches come out of the kitchen, with diners simply selecting the ones they want as they go by. At the end of the meal, your bill is added up according to the number of empty bowls on your table.

Street-side stir-fry in Chinatown, Kuala Lumpur

Chinese herbal

The Chinese attitude to food has always been linked to physical health, with many dishes carefully balanced to ensure the right combination of *yin* (cool) and *yang* (hot). These concepts are taken a step further in herbal food, where all the dishes are planned with their medicinal value in mind. Very little salt or oil is used, and flavours are generally subtle and delicate. In genuine herbal restaurants, a qualified Chinese physician presides over a huge wooden cabinet with numerous drawers containing herbs, roots and fungi. On request, he will check your pulse and tongue and decide what your body needs. After he has carefully weighed and mixed the desired ingredients, they are dispatched to the kitchen to be added to the dishes you have ordered. The food is delicious and even if you are already in good health, a herbal restaurant is a novel experience.

Hokkien

The Hokkiens from Fukien province form the largest ethnic group in Singapore and have provided Singapore's most popular noodle dish, Hokkien fried noodles or *mee*, a tasty mixture of thick noodles fried with prawns, pork and vegetables. Hokkien dishes tend to be less sophisticated than food from neighbouring Canton, with robust, rich flavours based on garlic, soya-bean paste and soy sauces. Typical dishes include *poh piah* (soft spring rolls filled with prawns, cabbage, egg and sausage) and *khong bak* (a steamed bun containing pork).

Peking

The best-known of Beijing (Peking) food is of course Peking Duck, served in

Aromatic spices ready for the kitchen

two or three separate courses (the crispy skin comes first, layered between pancakes with spring onions and plum sauce for seasoning; the meat is then stir-fried with bean sprouts as a second course and, finally, the rest of the duck is served as soup). Lamb or mutton is a main feature of Beijing restaurants and baked freshwater tench is another popular dish.

Szechuan

Possibly the spiciest of Chinese foods, Szechuan (or Sichuan) cooking has a distinctive character, and as well as liberal doses of chilli paste or fried chillies it also incorporates aromatic ingredients such as star anise, dried tangerine peel and Szechuan pepper. Don't be put off by the fiery reputation of Szechuan food – the chilli is not always that overwhelming and other, less strongly-flavoured classics worth trying include duck smoked over jasmine tea leaves and camphor.

HAWKER FOOD

A *Bradshaw's Overland Guide* published in 1870 directs readers' attention to Objects of Notice in Singapore, which include 'Perambulating Restaurants'. In common with other Asian countries, Singapore and Malaysia have a long tradition of street vendors (hawkers) who wheel out their stalls every day to entice hungry passers-by with freshly cooked dishes.

In Malaysia, hawker stalls are still found on busy street corners, or sometimes grouped together at *pasar malam* (night markets). In Singapore, the government decided some time ago that street hawkers were cluttering up their vision of the perfect tropical city and encouraged them to set up

The raw material: chillies are an essential part of Szechuan food

permanently in purpose-built hawker centres where standards of cleanliness could be controlled.

Whether you are grabbing a quick bowl of *mee goreng* (fried noodles) fresh from the wok in the streets of Kuala Lumpur or enjoying charcoal-cooked fish in Marina Square in Singapore, hawker food is an essential part of the travel experience in these two countries. It is also exceptional value: if you're on a budget you could eat hawker food every day and still find there were dishes you hadn't sampled.

Whether it is in the air-conditioned comfort of a hawker centre in Singapore or the *pasar malam* of Malaysia, eating out follows the same pattern: find a convenient table and then wander round the stalls to see what's on offer. Once you have ordered, tell the stallholder where you are sitting and your food will be brought to you. You pay for each dish as it arrives (tipping is not expected).

The great thing about hawker food is that a group of people can each order exactly what they want from different stalls (no need to argue about whether to eat Indian or Chinese!). In Singapore, stalls often have menus, but if not simply ask what's on offer and choose something that looks good. Prices are so reasonable that it won't matter if you make the occasional mistake.

Most hawker centres will also have juice stalls or drinks (including beer) and these stallholders will often come to your table independently to see what you want. Hawkers almost everywhere are used to dealing with tourists, and most speak some English (if not, simply point – although using only the thumb in Malaysia).

INDIAN FOOD
Northern Indian

This is generally not too spicy, relying more on subtly flavoured, creamy sauces. Many of the more popular northern Indian dishes are baked in a *tandoor*, or clay oven, with the meat or chicken often having been marinated previously in spices and yogurt. Indian breads such as *parathas* and *chapatis* are more usually served instead of rice, with *naan* (baked in the tandoor with garlic and herbs) being one of the most popular.

South Indian

Tends to be highly seasoned, and is always served with rice. Many southern Indian and vegetarian restaurants serve rice dishes on a fresh banana leaf instead of a plate, with various curries and *dhals* (made from lentils) heaped up around the rice. This is always eaten with the right hand only (the left customarily being used for ablutions) and there are always wash-basins provided if you want to have a go and end up making a real mess of it; of course, you can always ask for a spoon and fork. A Kerala dish, fish-head curry, is very popular in Singapore and tastes a lot better than it sounds (in fact, it is made from the top end of the fish, not just the head).

Indian Muslim

Centres around delicious snacks such as *roti paratha* and *murtabak* (similar to a *roti* except filled with meat or vegetables), which you will see all over Singapore and Malaysia in cafés and street-stalls as the cook deftly swings the dough into bigger and bigger circles before slapping it on to a hot griddle plate. A popular staple is *biryani*, saffron-scented rice served with mutton or chicken.

Indian food is as varied as the peoples of India, and most varieties can be found in Singapore

INDONESIAN FOOD
Indonesian food is more often found in Singapore than Malaysia, although Malaysian menus will often include items such as *gado-gado*, which is a vegetable and beansprout salad with peanut sauce. Other common Indonesian specialities are *nasi padang* (a rice dish with a selection of meat, chicken and seafood accompaniments) and *beef rendang* (hot, with a coconut sauce) from Sumatra.

INTERNATIONAL FOOD
In Malaysia most resort hotels feature western menus as well as local cuisine, and outlets such as McDonalds as well as local fast-food chains can be found in nearly every town or city. The same is true of Singapore, with the additional bonus of a wide range of top-class international restaurants with French, Swiss or Austrian chefs. Almost every national cuisine is represented in Singapore, from Mexican to Danish, Italian and Russian.

JAPANESE FOOD
Sushi, tempura, teppanyaki and other classic Japanese dishes are all available in Singapore – at a price.

MALAY FOOD
Malay cuisine is very close to that of Indonesia, and is similarly rich in herbs, spices and coconut milk. Most dishes are rice-based, with the addition of chicken, fish, vegetables and meat (never pork, since Malays are Muslim). Fish (*ikan*) appears in many different guises, for instance as *ikan panggang* (baked in banana leaves), *ikan assam* (fried in a tamarind curry sauce) and *ikan bilis* (anchovies, often sprinkled on top of other dishes). Chicken (*ayam*) is also

Curry buffet in the restored splendour of the Tiffin Room at the Raffles Hotel

eaten widely, for instance as *ayam goreng* (fried chicken), or *ayam kapitan* (curried with chilli and lemon grass).

The most widely known Malay dish is *satay*, skewers of marinated beef or chicken grilled over charcoal and served with a tasty peanut sauce. It is usually eaten as a snack or starter. A popular breakfast dish is *nasi lemak*, coconut rice with peanuts, curry sauce and *ikan bilis*; visitors may find the strong flavours (particularly the anchovies) a little over-powering first thing in the morning.

Malaysians also eat a lot of noodle-based dishes, many of which are common to the rest of Asia, such as *mee goreng* (fried noodles). A dessert found nowhere else is *ali batu campur* (advertised simply as 'ABC'), a chilled mound of ice with beans, sweetcorn and palm sugar. Sickly and stodgy it may be, but you have to try it once.

Lobster and other seafood is abundant

NYONYA FOOD

Like Peranakan (or Baba Nyonya) culture itself, nyonya food is a unique cross-over, involving combinations of Malay spices and Chinese sauces, Chinese-style soups with Malay herbs and other unusual dishes. The result is a piquant, spicy (but never fiery) cuisine with flavours provided by coconut milk, lemon grass, chillies, and *belacan* (dried shrimp paste). One of the classic nyonya dishes is *laksa lemak*, a sweet-sour noodle soup that is now eaten all over Malaysia. Other specialities include *otak otak* (spicy barbecued fishcakes) and *bakwang kepiting* (crabmeat and pork-ball soup). Cakes and desserts, which tend to be fairly heavy, include specialities such as *bubor terigu* (wholewheat porridge) and *gula melaka* (sago, palm sugar and coconut milk).

SEAFOOD

The waters around Malaysia and Singapore produce an abundant harvest of seafood of every description, from gleaming snapper to mussels, lobsters, crabs, prawns and squid. In the quest for the freshest possible taste, many restaurants have fish-tanks where live crustaceans, prawns and fish await the journey to the kitchen at the last possible minute.

As well as appearing in regional specialities such as baked fish in banana leaves or fish-head curry, seafood is often served using Chinese cooking methods. Fish is usually steamed, while prawns are either steamed or appear on the menu as 'drunken', in which case they are doused in Chinese wine or cognac and simmered in herbs. In Singapore, probably the most popular seafood dish of all is chilli crab, stir-fried with chilli, garlic, tomato and egg. Other favourites include fried squid in black-bean sauce, black-pepper crabs, seafood *dim sum* and baked mussels.

VEGETARIAN FOOD

Vegetarians will have little difficulty in finding suitable food in either Singapore or Malaysia. One of the most popular options is Indian vegetarian food, which features plenty of vegetable curries, breads and *dhals* (lentil soups). Other vegetarian favourites include the southern Indian *masala dosa* (spicy vegetables inside a thin pancake, with soup on the side), Indonesian *gado-gado,* and the Indian Muslim snacks *murtabak* and *roti paratha*. Sometimes the latter are served with meat, but you can simply ask for one without. In Singapore, there are a number of excellent restaurants serving all-you-can-eat salad buffets.

DRINKS

As in most tropical climates, the most effective way of quenching your thirst and cooling off is – paradoxically – a hot drink such as tea. In Malaysia, tea in local cafés is usually served with dollops of sickly condensed milk, and if you would prefer black tea you have to ask for *teh-o* (without milk). Chinese restaurants and cafés serve refreshing and fragrant Chinese teas. Except in hotels, coffee is likely to taste fairly weak (the best beans go for export). Soft drinks such as Coca-Cola, Fanta and 7-Up are widely available in restaurants and supermarkets.

For visitors, one of the delights of the region is the enormous variety of fresh fruit juices, which can be found almost everywhere. Street-stalls equipped with blenders will whizz up mango, watermelon, orange, starfruit or any other juice within seconds.

Alcohol is relatively expensive and is not always available outside tourist hotels everywhere in Malaysia (Muslims are forbidden to drink alcohol). Chinese restaurants and cafés usually have cold beer, with good local brands including Anchor and Tiger; bottled Guinness is also surprisingly popular. Imported spirits are expensive, although local brandies and whiskies can be found at a fraction of the cost (if you can stand the taste), usually in Chinese shops.

Fresh vegetables are piled high in every market

Dried fish features in many Malay dishes

TROPICAL FRUITS

The hot, damp climates of Singapore and Malaysia are well suited to the cultivation of many exotic tropical fruits. If you haven't ventured beyond pineapples before, now is the time to indulge yourself and experiment. Street markets usually have fruit stalls where you can sample slices of a whole variety of fruits, temptingly laid out on ice, or they can make up fruit salads

from any combination of your choosing.

Apart from the more familiar fruits such as bananas, pineapples, coconuts, watermelons and oranges, others worth trying include the following:

Custard apple: squeeze the fruit to reveal soft, white flesh with a delicious, lemon-tinged flavour.

Durian: crowned the 'King of Fruits', this thorny, football-sized fruit has an

Pomelos (above) and papaya (top) are among the many succulent fruits to tempt taste-buds

overpoweringly pungent smell, principally reminiscent of open sewers, which is why it is banned on all airplanes and in hotel rooms. The flesh inside has a rich/creamy, strong/sweet flavour that is very hard to describe, but suffice to say that it is considered an aphrodisiac and connoisseurs are willing to pay top

As well as the more familiar bananas and watermelons, exotic fruits such as the rambutan (top, inset) are worth trying

Mango: the appetising orange or yellow flesh of the mango varies in flavour between the huge number of varieties available.

Mangosteen: quite different from the mango, the mangosteen has a hard, purple skin, inside which are segments of white, juicy flesh with a sweet-sour flavour.

Papaya: the perfect breakfast fruit, served with a slice of lemon. The smooth, sweet flesh is rich in vitamins A and C.

Pomelo: resembling a pendulous grapefruit, the pomelo is not as tart. It is rich in vitamin C.

Rambutan: literally 'hairy fruit' in Malay, the red or yellow spines of the rambutan peel away to reveal sweet white flesh that tastes very much like the lychee.

prices for wild fruits.

You will either love it or hate it.

Jackfruit (or nangka): an enormous fruit that opens up to reveal yellow, rubbery but sweet-tasting segments of flesh.

Guava: the raw fruit tastes nothing like the tinned version often sold in the west, and is usually served with a seasoning of ground sour plums from stalls. It is extremely rich in vitamin C.

Restaurants

SINGAPORE

Eating out in Singapore can be as cheap or as expensive as you want it to be. On the one hand, you can get by very well eating from hawker centres, where basic dishes such as a bowl of tasty noodles cost as little as S$3 and more elaborate meals between S$10–20. On the other hand, you can spend upwards of S$100 or more for two people in any number of interesting and unusual restaurants.

The listings below represent an initial taste of the hundreds of restaurants in the city. The following symbols have been used to indicate the average cost per person, not including alcohol.

$	= up to S$20
$$	= S$20–50
$$$	= over S$50

A 10 per cent service charge and 3 per cent government tax is levied in all 'tourist class' restaurants (including all hotel restaurants). In coffee-shops and other simple eating places (including hawker centres) no charge is imposed, and a tip is not expected. Note that there is no smoking in air-conditioned restaurants.

CHINESE
Cantonese
Fook Yuen Seafood $$
Busy at lunchtimes for the popular *dim sum* in particular. *03–05/08 Paragon Shopping Centre, 290 Orchard Road (tel: 235 2211).*
Lei Garden $$$
Classic Cantonese cuisine, rated among the best in Singapore. Huge selection of *dim sum* on Sundays. Reservations advisable. *Boulevard Hotel, 200 Orchard Boulevard (tel: 235 8122).*

Chinese herbal
Imperial Herbal Restaurant $$
Excellent food with medicinal herbs added to suit the requirements of individuals by a qualified Chinese herbalist. *Metropole Hotel, 41 Seah Street (tel: 337 0491). Close to Raffles Hotel.*

Hokkien
Beng Hiang $$
Serves traditional Hokkien specialities such as fried oysters and deep-fried liver rolls, in unpretentious surroundings. *112 Amoy Street (tel: 221 6684). Off Maxwell Road.*

Peking
Pine Court $$$
Traditional Peking specialities such as duck and baked tench, in a palatial setting. Excellent lunchtime buffet. *Mandarin Hotel, 333 Orchard Road (tel: 737 4411).*
Prima Tower Revolving Restaurant $$
Panoramic views of the harbour. House specialities include Peking duck and braised beancurd in claypot. *201 Keppel Road (tel: 272 8822).*

Szechuan
Golden Phoenix $$
Singapore's first Szechuan restaurant, informal and always busy – reservations advisable. *Hotel Equatorial, 429 Bukit Timah Road (tel: 732 0431).*
Min Jiang $$
Classic Szechuan cuisine such as camphor and tea smoked duck and drunken chicken. Reservations essential. *Goodwood Park Hotel, 22 Scotts Road (tel: 730 1704).*

HAWKER CENTRES
Lau Pa Sat Festival Market $
Neat, clean food stalls amid lovely
Victorian cast-iron work. *18 Raffles
Quay.*
Newton Circus $
The biggest in Singapore, with a huge
choice. *Corner of Bukit Timah, Scotts
and Newton, 10 minutes from Orchard
Road.*
Orchard Emerald Food Court $
Local specialities as well as frozen
yoghurts and fruit salads. *Basement,
Orchard Emerald, 218 Orchard Road.*
Picnic Food Court $
Air-conditioned, with a good selection
of Indian, vegetarian and Chinese
food.
Scotts Shopping Centre, 6 Scotts Road.

INDIAN
Northern Indian
Kinara $$
Punjabi cuisine with river views and
Rajastani décor *(tel: 533 0412).*
Orchard Maharajah $$
Good selection of well-cooked dishes.
25 Cuppage Road (tel: 732 6331).

South Indian
Banana Leaf Apollo $$
Near Serangoon Road. Casual, canteen-
type atmosphere. Famous for fish-head
curry served on banana leaves. *56
Racecourse Road (tel: 293 8682).*
Bombay Woodlands $$
Convenient location, set meals and a
good range of desserts. *B1–01 Tanglin
Shopping Centre, 19 Tanglin Road (tel:
235 2712).*

INDONESIAN
Alkaff Mansion $$$
Fabulous restored 1920s mansion famed
for its *rijstaffel* (Indonesian 'rice table'

Follow the locals, eat with chopsticks

buffet). *10 Telok Blangah Green, Telok
Blangah Hill Park (tel: 278 6879). Off
Henderson Road.*
Tambuah Mas Café $
Good-value Javanese and Padang dishes.
Very busy at lunchtimes. *04–10 Tanglin
Shopping Centre, 19 Tanglin Road (tel:
733 2220).*

INTERNATIONAL
Chico's N Charlie's $$
Friendly and fun, with all the usual Tex-
Mex favourites and Margarita cocktails.
*05–01 Liat Towers, 541 Orchard Road
(tel: 734 1753).*
Hard Rock Café $$
Good steaks and burgers; open till 2am.
*02–01 HPL House, 50 Cuscaden Road
(tel: 235 5232).*
Emerson's Tiffin Rooms $$
Atmospheric re-creation of the original
Emersons (1886). The food blends east
and west with some interesting results.
51 Neil Road (tel: 227 7518).
Prego $$
Cheerful Italian atmosphere, with home-
made pasta. *Westin Plaza Hotel, 2
Stamford Road (tel: 431 5156).*
Zouk $$$
Greek, Spanish or Turkish dishes in a
Mediterranean-style atmosphere. *17–21
Jiak Kim Street (tel: 738 2988). Off Kim
Seng Road.*

A floating restaurant in Kuala Lumpur

JAPANESE

Hisamoto Family Restaurant $$
Busy, casual restaurant inside a
department store. Good-value set meals.
*03–16 Raffles City Shopping Centre, 250
North Bridge Road (tel: 339 6872).*

Suntory $$$
Part of an international chain, with a
wide range of *teppankyaki, sushi, shabu-
shabu* and *tempura. 06–01/02 Delfi
Orchard, 402 Orchard Road (tel: 732
5111).*

MALAY

Aziza's $$
Up-market setting, with authentic Malay
dishes such as *beef redang* (beef cooked
in coconut milk) and *ikan terutop* (spiced
fish). *02–05 Albert Court, 180 Albert
Street (tel: 235 1130).*

Sabar Menanti $
Typical, Malay-style coffee-shop, very
busy at lunchtimes serving specialities
such as *beef redang* and *ikan bakar*
(barbecued fish). *62 Kandahar Street.
Near Arab Street.*

NONYA

Nonya and Baba Restaurant $
Authentic atmosphere with reasonably
priced dishes such as *ayam buah keluak*
(chicken with black nuts) and *otak-otak.
262–264 River Valley Road (tel: 734
1382).*

Oleh Sayang $$
Small restaurant with a wide selection of
home-cooked *nonya* dishes. *Block 1018,
01–308 Woodlands Industrial Park D
(tel: 368 6009).*

SEAFOOD

Garden Seafood $$$
Cantonese and seafood dishes,
particularly recommended for the
popular, reasonably priced seafood
dim sum at lunchtimes. *Goodwood
Park Hotel, 22 Scotts Road (tel: 737
7411).*

Long Beach Seafood $$
Long-established seafood restaurant
with an outdoor section, famous for its
very fiery black-pepper crab. *Planet
Marina, 01–31 Marina Park (tel: 323
2222).*

Palm Beach Seafood $$
Huge and popular place with good-value
shellfish. *Palm Beach Leisure Park, 01–16
Stadium Walk (tel: 344 3088).*

VEGETARIAN

Kingsland Vegetarian $
Very popular Chinese vegetarian
restaurant with an innovative menu.
03–23, 60 Albert Street (tel: 338 2947).

Pete's Place $$
'Pasta e Basta' buffet at lunchtimes with
soups, 13 vegetable salads and pasta
station with cooked-to-order dishes.
*Hyatt Regency, 10–12 Scotts Road (tel:
730 7113).*

Ponderosa $
This chain is in fact a steak house, but
good value for all-you-can-eat salad
buffets. *02–13/15/17 Plaza Singapura
(tel: 336 0139); other outlets in Raffles
City and Marina Square.*

Sizzler $
Similar to the above.
13–00, 302 Orchard Road (tel: 738 6662).

MALAYSIA

As in Singapore, eating out in Malaysia is an adventure where even those on a tight budget will not find themselves constrained by lack of a credit card. Indeed, some of the best food in Malaysia is to be found at street-side food-stalls where fresh ingredients are thrown together to create mouth-watering dishes that cost no more than a few *ringgit*. The following is therefore no more than a sampling from the main tourist centres of the many thousands of places where you can indulge in the culinary delights of the region.

The average cost per person, not including alcohol, is indicated as follows:

R   = up to RM10
RR   = RM10-40
RRR   = RM40+

KUALA LUMPUR

Chinese

Golden Phoenix RRR
Traditional Cantonese dishes in a majestic setting. *Hotel Equatorial, Jalan Sultan Ismail (tel: 261 7777).*

Ming Palace RRR
Specialities include Szechuan dishes. *Ming Court Hotel, Jalan Ampang (tel: 261 1888).*

Shang Palace RRR
A wide range of Cantonese cuisine prepared by Hong Kong chefs. Popular for *dim sum. Shangri-la Hotel, 11 Jalan Sultan Ismail (tel: 232 2388).*

Xin Cuisine RR
Large restaurant popular for Cantonese food and *dim sum. Concorde Hotel, 2 Jalan Sultan Ismail (tel: 244 2200).*

Indian

Annalakshmi R
One of the best Indian vegetarian restaurants in Kuala Lumpur; excellent buffet. *44/46 Jalan Maroof, Bangsar Park (tel: 282 3799).*

Bangles RR
Reasonably priced authentic north Indian food. *60–A Jalan Tunku Abdul Rahman (tel: 298 6770).*

Bombay Palace RR
Good North Indian food in traditional setting. *388 Jalan Tun Razak (tel: 245 4241).*

The Taj RRR
Award-winning Indian cuisine in stylish Anglo-Indian surroundings. *Crown Princess Hotel, City Square Centre, Jalan Tun Razak (tel: 262 5522).*

International

Coliseum Cafe RR
A Kuala Lumpur institution, this old-fashioned café serves sizzling steaks on a platter, and western foods. *98–100 Jalan Tuanku Abdul Rahman (tel: 292 6270).*

Coq D'Or RRR
European/Malay food in the faded grandeur of a tin millionaire's mansion. *121 Jalan Ampang (tel: 242 9732).*

Malay

Bunga Raya RR
Good traditional Malaysian food. *Level 2, Putra World Trade Centre (tel: 442 2999).*

Rasa Utara RR
Bukit Bintang Plaza, Jalan Bukit Bintang (tel: 248 8639).

Satay Anika R
Highly recommended for their excellent *satay. Ground floor, Bukit Bintang Plaza, Jalan Bukit Bintang (tel: 248 3113).*

Yazmin Restaurant RRR
One of the city's best-known Malay restaurants, with dance performances in the evenings. *6 Jalan Kia Peng (tel: 241 5655).*

Seafood
Eden Village RR
Large, seafood restaurant with an
outdoor terrace, dance show indoors.
260 Jalan Raja Chulan (tel: 241 4027).

MELAKA
Chinese
Hoe Kee Chicken Rice R
Typical Chinese coffee-shop serving
Hainanese chicken rice. *Jalan Hang
Jebat.*
UE Teahouse R
Good *dim sum* at reasonable prices.
20 Lorong Bukit China.

Indian
Banana Leaf R
Very popular for *roti canai*, vegetarian
curries and *biriyanis. 42 Jalan Munshi
Abdullah.*

Nyonya
Jonkers RR
Pleasant restaurant in an old nonya
house, excellent lunchtime menu
(European as well as nonya food).
17 Jalan Hang Jebat (tel: 235 578).
Nyonya Makko RRR
Traditional nonya food. *123 Taman
Melaka Raya (tel: 283 0737).*
**Restoran Peranakan Town House
RRR**
*107 Jalan Tun Tan Cheng Lock
(tel: 284 5001).*

International
Kim Swee Huat R
Inexpensive breakfasts and western
food, as well as Asian staples. *38 Jalan
Laksmana.*
Pandan RR
Asian and Western food in a pleasant
outdoor setting. *Jalan Kota. Behind the
tourist office (tel: 283 6858).*

PULAU PINANG
Chinese
Holoman RR
Highly recommended for lunchtime *dim
sum. L43 Jalan Anson.*
Sin Kheng Hooi Hong RR
Chicken and other Hainanese dishes.
350 Lebuh Pantai.

Indian
Dawood RR
A popular spot for Indian Muslim food
including the Pinang speciality, *curry
kapitan. 63 Lebuh Queen (tel: 261 1633).*
Kaliaman RR
South Indian banana-leaf meals. *43
Lebuh Penang.*

Malay
Eliza City RRR
Traditional Malay food with views over
the sea. *Bayview Hotel, 25a Lorong
Farquhar (tel: 263 3161).*

Seafood
Eden RR
Reasonable prices for steaks and seafood
(also branches at Batu Ferringhi).
11B Lorong Hutton.
Sea Palace RR
Excellent range of seafood dishes. Often
very crowded. *50 Jalan Penang.*

EAST MALAYSIA
KUCHING
Chinese
Beijing Riverbank RR
Riverside location in a circular pavilion.
*Jalan Tunku Abdul Rahman (opposite
Riverside Majestic Hotel).*
Mei-San RR
Szechuan specialities and *dim sum* (good
value for Sunday set-price *dim sum*).
*Holiday Inn, Jalan Tunku Abdul Rahman
(tel: 423 111).*

Indian
Duffy Banana-Leaf Restaurant R
Curries served on banana-leafs; good
value. *Jalan Ban Hock.*

International
Café Majestic RR
International standards and Malay
snacks. *Riverside Majestic, Jalan Tunku
Abdul Rahman (tel: 247 777).*
Steak House RRR
Air-freighted sirloin steaks and western
specialities. *Hilton Hotel, Jalan Tunku
Abdul Rahman (tel: 248 200).*

Malay
Jubilee R
Good value Malay dishes. *Jalan India.*
Malay Restaurant RR
Lunchtimes only. *Jalan Kulas.*
National Islamic Café R
Rotis and *murtabak* as well as Malay
staples. *Jalan Carpenter.*
Sri Sarawak RRR
Authentic Malay dishes plus seafood.
*Riverside Majestic, Jalan Tunku Abdul
Rahman (tel: 247 777).*

SABAH
KOTA KINABALU
Chinese
**Avasi Cafeteria & Garden
Restaurant R**
Recommended for seafood and
steamboat dishes. *11 Kompleks Kuwasa.*
Nan Xing R
Good *dim sum* and Cantonese. *Jalan
Datuk Saleh Sulong.*
Phoenix Court RR
Dim sum and other Cantonese
specialities. *Hyatt Kinabalu, Jalan Datuk
Salleh Sulong (tel: 221 234).*
Restoran Tioman R
Good value for Chinese specialities; also
Malay food. *56 Bandaran Berjaya.*

A selection of Indian snacks and sweets

Indian
Bilal R
Tasty Indian Muslim food. *Block B, Lot
1 Segama Kompleks.*

International
Peppino RR
Very good but pricey Italian food.
*Shangri-La Tanjung Aru Resort (tel:
225 800).*
Semporna Grill RR
International and local dishes with
panoramic views across the harbour.
*Hyatt Kinabalu, Jalan Datuk Salleh
Sulong (tel: 221 234).*

Malay
Hot Chilli Café R
Excellent Malay dishes such as *beef
redang. Block BC, 3 Sadong Jaya
(tel: 239 242).*
New Arafat Restaurant R
Good value, recommended. *Block 1,
Sinsuran Kompleks.*

Seafood
Garden Restaurant RRR
Expensive but good. Pleasant outdoor
setting. *Tanjung Aru Beach Resort,
Tanjung Aru (tel: 225 800).*
Port View RR
Popular for chilli crab and other seafood
specialities. *Jalan Haji Saman.*

Hotels and Accommodation

SINGAPORE

Singapore has an extremely high standard of hotel accommodation with dozens of international-class hotels offering every conceivable luxury and high standards of service. Where the city doesn't score so well is in the budget accommodation category. Although there are cheaper hotels they are poor value compared to elsewhere in Asia.

Just a few years ago Singapore represented one of the best bargains in Asia for hotel rooms, since a glut of new hotels meant that you could expect an almost automatic discount of up to 40 per cent on published rates for the top hotels. However, occupancy rates have now caught up with the rooms available and the days of big discounts have gone – until the next building boom.

With hotels now competing in terms of the services they offer rather than price, they are often in the process of upgrading or renovation, so try and find out beforehand to avoid being disturbed by construction work.

All hotel rooms are subject to a 10 per cent service charge and government tax of 4 per cent (expressed as '++').

Deluxe accommodation

The majority of deluxe hotel rooms in Singapore come with all the standard facilities. Most hotels have 24-hour room service, hairdressing or beauty salons, news kiosks, and a travel desk for booking tours, entertainments or restaurants.

In the standard deluxe hotels such as the **Hyatt Regency**, the **Hilton**, the **Pan Pacific** and the **Oriental**, room rates hover around S$300–350++.

Apart from the normal deluxe hotels, there are several other options if you want somewhere with historic atmosphere. Foremost among them is the majestic **Raffles Hotel**, where all the rooms have now been converted into suites and furnished in colonial style. Rates start at around S$650–700++. Another elegant historic building is the **Goodwood Park Hotel**, built in 1900 (rooms cost S$350–400++). In complete contrast to the high-rise hotels that predominate in Singapore, **The Duxton** is an intimate but luxurious conversion of former homes in the heart of Tanjong Pagar (from S$290–380++).

Standard accommodation

Just below the deluxe category there are plenty of options for mid-range hotels, with rooms costing S$100–200++. Most of these have clean, air-conditioned rooms with the usual facilities.

In this category are hotels such as the **Amara** and the **Apollo**, both near Chinatown and the business district. On Orchard Road itself, one of the better-value hotels is the **Cockpit**. Set amid gardens just a few minutes walk from Orchard Road is the **Ladyhill**, which is also reasonably priced. Not all hotels in this category have swimming-pools. The savings to be made from being outside the Orchard Road district are considerable, and the inconvenience is offset by the fact that many hotels offer a free shuttle service to the shops.

Budget accommodation

It is still possible to find somewhere to stay in Singapore for as little as S$10 per night, although this will probably be in

The bright white interior of Raffles Hotel, restored after a S$160 million face-lift

one of the 'crash pads' popular with backpackers – usually, several bunk-beds squeezed into a private apartment that is operating as an unofficial hostel. The main centre for budget accommodation is in the Bencoolen Street area. A notch above the crash-pads are cheap, Chinese-run hotels, where a basic room with fan or air-conditioning costs S$20–50 (taxes are usually included in the price). A useful STPB leaflet, *Budget Hotels*, lists around 50 possibilities for under S$120.

THOMAS COOK
Traveller's Tip

Travellers who purchase their travel tickets from a Thomas Cook network location are entitled to use the services of any other Thomas Cook network location, free of charge, to make hotel reservations.

MALAYSIA

Malaysia has a wide range of accommodation available to suit every budget, from simple thatch huts on the beach for a few *ringgit* a night to luxury hotels with swimming-pools and full facilities. The international chains such as **Hyatt**, **Hilton** and **Holiday Inn** are well represented in major cities and in the larger resorts, with room prices that are generally lower than in Singapore. Local chains such as the **Merlin Hotels** also offer high standards of accommodation in many locations throughout Malaysia (central bookings in Kuala Lumpur, tel: (03) 783 8854; in Singapore, tel: (02) 338 1998). Other possibilities include government rest houses and youth hostels. National parks have a range of chalets etc; for bookings, see individual park entries under **What to See**.

All hotels are subject to a service charge of 10 per cent and 5 per cent government tax (expressed as '++'). Cheaper hotels do not generally add service charges, and the price is usually quoted net, ie, tax included.

Deluxe accommodation
Kuala Lumpur has the greatest range of international-class hotels, with rooms costing from between RM350–500++ in hotels such as the **Shangri-La**, **Hilton** or the **Regent**. These hotels offer all the amenities you would expect, such as comfortable, air-conditioned rooms, IDD telephones, shopping arcades and restaurants.

Outside Kuala Lumpur the cost of similar rooms tends to be less expensive (RM250–350++). At least two or three international-standard hotels can be found in major tourist centres such as Melaka, Pulau Pangkor, Kuching and Kota Kinabalu. For a taste of the South

The old Cathay Hotel in George Town, faded splendour at budget prices

Pacific, Pulau Pangkor Laut has the exceptional **Pangkor Laut Resort**, with water villas on stilts out over the sea. Pulau Pinang has a half-dozen good beach hotels, plus the venerable **E & O Hotel** in George Town if you want somewhere with a bit of atmosphere and old-world charm.

In the hill resorts you will find local chains, such as the Merlin Hotels, with adequate, comfortable rooms. For colonial nostalgia there is **Ye Olde Smokehouse** in both the Cameron Highlands and at Fraser's Hill.

Cooling off in a hotel pool at Batu Feringgi

Standard accommodation

In Kuala Lumpur, mid-price hotels tend to be fairly basic, offering clean, comfortable rooms with air-conditioning and a telephone, but otherwise very few frills. Hotels in this category include places such as the **Hotel Chamtan** and the **Hotel Malaya** in the downtown area, where rooms cost from RM80–160++. In most towns and cities outside Kuala Lumpur you can find similar-standard hotels for RM60–120++.

Government rest houses (*rumah rehat*) are another option, often situated in pleasant surroundings just outside town. The simple, old-fashioned rooms cost, on average, RM40–60++.

National parks usually have a range of chalets and bungalows, with prices from around RM30 for a simple, twin-bed cabin with shower, up to RM300 for a deluxe cabin sleeping four or more.

Budget accommodation

The standard budget accommodation in Malaysia is usually a Chinese-run hotel, often over a café or restaurant. Rooms are likely to be very basic indeed, with the minimum of furniture and probably just a wash-basin – showers and toilets are normally shared. Sometimes they have air-conditioning, sometimes just a fan. Often the rooms have been partitioned off inside the house with thin walls, which can make them very noisy. Standards of cleanliness also vary widely. Rooms generally cost RM25–50.

Most of the islands (except Pulau Pinang) have one or more beaches where you can stay in simple, thatched A-frame huts in Robinson Crusoe style for around RM20–40. Popular islands such as Pulau Tioman have the greatest choice at budget prices, while the other east-coast islands tend to be more expensive.

Kuala Lumpur is the most difficult place to find decent budget rooms, since the Chinese hotels tend to be of a lower standard and more expensive than elsewhere. However, there is a YMCA and a YWCA, which cost RM30–50 per person.

National parks almost invariably have dormitory accommodation with cooking facilities and communal bathrooms, generally costing around RM15–25 per person.

On Business

Singapore and Malaysia are both members of ASEAN (the Association of South East Nations) which, collectively, are among the fastest-growing economies in the world, with average annual growth rates of over 6 per cent.

In Singapore, manufacturing currently accounts for 30 per cent of GDP, with the emphasis on hi-tech industries such as biotechnology, aerospace, petrochemicals and information technology. There has been enormous growth in the services sector, with financial services growing at the rate of more than 20 per cent per annum in the early 1990s. Other service industries include agrotechnology, software development, conferences and exhibitions, consultancy, medical services and tourism.

In Malaysia, the economic picture is changing rapidly as the country becomes less dependent on commodity exports, the traditional mainstay of the economy. Political stability has attracted considerable foreign investment in the manufacturing sector, and manufactured goods now account for 60 per cent of export earnings. Labour shortages have also affected Malaysia, with the result that the emphasis is now on hi-tech industries and value-added products.

BUSINESS ETIQUETTE

Commerce and trade is the lifeblood of Singapore and it is an easy place to do business in. Services are excellent and people are friendly with a pragmatic, no-nonsense attitude to business dealings: there are no 'hidden agendas' or other pitfalls for the visiting business person.

In Malaysia business is approached in a more cautious fashion, and after the initial approach your Malaysian counterpart may indicate that he would like to discuss matters with his partners – whether he has partners or not is irrelevant, since Malaysians are reluctant to commit themselves without considerable forethought. Don't try and push for a quick decision, since this may lead to a negative answer.

In terms of bribery and corruption Malaysia is one of the 'cleanest' countries in Southeast Asia after Singapore (where they don't exist at all) although that's not to say that a 'contribution' to a favoured charity would go amiss in swinging a deal.

In Singapore business style is similar to that in the US or Europe and the exchange of business cards is usually casual. In Malaysia exchanging cards is more formal, and you should pay some attention to details on the card before pocketing it – remember also to offer yours with the right hand only. Malaysians set great store by titles, and Tuan Haji, Dato, Tan Sri and Tun feature on many people's cards: always address a Malaysian by his title, even if it takes you a while to master them (and no-one will be upset if you ask exactly how they wish to be addressed). Despite the emphasis on formalities, you will certainly be made to feel welcome doing business in Malaysia.

In Singapore dress style is casual, although business suits are usually worn at first meetings and in legal circles. In Malaysia dress codes are more formal.

In Kuala Lumpur most offices are convenient and easily reached but if you're planning a business trip outside the capital a flexible itinerary is advisable, bearing in mind the distances involved and possible transport delays. Remember that in Kelantan, Terengganu, Perlis, Johor and Kedah Thursday is a half-day and Friday a holiday (Saturday and Sunday are normal working days).

If possible avoid travelling on business around national holidays (see page 186) since flights may be heavily booked months in advance.

CONFERENCE FACILITIES

Singapore and Malaysia have first-rate facilities for international conferences and exhibitions with an enormous choice of venues and full back-up facilities.

In Kuala Lumpur the main conference venue is the modern, 3,500-seater Putra World Trade Centre. The numerous facilities in Singapore have increased with the addition in 1994 of the ultra-modern Singapore International Convention and Exhibition Centre, Suntec City, whose main hall seats up to 13,000 people.

While Singapore may have the edge in terms of centralised locations and convenience, Malaysia has the advantage of a wide range of inspiring locations, with convention facilities available in hill stations, beach resorts and elsewhere.

Full details on conference and exhibition facilities are available from the following organisations: Singapore Convention Bureau, Raffles City Tower 37–00, 250 North Bridge Road, Singapore (tel: 339 6622); and STPB offices overseas (see page 189). Convention Division, Malaysia Tourism Promotion Board (MTPB), Putra World Trade Centre, 45 Jalan Tun Ismail,

Kuala Lumpur (tel: (03) 293 5188); and MTPB offices overseas (see page 189).

SECRETARIAL AND TRANSLATION SERVICES

International-standard hotels in Singapore and Malaysia usually have a business centre providing secretarial assistance, translation, courier and facsimile services. Other suppliers of business services, as well as professional conference organisers, may be contacted through the relevant convention bureaux (see opposite).

TRADE DEVELOPMENT AGENCIES

Assistance and information on all matters relating to setting up business or sourcing products and services are available from: Singapore Trade Development Board, 230 Victoria Street, 07–00 Bugis Junction Office Tower (tel: 337 6628). STDB also maintains a network of offices worldwide. Malaysia Industrial Development Authority, 3rd–6th floor Wisma Damansara, Jalan Semantan, Damansara Heights, Kuala Lumpur (tel: (03) 255 3633).

Ministry of International Trade and Industry, Block 10 Kompleks Kerajaan, Jalan Duta, Kuala Lumpur (tel: (03) 254 0033).

Thomas Cook in Singapore offer facilities for commercial foreign exchange (tel: 221 9285).

TELECOMMUNICATIONS

Telecommunications services including international direct-dial, telefax/facsimile and video-conferencing are available in convention hotels and exhibition centres in Singapore and Kuala Lumpur. See also **Telephones**, page 189.

Practical Guide

Contents

ARRIVING

For social visits of under three months to Singapore or Malaysia, no visas are required for citizens of most European and Commonwelath countries (with the exception of the Indian sub-continent), the US or Japan. That includes Britain, Ireland, Canada, Australia, all EU countries and Switzerland. Other nationalities should consult their nearest embassy before departure. Visitors to Malaysia should ensure their passport is valid for at least six months beyond the period of intended stay.

By air

Singapore's Changi International Airport is generally recognised as one of the most efficient and well-equipped airports in the world.

Foreign exchange counters and telephone bureaux are open 24 hours. Disabled travellers are provided with adapted toilets and telephones as well as ramps and lifts for wheelchairs. The time taken from aircraft door to kerbside is swift (half-an-hour or less is normal), but don't neglect the duty-free arrival shops, which are in the arrivals area.

Changi has two terminals connected by a monorail. Most international carriers use Terminal 1; the ten which use Terminal 2 include Singapore Airlines, Swissair, Air France and Malaysia Airlines. Transport from Changi Airport to the city is swift and efficient either by taxi or by one of the three Airbus services which call at many major central hotels. The small military airport of Seletar, on the north coast of Singapore, is used for some local regional flights.

Malaysia's main gateway is Subang International Airport, 24km from Kuala Lumpur, which is served by over 20 airlines. Terminal 1 takes international traffic; Terminal 2 handles services to and from Singapore; Terminal 3 is for

Arrive in style at Kuala Lumpur's railway station

domestic flights. A new airport is being constructed at Sepang, Sengalor, and is scheduled for completion in 1998. Buses 47 and 343 operate between central Kuala Lumpur and Subang. The slightly quicker taxi-ride takes about 45 minutes (fixed charge). Some international airlines fly direct to other Malaysian destinations, including Pulau Pinang, Kota Kinabalu and Kuching. International airlines also fly direct into Pulau Pinang, Kota Kinabalu and Kuching.

By train
The main railway route from Thailand runs down the west coast of Malaysia, connecting Bangkok with Butterworth and Kuala Lumpur, terminating at Singapore's Keppel Road Station.

By road
Long-distance express buses link Singapore with Kuala Lumpur and other destinations in Malaysia. There are also frequent shuttle buses and shared taxis to and from Johor Bahru, across the causeway. Express buses and shared taxis also operate across the border between Thailand and Malaysia.

By sea
Ferries from the World Trade Centre link Singapore with the Riau Archipelago in Indonesia. Cruise ships arrive at International Cruise Ship Terminal next to the World Trade Centre. A high-speed catamaran links west-coast resort islands in Malaysia with Thailand and Indonesia. The ferry runs from Medan in Sumatra to Pulau Pinang, Pulau Langkawi and then on to Phuket in Thailand.

Timetables and further details of most of the above transport can be found in the *Thomas Cook Overseas*

Timetable, published bi-monthly.

CAMPING
There is a campsite on Sentosa Island, with tents and camp beds for hire. In Malaysia you can sometimes camp in national parks and nature parks.

CHILDREN
Baby foods, nappies and so on are available in supermarkets and shops. Most tourist hotels have reliable baby-sitting services (24 hours notice required). See also **Children**, pages 148–9.

CLIMATE
Hot and humid all year round, average temperatures range from 20°C (68°F) to 30°C (86° F). It can rain at any time of year, usually in short, heavy downpours.

Singapore has the most rain between November and January. In Malaysia the west coast is affected by the southwest monsoon, which brings rainfall mostly between September to December. The northeast monsoon arrives on the east coast slightly later, from October through to February. The east coast should be avoided during this time, since roads can be flooded, ferry services stop operating and many island resorts are closed. Sarawak and Sabah are also affected by the northeast monsoon, but travelling is not usually restricted.

CRIME

Singapore is one of the safest cities in Asia and crimes against tourists are rare; sexual harassment of women is likewise almost unheard of. However, take common-sense precautions.

Malaysia is also a safe destination for tourists. There have been occasional reports of bag-snatchers in Kuala Lumpur and Kota Kinabalu, but otherwise theft from tourists is unusual. Carry your own padlock if you are staying in beach huts or cheap Chinese hotels.

CUSTOMS REGULATIONS

There are no restrictions on the amount of currency imported or exported from Singapore and Malaysia.

Travellers arriving in Singapore from countries other than Malaysia may bring in 1 litre each of spirits, beer and wine free of duty. Controlled or prohibited items include pornography, weapons, endangered wildlife products, firecrackers and chewing gum. Pirated tapes, videos and other material that infringes international copyright laws is liable to confiscation.

Travellers arriving in Malaysia are allowed to import 1 litre of wine or spirits, 200 cigarettes and perfume not exceeding RM200 in value free of duty. Weapons and pornography are prohibited.

As the message on every tourist pamphlet and lurid billboard posted all over the country will remind you, the penalty for importing or dealing in *dadah* (drugs) in Malaysia is death. Severe penalties also apply in Singapore.

DISABLED TRAVELLERS

In Singapore, good facilities are available for the disabled traveller. A detailed

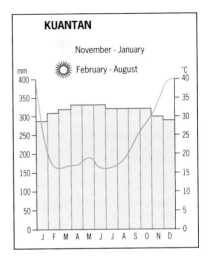

guide to easily accessible attractions, *Access Singapore*, is available from the Singapore Council of Social Services, 11 Pinang Lane (tel: 336 1544).

Malaysia is not an easy destination for disabled travellers; very few tourist attractions cater for wheelchairs. However, lift services are available in major hotels.

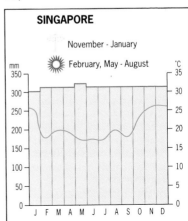

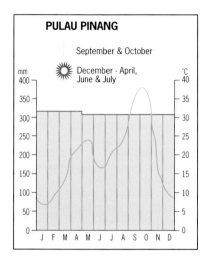

PULAU PINANG

September & October

December - April,
June & July

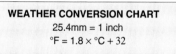

WEATHER CONVERSION CHART

25.4mm = 1 inch

$°F = 1.8 × °C + 32$

DRIVING

There is very little point in hiring a car in Singapore since taxis are relatively cheap and public transport is excellent.

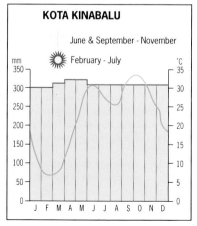

KOTA KINABALU

June & September - November

February - July

Conversion Table

FROM	TO	MULTIPLY BY
Inches	Centimetres	2.54
Feet	Metres	0.3048
Yards	Metres	0.9144
Miles	Kilometres	1.6090
Acres	Hectares	0.4047
Gallons	Litres	4.5460
Ounces	Grams	28.35
Pounds	Grams	453.6
Pounds	Kilograms	0.4536
Tons	Tonnes	1.0160

To convert back, for example from centimetres to inches, divide by the number in the third column.

Men's Suits

UK	36	38	40	42	44	46	48
Rest of Europe	46	48	50	52	54	56	58
US	36	38	40	42	44	46	48

Dress Sizes

UK	8	10	12	14	16	18
France	36	38	40	42	44	46
Italy	38	40	42	44	46	48
Rest of Europe	34	36	38	40	42	44
US	6	8	10	12	14	16

Men's Shirts

UK	14	14.5	15	15.5	16	16.5	17
Rest of Europe	36	37	38	39/40	41	42	43
US	14	14.5	15	15.5	16	16.5	17

Men's Shoes

UK	7	7.5	8.5		9.5	10.5	11
Rest of Europe	41	42	43	44	45	46
US	8	8.5	9.5	10.5	11.5	12

Women's Shoes

UK	4.5	5	5.5	6	6.5	7
Rest of Europe	38	38	39	39	40	41
US	6	6.5	7	7.5	8	8.5

Peninsular Malaysia has a good network of well-maintained and usually well-signposted roads. If starting out from Singapore, it is cheaper to cross into Malaysia and hire a car from there.

In general, the west-coast trunk routes are very busy. The new north–south expressway which runs all the way from the Thai border down to Johor Bahru, should relieve pressure on the main roads. At the top of the peninsula, the East–West Highway connects the two coasts.

Driving is on the left, with a speed limit of 110kph on expressways, 80kph on trunk roads and 50kph in towns and cities. An international driving licence is required. Seat-belts are compulsory for the driver and front-seat passenger.

Car rental companies
Avis Rent-A-Car, 40 Jalan Sultan Ismail, Kuala Lumpur (tel: (03) 242 3500).
Budget Rent-A-Car, 29 Jalan Yap Kwan Seng, Kuala Lumpur (tel: (03) 262 5116).
Hertz Rent-A-Car, Lot 214A Kompleks Antarabangsa, Jalan Sultan Ismail, Kuala Lumpur (tel: (03) 248 6433).
Mayflower Angkasaraya, Angkasaraya Building, 123 Jalan Ampang, Kuala Lumpur (tel: (03) 241 1400).

ELECTRICITY
The voltage is 220-240 volts AC. Hotels can supply transformers or adaptors to reduce the voltage if necessary.

EMBASSIES AND CONSULATES
Australia: 25 Napier Road, Singapore (tel: 737 9311); 3 Jalan Semantan 2, Damansara Heights, Kuala Lumpur (tel: 255 0176).
Canada: 80 Anson Road, 14-00 IBM Towers, Singapore (tel: 325 3200); 7th floor, Plaza MBF, Kuala Lumpur (tel: 261 2000).
Ireland: 298 Tiong Bahru Road, 08–06 Tiong Bahru Plaza, Singapore (tel: 276 8935); Bangunan Straits Trading, Kuala Lumpur (tel: 298 5111).
New Zealand: 391A Orchard Road, 15–06 Ngee Aun City Tower A, Singapore (tel: 235 9966); 193 Jalan Tun Razak, Kuala Lumpur (tel: 248 6422).
UK: Tanglin Road, Singapore (tel: 473 9333); 185 Jalan Ampang, Kuala Lumpur (tel: 248 2122).
US: 27 Napier Road, Singapore (tel: 476 9100); 376 Jalan Tun Razak, Kuala Lumpur (tel: 248 9011).

EMERGENCY TELEPHONE NUMBERS
Singapore
Police: 999; ambulance and fire: 995
Malaysia
Police, ambulance and fire: 999
Thomas Cook MasterCard Travellers' Cheque refund (24-hour service, report loss or theft within 24 hours): 800 4481–115. MasterCard card loss or theft: 800 1100 113.

ETIQUETTE
Singapore takes great pride in the cleanliness of the city. There is a hefty fine of up to S$1,000 for littering. Smoking in public buses, taxis, lifts, theatres, cinemas and government offices is also banned (punishable by a S$500 fine). Smoking in many private offices is usually frowned on – always ask first. Smoking in restaurants is also banned.

Eating, drinking and smoking is prohibited on the whole of the MRT system. Jaywalking is theoretically an offence within 50m of a pedestrian crossing, underpass or bridge, but is rarely enforced. The latest regulations concern chewing gum, which is now banned altogether since the authorities decided it is too difficult to clean up.

In Malaysia, pointing with the forefinger (or any finger) is considered rude. This applies to inanimate objects, animals and especially to people. The polite way to point at something is with your whole hand or with your hand loosely clenched in a fist with the thumb sticking forward.

Touching people is definitely not acceptable, particularly if they are of the opposite sex. Friendly gestures such as laying a hand on the shoulder or taking someone's arm during a walk or a conversation are considered impolite.

HEALTH

No vaccinations are required to enter either Singapore or Malaysia, unless you have visited an area where cholera or yellow fever is endemic within the previous six days.

Singapore is one of the healthiest cities in Asia. Tap water is safe to drink. In Malaysia water is safe to drink in major towns and cities, but elsewhere ensure that it has been purified.

One major hazard is dehydration from the tropical heat. Make sure you drink plenty of fruit juices and water to compensate for fluid loss. If outdoors for extended periods or relaxing by the hotel pool, remember that the equatorial sun burns skin very quickly.

Another common health problem is an upset stomach. In general, choose restaurants or cafés that look clean and are busy. Avoid food-stalls or restaurants where there are flies near the food. Avoid undercooked meats. Wash fruit in purified water and peel it yourself. Never eat raw seafood.

Diarrhoea can result from either unsanitary food or contaminated water. Rest and rehydration are important. There are several different causes of diarrhoea, so contact the hotel doctor if you are at all worried or if symptoms persist for more than three days.

Medical facilities in clinics and hospitals are of a high standard with well-qualified, English-speaking medical personnel.

There is no risk of malaria in Singapore. Dengue fever is known to occur – this is mosquito-borne and there is no vaccine, so take care to avoid insect bites. In Peninsular Malaysia, malaria exists in limited pockets only in the deep hinterland; if exploring rural areas anti-malarial precautions are advisable. In Sarawak and Sabah (except in the coastal areas of Sarawak) there is an all-year malarial risk and precautions are recommended. Precautions should also be taken against typhoid, polio, tetanus and hepatitis A.

HITCH-HIKING

In Malaysia hitch-hiking is acceptable, and it is usually fairly easy to get rides as long as you look presentable. There are few dangers involved, although women should not hitch-hike alone.

INSURANCE

Comprehensive insurance covering medical expenses and theft or loss and damage to your belongings is recommended.

LANGUAGE

There are four official languages in Singapore (English, Mandarin, Malay and Tamil), although English is the most widely used and is understood by almost everybody.

The official language of Malaysia is Bahasa Malaysia, although you will also come across a multitude of other languages in the country that reflect its ethnic diversity. English is widely spoken, and even in remote areas you will be able to find someone who knows a few words and can help you out. However, even a smattering of Bahasa Malaysia will prove useful.

LOST PROPERTY

In Singapore you have a good chance of recovering lost items. Contact the restaurant, shop or transport authority where the loss might have happened, asking the hotel concierge for assistance with telephone calls if necessary. In both countries the same procedures apply for lost property. Report it to the hotel management and the police, and obtain a copy of the report if you need to make a claim on your insurance.

MEDIA

Singapore's leading English-language newspapers are the *Straits Times* and the *Business Times*. There is one afternoon English-language paper, the *New Paper*. Singapore also provides Chinese, Malay and Tamil daily papers.

BASIC PHRASES

Basics

good morning	*selamat pagi*
good afternoon	*selamat petang*
goodnight	*selamat malam*
please	*silakan*
thank you	*terima kasih*
sorry	*maaf*
excuse me	*maafkan saya*

Questions

How much?	*berapakah harganya?*
What is this?	*apa ini?*
What is your name?	*siapa nama awak?*
How are you?	*apa khabar?*
Where is....?	*di mana......?*
When?	*bila?*
Why?	*mengapa?*

Time

today	*hari ini*
tomorrow	*esok*
yesterday	*semalam*
hour	*jam*
week	*minggu*
month	*bulan*
year	*tahun*
weekend	*hujung minggu*

Places

airport	*lapangan terbang*
beach	*pantai*
hill	*bukit*
island	*pulau*
mountain	*gunung*
lake	*tasik*
river	*sungai*
road	*jalan*
town	*bandar*
village	*kampung*

Useful words

good	bagus
bathroom	bilik mandi
drink	minuman
eat	makan
expensive	mahal
hot water	air panas
room	bilik
shop	kedai
sleep	tidur

The main national English-language newspaper in Malaysia is the *New Straits Times*. Other national papers include the *Star, Business Times* and the *Malay Mail*. In East Malaysia, regional papers include the *Borneo Post, Sabah Times* and the *Sarawak Tribune*.

For entertainment information, check the local newspapers. The MTDC publishes *Kuala Lumpur This Month*. A monthly diary is also issued by the Central Market (see page 140).

MONEY MATTERS
In Singapore the unit of currency is the Singapore dollar. Coins are issued in denominations of 1, 5, 10, 20 and 50 cents, notes in units of $1, 2, 5, 10, 20, 50, 100, 500, 1,000 and 10,000.

In Malaysia the unit of currency is the Malaysian *ringgit*, until recently symbolised by a dollar sign '$'. You may still see '$' used to denote *ringgit*, but the officially correct symbol is RM, for Ringgit Malaysia. The *ringgit* is divided into 100 *sen*, with notes in denominations of RM1, 2, 5, 10, 50, 100, 500 and 1,000. Coins are in denominations of 1 *sen*, 5 *sen*, 10 *sen*, 20 *sen*, 50 *sen* and RM1. Major credit cards are widely accepted.

Thomas Cook MasterCard travellers' cheques are the safest way to take large amounts of money; if lost they can easily be replaced (see **Emergency Telephone Numbers**, page 182, and **Thomas Cook**, page 189). Shops and restaurants in Singapore and in the main cities in Malaysia will accept them denominated in any major currency, and they can be cashed commission-free at Thomas Cook locations and at the following banks: Overseas-Chinese Banking Corp, United Overseas Bank, Chung Khiaw Bank, Far Eastern Bank.

NATIONAL HOLIDAYS
1 Jan New Year's Day; **Jan/Feb** Chinese New Year; **Mar/Apr** Hari Raya Puasa;

toilet	tandas
Food and drink	
beef	daging lembu
chicken	ayam
coffee	kopi
drinking water	air minuman
egg	telur
fish	ikan
pork	daging babi
rice	nasi
fried rice	nasi goreng
fried noodles	mee goreng
tea	teh
black tea	teh-o
vegetables	sayur

Numbers		
1	satu	7 tujuh
2	dua	8 lapan
3	tiga	9 sembilan
4	empat	10 sepuluh
5	lima	50 lima puluh
6	enam	100 seratus
		1000 seribu

Multilingual signs

1 May Labour Day; **27 May** Vesak Day; **5 Jun** Birthday of the Yang Di-Pertuan Agong (Malaysia); **Jul/Aug** Hari Raya Haji; **9 Aug** National Day (Singapore); **31 Aug** National Day (Malaysia); **Oct/ Nov** Deepavali; **17 Dec** Birthday of the prophet Mohammed (Malaysia); **25 Dec** Christmas Day.

In Singapore, offices and government departments are closed on national holidays, but many shops stay open.

During national holidays in Malaysia, hotels in resort areas are likely to be heavily booked, so make sure you have a reservation before arriving. The same applies to school holidays, which are the last week in January, March and August and the whole of November.

OPENING HOURS
Singapore
Official hours for government offices are 8am–5pm weekdays, 8am–1pm Sat. Shops are open from around 10am to 8–9pm, many until 10pm or later. Most banks are open from 10am–3pm weekdays, 9.30am–1pm Sat (some banks in Orchard Road are also open from 9.30am–3pm on Sun). Money-changers are usually open from 10am–10pm daily.

Malaysia
Government offices are open daily from around 8.30am–12.30pm and 2pm–4.30–5pm, on Saturdays from 8.30am to 12.30–1pm. Shops are usually open from around 9–10am to 6–7pm, with department stores and supermarkets in cities often open until 10pm. Chinese shops and those in tourist areas are also often open until 9pm or later. Banks are open Mon–Fri 10am–3pm, Sat 9.30–11.30am.

In Johor, Kedah, Perlis, Kelantan and Terengganu, shops, banks and offices are closed on Thu afternoon and all day Fri. In all states, the lunch hour on Fri lasts from 11.30am–2.30pm.

PHARMACIES
Western medicines are widely available in pharmacies. In Singapore, pharmacies are found in most shopping malls and department stores.

PLACES OF WORSHIP
Visitors are welcome during ceremonies in Chinese, Buddhist or Hindu temples and in mosques outside prayer times. There are several Christian churches and a synagogue in Singapore, and Christian churches in most large towns and cities in Malaysia.

POLICE
Singapore has no separate tourist police force (dial 999 for emergencies). In case of trouble in Malaysia, contact any police station, or in Kuala Lumpur one of the numerous *Pondok Polis* (mini police stations). Kuala Lumpur also has a special Tourist Police unit (tel: (03) 249 6593).

POST OFFICES
In Singapore, post offices are located in several shopping malls (such as Raffles City, Specialists Centre), open 8.30am–5pm weekdays, 8.30am–1 pm Sat. Twenty-four-hour facilities are available at the General Post Office, Fuller Building, Fullerton Road and the Comcentre, 31 Exeter Road.

In Malaysia, post offices are open from 8am–5pm Mon–Fri, 8am–noon Sat. The cost of a postcard to anywhere in the world is 50 *sen*. In Kuala Lumpur, the central post office is on the second floor of the huge Dayabumi complex (tel: (03) 274 1122).

PUBLIC TRANSPORT

Singapore
MRT (Mass Rapid Transport)
The fastest way to get around is on the MRT, with trains operating from 6am to midnight. There are two main routes, the north–south line and the east–west line. Fares are low. The easiest way to use the MRT is to buy a TransitLink Farecard. This has the additional advantage of being valid for travel on Singapore Bus Services (SBS) and Trans-Island Bus Service (TIBS).

Farecards can be obtained from TransitLink counters in MRT stations and at bus interchanges.

Buses
Bus services are frequent and fares cheap. Buses are driver-only, with fares either flat rate or based on distance. The exact fare must be paid. Alternatively, you can use a TransitLink card on some buses, or a Singapore Explorer ticket.

Taxis
Fares are metered, and surcharges apply for journeys between midnight–6am (50 per cent of the fare), those starting at Changi Airport, for telephone bookings, and for trips to and from the Central Business District during peak hours.

Malaysia
Air
Malaysia Airlines (MAS) operate a network of domestic flights. Special fares are available on some routes for night flights and 14-day advance purchase. MAS and Singapore Airlines operate a joint shuttle service between Kuala Lumpur and Singapore. Domestic flight tickets are available at travel agents or MAS booking offices.

Traffic police in Kuala Lumpur

Bus
The country has a huge network of long-distance and local buses, providing a cheap, fast and fairly reliable service.

Trains
Malaysian Railways (KTMB – Keretapi Tanah Melayu Berhad) operates two

Visitors are usually welcome in temples

main lines. The west-coast line runs down from the Thai border to Kuala Lumpur and Singapore. The other line branches off from this one south of Kuala Lumpur and travels up through the centre of the country to Kota Bharu on the east coast. For overseas visitors, a Railpass is available allowing unlimited travel for either 10 or 30 days.

Up-to-date information for Malaysian trains, long-distance buses and ferries can be obtained in the bi-monthly *Thomas Cook Overseas Timetable*. It can be purchased from branches of Thomas Cook in the UK and in some other parts of the world, or by phoning 01733 (+44 1733) 503571/2. In the US contact Forsyth Travel Library Inc (tel: (1–800) 367–7984 (toll-free).

Taxis

One of the best ways to travel between major towns is by long-distance taxi, sharing the cost between passengers.

Ferries

Regular ferries operate between mainland ports and offshore islands in Peninsular Malaysia.

TELEPHONES
Singapore

Public pay-phones accept either coins or phonecards. For overseas phone calls, all major hotels provide IDD facilities, but the costs will be much higher than calling from a public phone. IDD calls can be made from phone booths or Telecom centres (open 24 hours) such as those in the GPO on Fullerton Road.
Directory enquiries   103
Overseas operator   104
International access code   055+
International dialing codes:
Australia 061; Canada 001; Ireland 353;

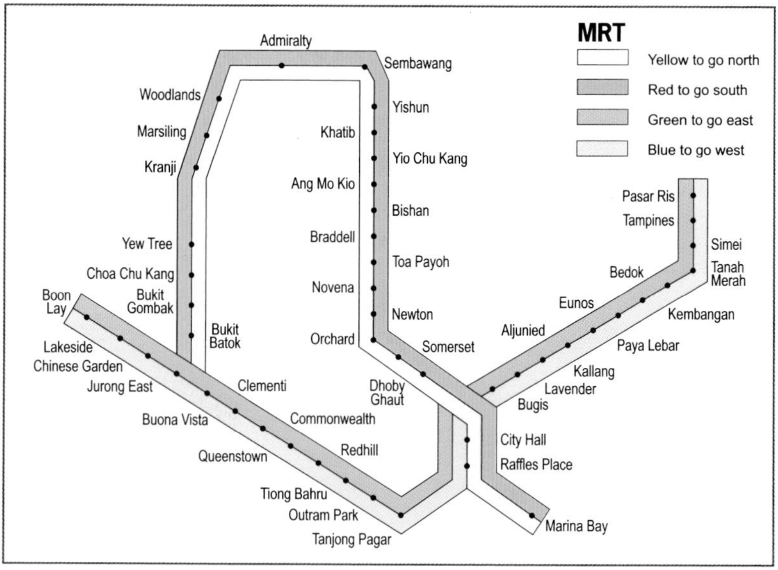

MRT

Yellow to go north
Red to go south
Green to go east
Blue to go west

New Zealand 064; UK 044; US 001.
Malaysia
Public pay-phones accept coins or
phonecards. International calls can be
made from any Kedai Telecom during
office hours.
Enquiries 102
Directory 103
International 108
International access code 007+
International dialing codes: Australia 61;
Canada 1; Ireland 353; New Zealand
64; UK 44; US 1.

THOMAS COOK
Singapore
★Thomas Cook Travel Services, 79
Anson Road, 22–03, Singapore 079906
(tel: 221 9285. Open Mon–Fri
9am–5pm, Sat 9am–12.30pm.
Malaysia
Boustead Travel Services are the local
Thomas Cook Worldwide Network
Licensee, with travel agencies at the
following locations (all open Mon–Fri
9am–5pm, Sat 9am–1pm).
★13th Floor, Menara Boustead, 69 Jalan
Raja Chulan, Kuala Lumpur 5200 (tel:
241 7022.
Pengkalan Weld, Penang 0300 (tel: 261
0511.
11 A/B Jalan SS2/3, Selangor Darul
Ehsan, Petaling Jaya 47300 (tel: 777
7148.
No 6, 1st Floor, Jalan Utas D 15/D,
Selangor Darul Ehsan, Shah Alam (tel:
559 7408.
The above branches provide a range of
travel services to visitors, and those
marked ★ also cash travellers' cheques
(Thomas Cook cheques commission-
free). All offer emergency assistance in
the case of loss or theft of Thomas Cook
MasterCard travellers' cheques or
CarsterCard cards. Travellers who have

purchsed their tickets at another
Thomas Cook location are also entitled
under the Thomas Cook Worldwide
Network Customer Promise to receive
services free of agency charges, such as
airline ticket re-routing or revalidation,
and hotel and car rental reservations.

Web site
Thomas Cook's World Wide Web site,
at www.thomascook,com, provides up-
to-the-minute details of Thomas Cook's
travel and foreign money services,
including its unique on-line Currency
Converter.

TIME
Australia +2; Canada -13– -16; Ireland
-8; New Zealand +4; UK -8; US (EST)
-13; US (WST) -16.

TIPPING
This is not expected at hotels and restaurants that levy a 10 per cent service
charge. Taxis will expect to keep change
rounded up to the nearest dollar or
ringgit.

TOILETS
In Singapore, toilets are found in
shopping malls, hotels and restaurants.
In Malaysia, they are found in towns
and tourist areas.

TOURIST OFFICES
Singapore
Head Office Tourism Court, 1 Orchard
Spring Lane (tel: 736 6622).
Malaysia
Local and regional MTDC offices
provide the usual services.
Kuala Lumpur
Head Office, 17th floor, Putra World
Trade Centre, 45 Jalan Tun Ismail, tel:
(03) 2935188.

ACKNOWLEDGEMENTS

The Automobile Association wishes to thank the following organisations, libraries and photographers for their assistance in the preparation of this book.
FOOTPRINTS 94 (N Hanna), 95a (A Dalton), 95b (A Misiewicz), 95c (E Lonsdale), 95d (A Misiewicz)
NICK HANNA 11a, 15a, 97, 98, 99, 100, 101, 102, 103, 107, 108, 109, 110, 111, 113a, 113b, 114, 115, 121, 123, 124, 145a,145b, 145c, 147.
MALAYSIA TOURISM PROMOTION BOARD 144, 150, 150/1.
SINGAPORE TOURIST PROMOTION BOARD 20b, 21b, 143.
SPECTRUM COLOUR LIBRARY spine.
The remaining photographs are held in the AA Photo Library and were taken by Ken Paterson, with the exception of the back cover (b) taken by Alex Kouprianoff and page 153 taken by Paul Kenward.

CONTRIBUTORS
Series advisor: Melissa Shales   **Copy editor:** Helen Douglas-Cooper   **Indexer:** Marie Lorimer
Thanks to **Lindsay Hunt** for her updating work on this revised edition.